THE
sweet as
BAKING
COOKBOOK

CONTENTS

WELCOME

If there is one thing taste.com.au has been famous for over the years, it's got to be its sweet bakes. I don't think we've ever counted them, but they'd have to number in the several thousand at least by now.

While it's exciting to have so many baking recipes to choose from (and you know taste can always be relied on for guaranteed winners that are great every time), sometimes you just want the taste experts to fess-up on their own personal favourites in every sweet baking category. And that's exactly what this book is all about. Finally, our taste experts are spilling the beans – or should that be spilling the flour?

In fact, this really is the big baking book all of us at taste have been dreaming about – of hand-selected all-time favourites the taste.com.au food experts themselves love to cook again and again... and the ones that tasties, such as yourself, have raved about again and again.

Bakers have so many moods and motivations, from simple to sensational, from whip-it-up to wondrous, from biscuits to birthday cakes, and everything in between. It's all covered here.

Best of all, the book itself is built to live in the kitchen, sturdy and trusty, right at your fingertips, always at the ready for that moment when the baking bug bites.

We hope you enjoy pulling it down from the shelf and flipping it open and cooking along, with the book right in front of you, old-school style, perhaps even channelling some of the great bakers from your family past.

I do like to think that this beautiful book may even pass on that taste mantle for famous bakes to you! That really would be, just as the name says, sweet as.

Brodee

BRODEE MYERS,
EDITOR-IN-CHIEF

The sweet as
BAKING COOKBOOK

Welcome to taste.com.au's *The Sweet As Baking Cookbook*. Your ultimate collection of baking greats, from biscuits and slices to pies, tarts and party cakes. Plus hot tips and a step-by-step icing guide.

AMAZING FEATURES

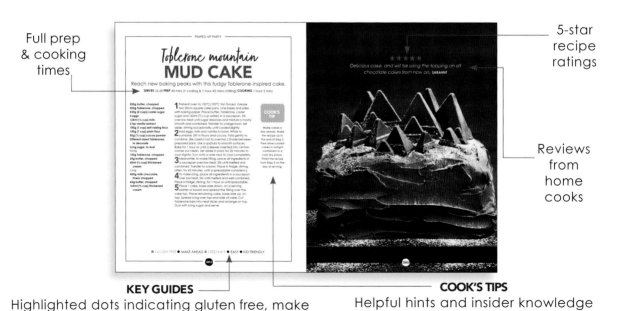

Full prep & cooking times

5-star recipe ratings

Reviews from home cooks

KEY GUIDES
Highlighted dots indicating gluten free, make ahead, freezable, easy and kid-friendly

COOK'S TIPS
Helpful hints and insider knowledge courtesy of our expert food team

COOK'S TIP

Keep an eye out for our handy ingredient swaps, storage tips and serving tricks.

INFO AT A GLANCE

Use our highlighted dots to find the best baking choices to suit you and your family (such as gluten free, make ahead, freezable, easy and kid-friendly – or all five!). The dots are featured under each recipe.

● GLUTEN FREE ● MAKE AHEAD ● FREEZABLE ● EASY ● KID-FRIENDLY

Baker's SECRETS

Whether you're a seasoned baker or just starting out on your baking journey, these are our expert tips to set you up for success and the perfect cake.

Baking is a wonderful blend of art and science. Once you've mastered some of the more hard and fast rules to baking, you can draw upon creative expression, and a little crafty know-how, to decorate or create the sweet masterpiece you've dreamed of.

Of course following the tried and tested recipe directions also helps! Just in case, here are some of our foodie's expert secrets to sweet success, all in one place, as well as a handy guide to prepping your baking tin before you start. Happy baking!

STEPS TO SUCCESS

GET READY
Make sure all ingredients are at room temperature before starting.

WEIGH IT UP
Measure dry ingredients in measuring cups and wet ingredients in measuring jugs.

STAY CENTRED
Check the oven rack is in the centre of the oven before preheating it.

MAKE TIME
To preheat the oven to the correct temperature, turn it on 20 minutes before baking.

TWO IN ONE
When mixing ingredients for two cakes (packet or homemade), make them both in one large bowl.

SLICK TO STICK
Grease cake pans with melted butter or spray oil before lining with non-stick baking paper to help secure the baking paper.

SHELF SHARE
If making two cakes at the same time, bake them on the same shelf in the oven to ensure even cooking.

HOT SPOTS
Don't allow cake pans to touch each other or oven walls during baking as this can cause hot spots on the cakes.

SWAP IT
When you're baking two cakes at the same time, make sure that you gently swap the pan positions after two-thirds of the baking time for even cooking.

KEEP IT SHUT
During baking, don't open the oven door during the first half of cooking time as this can cause cakes to sink.

HEAT PROTECTION
If you notice that your cake is over-browning, cover it loosely with foil.

GOLDEN RULE
As a general rule bake cakes until golden and a skewer inserted into the centre comes out clean.

SHELL FREE
Crack eggs into a small bowl before adding to any cake mix. This ensures that the egg is

fresh and without any blood. It also helps to prevent egg shell getting cracked into the cake.

TAKE TURNS
When adding flour and milk to the cake mixture, always add them in alternating batches, and stir gently with a wooden spoon. This is so you don't overwork the flour which can result in a rubbery cake.

FLAVOUR HIT
If adding flavours to your cake, such as citrus rinds or vanilla extracts or pastes or spices such as cinnamon, add them when you are beating together the butter and sugar so that they are well distributed throughout your batter.

CAKE TIN TIPS!

Avoid leaks, drips and cracked cakes with this handy guide to lining a cake tin.

LINE IT UP
Place a sheet of baking paper on the table and lie the cake tin on its side (the long side if it's a rectangular tin) up against one edge of the paper. Measure 2cm above the height of the tin and mark it with a pencil. Using a ruler as a guide, cut the paper at the level of the mark. Repeat on a second piece of baking paper for a round tin, and three times for a square or rectangular one.

THE RIGHT FIT
Place the cake tin flat on another piece of baking paper and trace around the base with a pencil. Then, carefully cut out the shape. Grease the base and sides of the baking tin well with butter. Place the base piece of baking paper in the bottom of the pan, making sure to press it well into the edges. Place the other pieces along the sides of the cake tin, allowing them to overlap slightly.

HANDLES WELL
Leaving a 2cm overhang will help you to remove the cake or slice more easily from the tin.

STAY DRY
Always dry a cake tin completely after washing to prevent it from rusting.

COOL OFF
When the cake is finished baking, remove from oven and leave it in the tin for 5 minutes so that it doesn't crack when your turning it out – a very hot

cake can ruin the risk of splitting. However, don't leave the cake in the tin too long or it will sweat and go soggy.

STUCK IN
If cake gets stuck, run a flat-bladed knife around the inside of the pan and Remove the baking paper immediately. Recipes are designed for specific cake tins, so it's important to use the stated size or you run the risk of the cake being over or under-cooked.

BAKER'S SECRETS

Wherever you are on your baking journey, it helps to keep these expert baking tips on hand for your best chance at sweet success every time. Plus our trusty guide to lining a cake tin.

taste.COM.AU
TRIPLE-TESTED TRUSTED & RATED

THE TASTE.COM.AU GUARANTEE

All taste.com.au recipes are triple-tested, rated and reviewed by Aussie cooks just like you. Plus, every ingredient is as close as your local supermarket.

9

Baker's
SECRETS

Whether you're a seasoned baker or just starting out on your baking journey, these are our expert tips to set you up for success and the perfect cake.

Baking is a wonderful blend of art and science. Once you've mastered some of the more hard and fast rules to baking, you can draw upon creative expression, and a little crafty know-how, to decorate or create the sweet masterpiece you've dreamed of.

Of course following the tried and tested recipe directions also helps! Just in case, here are some of our foodie's expert secrets to sweet success, all in one place, as well as a handy guide to prepping your baking pan before you start. Happy baking!

STEPS TO SUCCESS

GET READY
Make sure all ingredients are at room temperature before starting.

WEIGH IT UP
Measure dry ingredients in measuring cups and wet ingredients in measuring jugs.

STAY CENTRED
Check the oven rack is in the centre of the oven before preheating it.

MAKE TIME
To preheat the oven to the correct temperature, turn it on 20 minutes before baking.

TWO IN ONE
When mixing ingredients for two cakes (packet or homemade), make them both in one large bowl.

SLICK TO STICK
Grease cake pans with melted butter or spray oil before lining with non-stick baking paper to help secure the baking paper.

SHELF SHARE
If baking two cakes at the same time, bake them on the same shelf in the oven to ensure even cooking.

HOT SPOTS
Don't allow cake pans to touch each other or oven walls during baking as this can cause burnt spots on the cakes.

SWAP IT
When you're baking two cakes at the same time, make sure that you gently swap the pan

positions after two-thirds of the baking time for even cooking.

KEEP IT SHUT
During baking, don't open the oven door during the first half of cooking time as this can cause cakes to sink.

HEAT PROTECTION
If you notice that your cake is over-browning, cover it loosely with foil.

GOLDEN RULE
As a general rule bake cakes until golden and a skewer inserted into the centre comes out clean.

SHELL FREE
Crack eggs into a small bowl before adding to any cake mix. This ensures that the egg is

fresh and without any blood. It also helps to prevent egg shell getting cracked into the cake.

TAKE TURNS
When adding flour and milk to the cake mixture, always add them in alternating batches, and stir gently with a wooden spoon. This is so you don't overwork the flour which can result in a rubbery cake.

FLAVOUR HIT
If adding flavours to your cake, such as citrus rinds or vanilla extracts or pastes or spices such as cinnamon, add them when you are beating together the butter and sugar so that they are well distributed throughout your batter.

CAKE PAN TIPS!

Avoid leaks, drips and cracked cakes with this handy guide to lining a cake pan.

LINE IT UP
Place a sheet of baking paper on the table and lay the cake pan on its side (the long side if it's a rectangular pan) up against one edge of the paper. Measure 2cm above the height of the pan and mark it with a pencil. Using a ruler as a guide, cut the paper at the level of the mark. Repeat on a second piece of baking paper for a round pan, and three times for a square or rectangular one.

THE RIGHT FIT
Place the cake pan flat on another piece of baking paper and trace around the base with a pencil. Then, carefully cut out the shape. Grease the base and sides of the baking pan well with butter. Place the base piece of baking paper in the bottom of the pan, making sure to press it well into the edges. Place the other pieces along the sides of the cake pan, allowing them to overlap slightly.

HANDLES WELL
Leaving a 2cm overhang will help you to remove the cake or slice more easily from the pan.

STAY DRY
Always dry a cake pan completely after washing to prevent it from rusting.

COOL OFF
When the cake is finished baking, remove from oven and leave it in the pan for 5 minutes so it doesn't crack when turning it out – a very hot cake can run the risk of splitting. However, if you leave the cake in the pan too long, it will sweat and go soggy.

STUCK IN
If the cake gets stuck, run a flat-bladed knife around the inside edge of the pan and remove the cake, then the baking paper immediately. Recipes are designed for specific pans, so use the stated size or you run the risk of the cake being over- or under-cooked.

BISCUITS & BITES

FROM LUXE TRIPLE-CHOCOLATE MELTING MOMENTS TO BETTER-FOR-YOU MADELEINES, TURN THE PAGES TO FIND THE PERFECT BISCUIT OR BITE FOR ANY OCCASION.

Choc-mint COOKIES

Get lost in the mo-mint with these mega chocolate cookies.

MAKES 6 **PREP** 20 mins (+ cooling & 20 mins resting) **COOK** 15 mins

125g unsalted butter, chopped, at room temperature
70g (⅓ cup) caster sugar
2 tbs brown sugar
1 tsp vanilla extract
1 egg, lightly whisked
200g (1⅓ cups) plain flour
35g (⅓ cup) cocoa powder, plus extra, to dust
65g (⅓ cup) dark choc chips
6 x 20g Nestlé Mint Patties
Dark chocolate, melted, to decorate
Nestlé Peppermint Crisp, crushed, to decorate

1 Use electric beaters to beat the butter, caster sugar, brown sugar and vanilla in a bowl until pale and creamy. Add the egg and beat until combined. Sift flour and cocoa over butter mixture. Add the choc chips. Stir until combined then turn onto a lightly floured surface. Knead gently until smooth. Shape into a disc and cover with plastic wrap. Place in the freezer for 20 minutes to rest.

2 Preheat the oven to 180°C/160°C fan forced. Line a baking tray with baking paper. Roll out the dough between 2 sheets of baking paper until about 1cm thick. Use a 9cm-diameter round pastry cutter to cut a disc from dough. Use fingers to shape into a 12cm disc. Top with a Mint Pattie, face-side down. Fold the dough over to enclose pattie and gently press to seal. Place, seam-side down, on prepared tray. Repeat with remaining dough and Mint Patties, rerolling scraps of dough, to make 6 cookies. Bake for 15 minutes or until just firm. Set aside to cool slightly.

3 Drizzle melted chocolate over each cookie then sprinkle with the crushed Peppermint Crisp. Allow chocolate to set before serving.

COOK'S TIP

To melt chocolate in the microwave, break chocolate into small pieces. Place in a large microwave-safe bowl. Microwave on high for 20 seconds. Stir and repeat 4 times to prevent seizing.

★★★★★

The crunch was amazing. One bite and you're in heaven!
ARTFULCHARLOTTE

● GLUTEN FREE ● MAKE AHEAD ● FREEZABLE ● EASY ● KID FRIENDLY

Hubba Bubba
DOUGHNUTS

Baked, not fried, these bubblegum doughnuts are ready to pop!

MAKES 15 **PREP** 30 mins (+ cooling) **COOK** 20 mins

250g (1²/₃ cup) plain flour
155g (¾ cup) caster sugar
2 tsp baking powder
½ tsp ground nutmeg
185ml (¾ cup) buttermilk
2 eggs, lightly whisked
2 tbs vegetable oil
Edible gold leaf, to decorate
glaze
35g pkt Hubba Bubba
   Groovy Grape Flavour,
   finely chopped
60ml (¼ cup) thickened
   cream
230g (1½ cups) pure icing
   sugar, sifted
Purple gel food colouring,
   to tint

1 Preheat oven to 220°C/200°C fan forced. Lightly grease two 7cm-diameter, 12-hole silicone doughnut pans.

2 Sift flour, sugar, baking powder and nutmeg into a large bowl. Add buttermilk, egg and oil. Stir until just combined. Spoon mixture into a piping bag fitted with a 1cm plain nozzle. Pipe into prepared pans until two-thirds full. Bake for 7-9 minutes or until doughnuts spring back when lightly touched. Set aside in pan for 1 minute before turning onto a wire rack to cool completely. Repeat with remaining mixture.

3 To make the glaze, place Hubba Bubba and cream in a heatproof bowl over a saucepan of simmering water. Stir until Hubba Bubba has softened. Cook, stirring, until smooth. Remove from heat. Set aside for 5 minutes to cool slightly. Stir in icing sugar and 1-2 tbs of water until glaze is thickened and a ribbon trail forms when the spoon is lifted.

4 Add food colouring to tint glaze mauve. Add a few extra drops then gently stir to create a ripple effect. Dip doughnuts in glaze. Allow excess to drip off. Place on wire rack to set. Decorate with gold leaf.

COOK'S TIP

Don't stop at grape! You can make the doughnut glaze with any bright bubblegum flavour.

● GLUTEN FREE ● MAKE AHEAD ● FREEZABLE ● EASY ● KID FRIENDLY

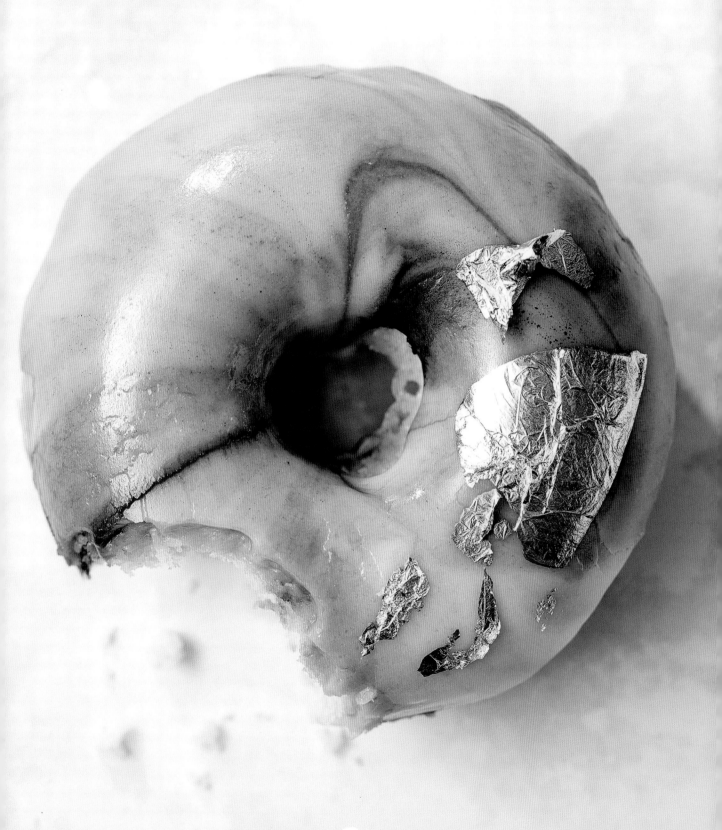

Passionfruit white-choc
GANACHE COOKIES

Passionfruit adds a hint of tang to these rich, buttery choc cookies.

MAKES 16 **PREP** 30 mins (+ chilling, cooling & setting) **COOK** 20 mins

250g unsalted butter,
  chopped, at room
  temperature
200g (1⅓ cups) plain flour
125g (¾ cup) icing sugar
  mixture
35g (⅓ cup) cocoa powder,
  plus extra, to dust
50g (⅓ cup) cornflour
1 tbs milk
passionfruit white choc
  ganache
150g white chocolate,
  chopped
2 tbs thickened cream
Pulp of 2 passionfruit (you'll
  need 2 tbs pulp, see note)

1 Preheat oven to 160°C/140°C fan forced. Line 2 baking trays with baking paper. Use electric beaters to beat the butter in a bowl until very pale and creamy. Sift over the flour, icing sugar, cocoa and cornflour. Add the milk. Use a wooden spoon to stir until combined.

2 Roll level tablespoonfuls of the mixture into balls. Place on the prepared trays, allowing room for spreading. Bake, swapping the trays halfway through cooking, for 20 minutes or until cooked through. Set aside on trays until cooled completely.

3 Meanwhile, make the ganache. Place the white chocolate and cream in a microwave-safe bowl. Microwave on Medium, stirring every 30 seconds, for 1 minute 30 seconds or until melted and smooth. Set aside for 10 minutes to cool. Stir through the passionfruit pulp. Place in the fridge for 1 hour or until thick and spreadable.

4 Place 1 heaped teaspoonful of the ganache on 1 cookie. Sandwich with another cookie. Repeat with remaining ganache and cookies. Set aside until set. Dust with cocoa, to serve.

COOK'S TIP

If you can't find fresh, canned or frozen passionfruit pulp will do the trick.

● GLUTEN FREE ● MAKE AHEAD ● FREEZABLE ● EASY ● KID FRIENDLY

Coconut & sesame
MADELEINES

Light on calories, packed full of flavour – the perfect guilt-free treat!

MAKES 16 **PREP** 10 mins (+ cooling) **COOK** 20 mins

2 tbs spelt flour, plus extra, to dust
2 eggs
1 tsp vanilla extract
55g (¼ cup) raw caster sugar
2 tbs desiccated coconut
2 tbs coconut flour
2 tsp black sesame seeds
½ tsp baking powder
60g butter, melted
Dark chocolate (70% cocoa), melted, to decorate

1 Preheat oven to 180°C/160°C fan forced. Lightly grease 12 madeleine pans. Dust with the extra spelt flour then shake out excess.

2 Use electric beaters to beat the eggs, vanilla and sugar in a large bowl for 5 minutes or until pale and creamy. Use a spatula to fold the spelt flour, desiccated coconut, coconut flour, sesame seeds and baking powder into the egg mixture until just combined. Fold in the butter until just combined.

3 Divide mixture among prepared pans. Bake for 8-10 minutes or until light golden and just cooked through. Carefully turn onto a wire rack to cool. Repeat with the remaining mixture, greasing moulds and dusting with flour between batches.

4 Drizzle the madeleines with the melted chocolate to serve.

COOK'S TIP

To stop them going soggy, make sure that you turn the madeleines onto a wire rack as soon as they're done baking. You can use a palette knife or spatula to help ease them out of their pans.

● GLUTEN FREE ● MAKE AHEAD ● FREEZABLE ● EASY ● KID FRIENDLY

Tahini crackle BISCUITS

Eeny, meeny, tahini! These basic bikkies will melt in your mouth!

MAKES 32 **PREP** 20 mins (+ cooling) **COOK** 15 mins

155g (1½ cups) almond meal
2 tbs coconut flour
½ tsp bicarbonate of soda
½ tsp ground cinnamon
150g (½ cup) tahini
80ml (⅓ cup) honey
55g (⅓ cup) sesame seeds

1 Preheat the oven to 180°C/160°C fan forced. Line 2 baking trays with baking paper.

2 Place the almond meal, coconut flour, bicarb and cinnamon in a large bowl and stir until combined. Add the tahini and honey and stir until well combined. Place sesame seeds in a separate bowl.

3 Roll 2 teaspoonfuls of the tahini mixture into a ball. Roll in the sesame seeds until coated then place on prepared tray. Flatten slightly. Repeat with the remaining tahini mixture to make 32 biscuits.

4 Bake for 12 minutes or until golden. Set aside on the trays to cool completely.

COOK'S TIP

To stop them sticking, use clean, damp hands to roll the tahini mixture into balls.

★★★★★

I could eat these all day – not overly sweet but more-ish. They are a hit!

JP93

● GLUTEN FREE ● MAKE AHEAD ● FREEZABLE ● EASY ● KID FRIENDLY

Red velvet biscuits
WITH GANACHE

Stack the deck with these impressive (but easy) biscuit towers.

MAKES 4 **PREP** 20 mins (+ cooling, resting, 20 mins freezing & 20 mins chilling) **COOK** 30 mins

125g unsalted butter,
  chopped, at room
  temperature
215g (1 cup) caster sugar
1 egg
1 tsp vanilla extract
265g (1¾ cups) plain flour
30g (¼ cup) Dutch process
  cocoa powder
3 tsp red liquid food
  colouring, to tint
½ tsp white vinegar
White chocolate curls,
  to serve
white chocolate ganache
360g white cooking
  chocolate, chopped
160ml (²/₃ cup) thickened
  cream

1 Use electric beaters to beat the butter and sugar in a bowl until pale and creamy. Beat in the egg and vanilla. Slowly beat in the flour until combined. Add the cocoa and beat until combined. Add food colouring to tint red. Beat until evenly coloured. Add the vinegar and beat until combined.

2 Transfer the mixture to a clean work surface. Knead until smooth. Divide into 2 portions. Shape each portion into a disc and cover with plastic wrap. Place in the freezer for 20 minutes or until firm.

3 Preheat oven to 180°C/160°C fan forced. Line a baking tray with baking paper. Roll out 1 portion of dough between 2 sheets of baking paper until 3mm thick. Use a 6.5cm-diameter round fluted pastry cutter to cut 8 circles from dough. Transfer to prepared tray. Bake for 15 minutes or until just firm. Set aside on tray for 5 minutes to cool slightly. Transfer to a wire rack to cool completely. Repeat with remaining dough.

4 To make the ganache, place the chocolate in a heatproof bowl. Place cream in a microwave-safe jug and microwave for 1 minute or until simmering. Pour cream over chocolate. Set aside for 5 minutes or until chocolate has melted. Stir until smooth. Place in the fridge for 20 minutes or until slightly firm. Use a fork to beat until smooth.

5 To assemble, spoon ganache into a piping bag fitted with a 5mm star nozzle. Pipe ganache onto 1 biscuit. Continue layering with another 3 biscuits, finishing with ganache. Top with white chocolate curls. Repeat with remaining biscuits and ganache.

COOK'S TIP

To make chocolate curls, run a vegetable peeler down the back (flat side) of a block of chocolate.

● GLUTEN FREE ● MAKE AHEAD ● FREEZABLE ● EASY ● KID FRIENDLY

Chamomile jam BISCUITS

Chamomile adds a delicate floral twist to traditional jam bikkies.

MAKES 8 **PREP** 50 mins (+ 2 hours resting, 30 mins chilling & cooling) **COOK** 25 mins

2 tbs chamomile loose leaf tea
120g caster sugar
250g unsalted butter, chopped, at room temperature
¼ tsp vanilla bean paste
Large pinch of salt
80g (²/₃ cup) almond meal
1 egg
340g (2¼ cups) plain flour, plus extra, to dust
Good-quality strawberry jam, to sandwich

1 Place chamomile in a small food processor and process until finely chopped. Pass through a coarse sieve and discard any large solids. Return the sieved chamomile to the food processor. Add the sugar and process until well combined.

2 Transfer sugar mixture to a large bowl. Add butter, vanilla and salt. Use electric beaters to beat until pale and creamy. Add almond meal and egg. Beat until combined. Add flour. Beat until just combined. Turn dough onto a lightly floured surface. Divide in half. Shape into discs. Wrap in plastic wrap and place in the fridge for at least 2 hours or overnight to rest.

3 Preheat oven to 180°C/160°C fan forced. Line 3 baking trays with baking paper. Roll out 1 portion of dough between 2 sheets of baking paper until 4mm thick. Use a 7cm round fluted cutter to cut 8 discs from dough, re-rolling scraps. Place on a prepared tray. Place tray in the fridge for 15 minutes to chill.

4 Roll out the remaining dough. Cut another 8 discs, re-rolling scraps. Use a 4cm-diameter flower-shaped cutter to cut out the centre of each disc. Place the discs on a prepared tray. Place the flower shapes on the remaining tray. Place the trays in fridge for 15 minutes to chill.

5 Bake discs, swapping trays halfway through cooking, for 12-14 minutes or until light golden. Bake flower shapes for 7-8 minutes or until light golden. Set aside on trays to cool completely.

6 Spread whole round biscuits evenly with spoonfuls of jam. Dust cut round biscuits with icing sugar. Sandwich together. Serve with the flower biscuits.

COOK'S TIP

To stop jam spilling out the sides, only spread until it almost reaches the edge of the biscuit, leaving a little border. It will spread to the edge when you sandwich the biscuits together.

● GLUTEN FREE ● MAKE AHEAD ● FREEZABLE ● EASY ● KID FRIENDLY

Chocolate melting MOMENTS

These triple-choc morsels are seriously decadent.

MAKES 14 **PREP** 40 mins (+ cooling) **COOK** 20 mins

250g unsalted butter, chopped, at room temperature

125g (¾ cup) icing sugar mixture, sifted

2 tsp vanilla extract

250g (1⅔ cups) plain flour, sifted, plus extra to dust

45g (¼ cup) rice flour, sifted

30g (¼ cup) dark cocoa powder, sifted

Melted dark chocolate, to serve

filling

100g unsalted butter, at room temperature

60g (⅓ cup) icing sugar mixture

100g dark chocolate, melted, cooled

1 Preheat oven to 180°C/160°C fan forced. Line 2 baking trays with baking paper. Use electric beaters to beat the butter and icing sugar in a large bowl until smooth and creamy. Beat in the vanilla.

2 Use a large metal spoon to fold the flours and cocoa into the butter mixture. Using lightly floured hands, roll tablespoonfuls of the mixture into balls. Place on the prepared trays, allowing room for spreading. Use a lightly floured fork to flatten. Bake for 15-20 minutes or until firm. Set aside to cool completely.

3 To make the filling, use electric beaters to beat the butter and icing sugar in a bowl until pale and creamy. Add the chocolate and beat until smooth. Spoon into a piping bag fitted with a 5mm star nozzle. Pipe mixture over half the biscuits. Top with remaining biscuits then drizzle over the melted chocolate.

COOK'S TIP

If your butter is still cold when you're ready to bake, place it in a microwave-safe dish and microwave on Medium-Low for 15-30 seconds, being careful not to melt it.

★★★★★

They were perfect! My mum and dad think they are great.

ICE4CREAM

● GLUTEN FREE ● MAKE AHEAD ● FREEZABLE ● EASY ● KID FRIENDLY

Hazelnut & fig CACAO BISCUITS

Hazelnut meal keeps these bikkies gluten-free.

MAKES 12 **PREP** 20 mins (+ cooling) **COOK** 20 mins

155g (1½ cups) hazelnut meal
80g dried figs, finely chopped
2 tbs raw cacao nibs
1¼ tsp gluten-free baking powder
¼ tsp ground cinnamon
Pinch of salt
60ml (¼ cup) melted coconut oil
2½ tbs maple syrup
maple drizzle
2 tsp solidified coconut oil
1¼ tsp maple syrup
1 tsp raw cacao powder

1 Preheat the oven to 175°C/155°C fan forced. Line a large baking tray with baking paper.

2 Place the hazelnut meal, figs, cacao nibs, baking powder, cinnamon and salt in a bowl and stir until combined. Make a well in the centre. Add the oil and maple syrup and stir until combined. Roll heaped tablespoonfuls of the mixture into balls. Place on the prepared tray. Flatten slightly. Bake for 20 minutes or until golden. Set aside on tray to cool.

3 Meanwhile, make the drizzle. Place oil and maple syrup in a microwave-safe bowl. Microwave on Medium-High for 30 seconds. Add cacao powder and stir until combined. Set aside for 10 minutes, stirring occasionally, until thickened slightly.

4 Drizzle over biscuits. Set aside until the drizzle hardens slightly before serving.

COOK'S TIP

Check the bottom of the biscuits – they'll turn dark golden once they're cooked, and will crisp up once they're cool.

★★★★★

OMG these are to die for!! Super easy to make, healthy and delicious!
MEGANHARRIS03

● GLUTEN FREE ● MAKE AHEAD ● FREEZABLE ● EASY ● KID FRIENDLY

Hot cross bun JAM DOUGHNUTS

Spiced hot cross doughnuts with a bursting berry jam centre.

MAKES 28 **PREP** 45 mins (+ 1 hour 50 mins proving) **COOK** 15 mins

1 tsp instant dried yeast
1½ tbs warm water
100g (½ cup) caster sugar
½ tsp mixed spice
350g (2⅓ cups) plain flour,
　plus extra, to dust
1 egg, lightly whisked
80ml (⅓ cup milk), warmed
50g butter, melted
½ tsp vanilla extract
115g (⅓ cup) strawberry jam
Vegetable oil, to shallow fry

1 Place the yeast, water and 1 tsp sugar in a small jug. Whisk until the yeast dissolves. Set aside in a warm, draught-free place for 5 minutes or until frothy.

2 Place mixed spice, 300g (2 cups) flour, 55g (¼ cup) remaining sugar and a pinch of salt in a large bowl. Stir until combined. Make a well in centre. Add yeast mixture, egg, milk, butter and vanilla. Stir until a dough forms. Turn onto a lightly floured surface. Knead for 2 minutes or until smooth. Transfer to a greased bowl. Cover with a damp tea towel. Set aside in a draught-free place for 1 hour 30 minutes or until doubled in size.

3 Line 2 baking trays with baking paper. Use your fist to punch back the dough. Turn onto a lightly floured surface and knead for 2 minutes or until smooth. Roll 1 tablespoonful of the dough into a ball and place on a prepared tray. Repeat with the remaining dough.

4 Place remaining flour in a small bowl. Add 2 tbs water. Whisk until smooth. Spoon mixture into a sealable plastic bag. Snip off 1 corner, 5mm from end. Pipe a cross onto each dough ball. Set aside in a warm, draught-free place for 20 minutes to prove.

5 Spoon jam into a piping bag fitted with a 7mm plain nozzle. Place remaining sugar in a shallow bowl. Add oil to a frying pan to come 2cm up side of pan. Heat over medium-high heat. Fry dough balls, in batches, for 1-2 minutes each side or until golden and puffed. Transfer to a tray lined with paper towel. Drain for 10 seconds. Make a small hole in each doughnut. Pipe jam into each hole. Toss doughnuts in sugar.

COOK'S TIP

Don't rush the resting and proving time: if they are under-proofed, the doughnuts may turn out dense.

● GLUTEN FREE ● MAKE AHEAD ● FREEZABLE ● EASY ● KID FRIENDLY

Honey jumble
BISCUITS

These simple spiced bikkies with royal icing are a classic!

MAKES 20 **PREP** 40 mins (+ cooling, 1 hour resting & 30 mins setting) **COOK** 15 mins

60g unsalted butter,
   chopped
125ml (½ cup) honey
55g (¼ cup, firmly packed)
   brown sugar
225 (1½ cups) plain flour
½ tsp bicarbonate of soda
1 tsp ground ginger
½ tsp mixed spice
¼ tsp ground cloves
2 tsp milk
icing
1 egg white
230g (1½ cups) pure icing
   sugar, sifted
2 tsp fresh lemon juice
Pink liquid food colouring,
   to tint

1 Place the butter, honey and sugar in a saucepan over medium heat. Cook, stirring, for 3 minutes or until melted and smooth. Bring to the boil. Remove from heat. Set aside for 10 minutes to cool slightly.

2 Sift the flour, bicarb, ginger, mixed spice and cloves over the butter mixture. Add the milk. Stir until combined. Cover and set aside for 1 hour or until thickened.

3 Preheat the oven to 180°C/160°C fan forced. Line 2 baking trays with baking paper. Turn the dough onto a lightly floured surface and knead until smooth. Divide the dough into quarters. Roll 1 quarter into a 25cm-long log. Cut into 5cm pieces. Place on the prepared trays, allowing room for spreading. Flatten each piece of dough until 5mm-thick. Repeat with the remaining dough quarters. Bake for 10-12 minutes or until light golden. Set aside on tray for 10 minutes to cool slightly before transferring to a wire rack to cool completely.

4 To make the icing, whisk the egg white in a bowl until foamy. Gradually whisk in the icing sugar until combined. Stir in the lemon juice. Spoon half the mixture into a separate bowl. Add food colouring to tint pink. Stir until evenly coloured. Top half the biscuits with the pink icing and half with the white icing. Set biscuits aside for 30 minutes or until set.

COOK'S TIP

These biscuits should still be a little soft when baked. Don't overbake – they will firm up once cooled.

● GLUTEN FREE ● MAKE AHEAD ● FREEZABLE ● EASY ● KID FRIENDLY

34

Healthier chocolate COOKIES

These better-for-you bakes make a nourishing lunch box treat.

MAKES 30 **PREP** 10 mins (+ 30 mins resting & cooling) **COOK** 15 mins

10 dates, pitted, finely
   chopped
60ml (¼ cup) boiling water
90g (1 cup) rolled oats
400g can chickpeas,
   drained, rinsed
45g (½ cup) desiccated
   coconut
2 tbs cocoa powder,
   plus extra
1 tsp baking powder
75g (⅓ cup) solid coconut
   oil, melted, cooled
1 egg
1 tsp vanilla extract

1 Preheat oven to 180°C/160°C fan forced. Line 2 baking trays with baking paper. Place dates in a heatproof bowl and cover with the water. Set aside for 2 minutes or until softened. Use a fork to mash.

2 Place oats in a food processor and process until chopped. Add the dates, chickpeas, coconut, cocoa powder, baking powder, coconut oil, egg and vanilla. Process until combined. Transfer to a bowl and set aside for 30 minutes or until thickened.

3 Roll level tablespoonfuls of the mixture into balls and place on prepared trays. Dip fork in extra cocoa. Press into cookie to flatten slightly. Turn the fork and gently press into cookie again to create a hash pattern. Repeat with remaining cookies.

4 Bake cookies for 12 minutes. Set aside on trays for 5 minutes cool slightly before transferring to a wire rack to cool completely. Store in an airtight container for up to 4 days.

COOK'S TIP

Dip your fork in cocoa after flattening each cookie, or as needed, to prevent the dough sticking.

★★★★★

They were soooo yummy! Not too sweet, which I love.

JUDYMG83

● GLUTEN FREE ● MAKE AHEAD ● FREEZABLE ● EASY ● KID FRIENDLY

10
minutes
prep

Double-choc
'WAGON WHEELS'

Get on a roll with these no-bake biscuits! They're ready in 20 minutes.

MAKES 14 **PREP** 20 mins (+ 10 mins setting) **COOK** 5 mins

2 x 250g pkt plain
   chocolate biscuits
2 tbs raspberry jam
7 white marshmallows,
   halved
400g dark chocolate melts,
   melted
Silver and red sprinkles,
   to decorate

1 Line 2 trays with baking paper. Place half the biscuits, base-side up, on 1 tray. Spread biscuits with ½ tsp jam. Place 3 of the remaining biscuits on a microwave-safe plate. Place half a marshmallow in the centre of each biscuit. Microwave on High for 10 seconds or until the marshmallows melt slightly.

2 Working quickly, top with a jam-covered biscuit, pressing lightly to sandwich together. Return the biscuits to the tray. Set aside for 5 minutes to set. Repeat with the remaining marshmallows, biscuits and jam-covered biscuits to make 14 sandwiches.

3 Use a fork to carefully dip the biscuits into the melted chocolate to coat. Tap on the edge of the bowl to remove excess chocolate. Place on remaining prepared tray. Top with sprinkles then set aside for 10 minutes to set.

COOK'S TIP

No sprinkles? Decorate these bikkies with desiccated coconut, pepitas, Smarties, lollies or anything your heart desires!

★ ★ ★ ★ ★

This is now a favourite birthday party treat for our family!

AGREAR

● GLUTEN FREE ● MAKE AHEAD ● FREEZABLE ● EASY ● KID FRIENDLY

20
minutes
prep

Anzac
BISCUITS

Whip up a batch of these simple bikkies and watch them disappear!

MAKES 26 **PREP** 15 mins **COOK** 15 mins

155g (¾ cup) caster sugar
150g (1 cup) plain flour
140g (1½ cups) rolled oats
55g (1 cup) McKenzie's
   Moist Flakes Coconut
120g butter, melted
60ml (¼ cup) golden syrup
½ tsp bicarbonate of soda
1 tbs boiling water

1 Preheat the oven to 180°C/160°C fan forced.
Line 2 baking trays with baking paper.

2 Place the sugar, flour, oats and coconut in a bowl
and stir until combined. Make a well in the centre.
Add the butter and golden syrup. Place the bicarb
and water in a small bowl and stir until combined.
Add to the well and stir until combined.

3 Roll tablespoonfuls of the mixture into balls and
place on prepared trays, 5cm apart. Flatten
slightly. Bake for 12-15 minutes or until golden brown.
Set aside on trays to cool completely.

COOK'S TIP

These biscuits
can be stored
in an airtight
container for
up to 2 weeks.

Quick and easy. Texture and taste was just superb. Will make again.
LEHA123123

● GLUTEN FREE ● MAKE AHEAD ● FREEZABLE ● EASY ● KID FRIENDLY

15
minutes
prep

Rainbow
SHORTBREAD

Twirl and swirl your way to the sweetest technicolour treats.

MAKES 40 **PREP** 30 mins (+ 5 mins resting & cooling) **COOK** 10 mins

185g butter, at room
   temperature
120g (²/₃ cup) icing sugar
1 tsp vanilla extract
1 egg, lightly whisked
265g (1¾ cups) plain flour,
   sifted, plus extra
½ tsp baking powder, sifted
Red, blue and yellow liquid
   food colouring

1 Preheat the oven to 180°C/160°C fan forced. Line 2 baking trays with baking paper. Place the butter, icing sugar and vanilla in bowl and stir until just combined. Add the egg and stir until combined (mixture may look curdled but will come together when flour is added). Add the flour and baking powder and stir until the dough comes together. If too soft to roll, add a little extra flour.

2 Divide the dough into 3 portions. Add red food colouring to 1 portion and knead gently until dough is bright red. Repeat with the remaining portions to make blue and yellow dough. Set aside for 5 minutes to rest. Roll each portion into marble-sized balls. Gently roll 1 ball of each colour together to form a tri-coloured ball. Gently roll each ball into a log about 8cm long. Coil into a snail shape. Tuck the end under and twist to create a swirl effect.

3 Bake, swapping trays halfway through cooking, for 8-10 minutes or until just cooked. Set aside on trays for 5 minutes to cool slightly before transferring to wire rack to cool completely.

COOK'S TIP

When combining the little dough balls, don't be tempted to dust with flour, or the balls won't stick together.

★ ★ ★ ★ ★

My kids loved them! Will make again.

NAOMISANJOSE

● GLUTEN FREE ● MAKE AHEAD ● FREEZABLE ● EASY ● KID FRIENDLY

Chocolate & cream
BISCUITS

Get ahead! Bake and freeze these bikkies then assemble on the day.

MAKES 36 **PREP** 40 mins (+ 40 mins chilling) **COOK** 30 mins

250g butter, at room
    temperature
215g (1 cup) caster sugar
1 tsp vanilla extract
1 egg
190g (1¼ cup) plain flour
115g (¾ cup) self-raising
    flour
70g (²/₃ cup) cocoa powder
filling
345g (2¼ cups) icing sugar
125g unsalted butter,
    at room temperature
1 tbs milk
1 tsp vanilla extract

1 Line 2 baking trays with baking paper. Use electric beaters to beat the butter, sugar and vanilla in a bowl for 3 minutes or until pale and creamy. Add the egg and beat until well combined. Sift flours and cocoa over butter mixture. Stir until combined. Turn mixture onto a lightly floured surface and shape into a ball. Divide dough in half. Cover with plastic wrap and place in the fridge for 10 minutes.

2 Preheat oven to 180°C/160°C fan forced. Roll out 1 dough portion between 2 sheets of baking paper until 5mm thick. Slide the paper with the dough onto a tray and place in the fridge for 10-15 minutes or until firm.

3 Use a 4.5cm-diameter round pastry cutter to cut discs from dough. Place on lined trays, about 2cm apart. Bake for 12-15 minutes or until just firm. Set aside on trays for 5 minutes to cool slightly before transferring to a wire rack to cool completely. Repeat with remaining dough. Re-roll scraps and place in fridge for 10-15 minutes. Repeat cutting and baking.

4 For the filling, use electric beaters to beat the icing sugar, butter, milk and vanilla in a bowl for 3 minutes or until pale and creamy.

5 Spoon filling into a piping bag fitted with a 1.5cm plain nozzle. Pipe a generous amount onto the base of half of the biscuits. Sandwich with remaining biscuits.

COOK'S TIP

Unfilled biscuits can be frozen in an airtight containers for up to 1 month.

● GLUTEN FREE ● MAKE AHEAD ● FREEZABLE ● EASY ● KID FRIENDLY

I made these for a family gathering. Everybody (young and old) LOVED them. Would definitely make again.

BEXMULLER

Lemon drop BISCUITS

Jam drops get a citrus twist! Custard powder makes them extra crisp.

MAKES 30 **PREP** 20 mins (+ 5 mins resting & 30 mins cooling) **COOK** 15 mins

125g unsalted butter, chopped, at room temperature
100g (½ cup) caster sugar
1 tbs finely grated lemon rind
1 egg, lightly whisked
150g (1 cup) self-raising flour
35g (¼ cup) custard powder
105g (⅓ cup) bought lemon curd

1 Preheat the oven to 180°C/160°C fan forced. Line 2 baking trays with baking paper.

2 Use electric beaters to beat the butter, sugar and lemon rind in a large bowl until pale and creamy. Add the egg and beat until well combined. Sift over the flour and custard powder. Stir until combined then set aside for 5 minutes to rest.

3 Use lightly floured hands to roll 2 teaspoonfuls of the mixture into balls. Place on prepared trays, about 5cm apart. Use a lightly floured finger to make an indent in the centre of each ball. Spoon ½ tsp lemon curd into each indent.

4 Bake, swapping trays halfway through cooking, for 12-15 minutes or until golden. Set aside on trays for 30 minutes or until cooled completely.

COOK'S TIP

Don't have any lemon curd? Swap it out for your favourite jam and omit the lemon rind from the dough.

★★★★★

When I make these there is never any leftovers. Easy and delicious.

ROBYNKIDDELL

 GLUTEN FREE ● MAKE AHEAD ● FREEZABLE ● EASY ● KID FRIENDLY

Mini jam
SHORTBREADS

These soft sandwich bikkies are light, fluffy and perfect with a cuppa.

MAKES 30 **PREP** 30 mins (+ cooling) **COOK** 10 mins

5 eggs, separated
70g (⅓ cup) caster sugar
150g (1 cup) plain flour
210g (⅔ cup) raspberry jam
icing
380g (2½ cups) icing
    sugar mixture
30g butter
2 tbs boiling water,
    plus 1 tsp extra
2 tsp cocoa powder

1 Preheat oven to 200°C/180°C fan forced. Line 2 baking trays with baking paper.

2 Use electric beaters to whisk the egg whites in a clean, dry bowl until firm peaks form. Gradually add the sugar, whisking constantly until thick and glossy. Whisk together the egg yolks in a bowl until pale and creamy. Add to the egg white mixture. Use a large metal spoon to fold until just combined. Sift flour over mixture. Fold until combined.

3 Spoon half the mixture into a piping bag fitted with a 1cm plain nozzle. Pipe 4cm discs onto the prepared trays, allowing room for spreading. Bake, swapping the trays halfway through cooking, for 7-10 minutes or until light golden. Transfer to a wire rack to cool. Repeat with the remaining mixture.

4 Make icing. Sift the icing sugar into a large bowl. Add the butter. Pour the boiling water over the butter and stir until well combined. Spoon half the icing into a separate bowl. Add cocoa and extra water to half of the icing. Stir until well combined.

5 Spread 1 tsp jam onto the base of half the cakes. Spread tops of half of the remaining cakes with the white icing and half with the chocolate icing. Sandwich with the jam cakes.

COOK'S TIP

If you don't have time to make the icing, try drizzling over melted chocolate instead.

★★★★★

Very tasty.

AVBSATHIK

● GLUTEN FREE ● MAKE AHEAD ● FREEZABLE ● EASY ● KID FRIENDLY

Brownie
DOUGHNUTS

Turn a box of brownie mix into these cheat's chocolate doughnuts.

MAKES 12 **PREP** 20 mins (+ 5 mins cooling & setting) **COOK** 15 mins

380g pkt Green's Chocolate
   Brownie mix
2 eggs, lightly whisked
80g butter, melted
100g dark chocolate,
   finely chopped
300g (2 cups) icing sugar
   mixture
2 tbs cocoa powder
2½ tbs boiling water
Milk and white chocolate,
   grated, to decorate

1 Preheat oven to 180°C/160°C fan forced. Spray two 7cm-diameter, 12-hole silicone doughnut pans with oil spray.

2 Place brownie mix, egg and butter in a bowl and stir until well combined. Add dark chocolate and stir until combined. Spoon mixture into prepared pans. Use a spoon dipped in water to smooth surface.

3 Bake for 10-15 minutes or until just firm. Set aside in the pans for 2 minutes to cool slightly. Transfer to a wire rack set on top of a tray to cool completely.

4 Meanwhile, sift icing sugar and cocoa into a large heatproof bowl. Add the boiling water, a little at a time, to make a spreadable icing (it should have the consistency of thickened cream). Place bowl over a saucepan of simmering water (make sure bowl doesn't touch the water) and stir until thin and pourable.

5 Drizzle the icing over the doughnuts. Immediately sprinkle with the grated chocolate. Set aside until the icing has set. Serve.

COOK'S TIP

Make sure you fill the doughnut pans right to the top (or as close as you can) as this will give your doughnuts a better shape!

● GLUTEN FREE ● MAKE AHEAD ● FREEZABLE ● EASY ● KID FRIENDLY

Buttery funfetti
BISCUITS

Dig into your sprinkle stash for these easy party-on-a-plate bikkies.

MAKES 45 **PREP** 1 hour (+ cooling) **COOK** 10 mins

225g (1½ cups) plain flour
½ tsp cream of tartar
½ tsp bicarbonate of soda
155g (¾ cup) caster sugar
115g butter, melted, cooled
1 egg, lightly whisked
1 tsp vanilla extract
¼ cup sprinkles, plus extra,
   to decorate

1 Preheat oven to 180°C/160°C fan forced. Grease 4 large baking trays. Line with baking paper.
2 Sift the flour, cream of tartar and bicarb into a large bowl. Add the sugar and stir until combined. Add the butter, egg and vanilla and stir until well combined. Stir in the sprinkles. Roll 2 teaspoonfuls of mixture into a ball. Place on 1 prepared tray. Repeat with remaining mixture, placing balls 5cm apart. Flatten slightly. Top with extra sprinkles.
3 Bake 2 trays at a time, swapping trays halfway through cooking, for 10 minutes or until just firm to the touch but not browned. Set aside on trays for 5 minutes to cool slightly before transferring to a baking paper-lined wire rack to cool completely.

COOK'S TIP

Store these biscuits in an airtight container for up to 1 week.

★★★★★

Great recipe for the kids to make. Yum!
CONOMY

● GLUTEN FREE ● MAKE AHEAD ● FREEZABLE ● EASY ● KID FRIENDLY

Spiced molasses
COOKIES

These gluten-free bikkies are loaded with better-for-you ingredients.

MAKES 20 **PREP** 20 mins (+ 20 mins chilling & cooling) **COOK** 20 mins

115g (¾ cup) buckwheat flour
45g (¼ cup) brown rice flour
40g (⅓ cup) almond meal
40g (¼ cup) quinoa flour
25g (¼ cup) quinoa flakes
35g (¼ cup) panela sugar, plus 1½ tbs, extra
2½ tsp ground ginger
1½ tsp ground cinnamon
1 tsp bicarbonate of soda
¼ tsp ground cloves
80ml (⅓ cup) molasses
60ml (¼ cup) melted coconut oil
1 egg

1 Preheat the oven to 180°C/160°C fan forced. Line 2 baking trays with baking paper. Place the buckwheat flour, rice flour, almond meal, quinoa flour, quinoa flakes, sugar, ginger, cinnamon, bicarb and cloves in a large bowl. Stir until combined then make a well in the centre.

2 Place the molasses, coconut oil and egg in a jug and use a fork to whisk until combined. Add to the well and stir until a sticky dough comes together. Place in the fridge for 20 minutes or until firm.

3 Place extra sugar on a plate. Roll tablespoonfuls of mixture into balls and then quickly roll in the sugar. Place balls on prepared trays, allowing room for spreading. Flatten slightly. Bake, swapping trays after 10 minutes of cooking, for 16 minutes or until crisp. Set aside on trays to cool completely.

COOK'S TIP

To prevent sticking, use slightly damp palms to gently flatten the cookies before baking.

● GLUTEN FREE ● MAKE AHEAD ● FREEZABLE ● EASY ● KID FRIENDLY

Choc-mint brownies
BISCUITS

10 minutes is all takes to prep these fudgy chocolate bikkies.

MAKES 24 **PREP** 10 mins (+ cooling) **COOK** 35 mins

40g unsalted butter, chopped
250g dark chocolate, chopped
2 eggs, lightly whisked
1 tsp vanilla extract
220g (1 cup) white sugar
40g (¼ cup) plain flour
30g (¼ cup) Dutch cocoa powder
½ tsp baking powder
Pinch of salt
mint filling
250g cream cheese, at room temperature
70g (⅓ cup) caster sugar
20g butter, at room temperature
2 drops peppermint essence
Green liquid food colouring, to tint

1 Preheat oven to 180°C/160°C fan forced. Grease 2 baking trays. Line with baking paper.

2 Place butter and chocolate in a heatproof bowl over a saucepan of simmering water (make sure the bowl doesn't touch the water). Use a metal spoon to stir until melted. Remove from heat. Quickly add egg, vanilla, sugar, flour, cocoa, baking powder and salt and stir until just combined. Place tablespoonfuls of mixture onto prepared trays. Bake for 12-15 minutes or until just set. Set aside on trays to cool.

3 Meanwhile, to make the mint filling. Place cream cheese, caster sugar, butter and mint essence in a bowl and stir until combined. Add food colouring to tint green and stir until evenly coloured. Pipe onto biscuits and sandwich together.

COOK'S TIP

These biscuits will spread while they bake, so make sure to allow plenty of room between them.

● GLUTEN FREE ● MAKE AHEAD ● FREEZABLE ● EASY ● KID FRIENDLY

10
minutes
prep

Chocolate & vanilla
ZEBRA BISCUITS

Earn your baking stripes with these magic mocha biscuits.

MAKES 30 **PREP** 40 mins (+ chilling & cooling) **COOK** 20 mins

200g butter, at room temperature
150g (1 cup) icing sugar mixture
1 tsp vanilla bean paste
1 egg
300g (2 cups) plain flour, sifted
75g (½ cup) self-raising flour, sifted
3 tsp espresso coffee granules
2 tsp cocoa powder, sifted
250g dark chocolate (70% cocoa)
50g Copha, chopped
60g chocolate-coated coffee beans

1 Use electric beaters to beat the butter, icing sugar and vanilla in a bowl until combined. Add the egg and beat until just combined. Add the flours. Stir until a soft dough comes together. Divide dough in half. Lightly knead coffee and cocoa into 1 half. Roll out between 2 sheets of baking paper into a 5mm-thick, 24cm square. Repeat the rolling with the plain dough. Transfer paper and dough to 2 separate baking trays. Place in the fridge for 20 minutes or until firm.

2 Preheat oven to 180°C/160°C fan forced. Line 2 baking trays with baking paper. Cut each square of dough into four 6cm lengths. Stack dough together alternately, brushing with a little water in between, to stick. Cut stack in half. Secure together to create a tall stack of 16 layers. Place in the fridge for 20 minutes or until firm. Trim the sides to make a rectangular shape. Place stack sideways on a clean chopping board (this makes it easier to slice the dough evenly). Cut into 5mm-thick slices.

3 Place the biscuits 1cm apart on prepared trays. Bake for 10-15 minutes or until lightly browned. Set aside on trays for 5 minutes to cool slightly before transferring to a wire rack to cool completely.

4 Place chocolate and Copha in a microwave safe bowl. Microwave on medium-high, stirring every 30 seconds, for 1-2 minutes or until smooth. Dip the biscuits at an angle into chocolate, allowing excess to drip off. Transfer to lined tray. Top with a chocolate coated coffee bean. Set aside to set.

COOK'S TIP

If you don't like chocolate coated coffee beans, you can swap them out. Try chocolate coated nuts, dried fruit or popcorn instead. Alternatively leave them out altogether.

● GLUTEN FREE ● MAKE AHEAD ● FREEZABLE ● EASY ● KID FRIENDLY

Anzac biscuits with BUTTERCREAM

Turn the classic biscuit up a notch with a lush golden syrup filling.

MAKES 10 **PREP** 25 mins (+ cooling) **COOK** 20 mins

150g (1 cup) plain flour
90g (1 cup) rolled oats
215g (1 cup) caster sugar
65g (¾ cup) desiccated
  coconut
125g butter, chopped
2 tbs boiling water
1 tbs golden syrup
½ tsp bicarbonate of soda
golden syrup buttercream
100g butter, at room
  temperature
1¼ cups icing sugar mixture
1½ tbs golden syrup

1 Preheat oven to 180°C/160°C fan forced. Line 2 baking trays with baking paper. Sift the flour into a bowl. Add the oats, sugar and coconut. Stir until well combined. Make a well in the centre.

2 Place the butter, water and golden syrup in a small saucepan over high heat. Cook, stirring, for 3 minutes or until melted and smooth. Remove from heat. Add the bicarb and stir until combined.

3 Add the butter mixture to the oat mixture and stir until well combined. Roll 2 rounded teaspoonfuls of the mixture into balls. Place the balls 3cm apart on prepared trays. Flatten slightly. Bake, swapping trays halfway through, for 12-14 minutes or until golden. Set aside on trays for 5 minutes to cool slightly before transferring to a wire rack to cool completely.

4 Meanwhile, make the buttercream. Use electric beaters to beat the butter until pale and creamy. Gradually add the icing sugar and golden syrup, beating constantly until well combined.

5 Sandwich the Anzac biscuits with the buttercream to serve.

COOK'S TIP

For perfectly thick and glossy buttercream, make sure to beat the butter for at least 4-5 minutes or until it is pale and aerated.

● GLUTEN FREE ● MAKE AHEAD ● FREEZABLE ● EASY ● KID FRIENDLY

Love this recipe. A favourite for my family and neighbours.

JDKINGSFORD

Cheesecake thumbprint
COOKIES

Cream cheese in the dough makes these cookies rich and moist.

MAKES 25 **PREP** 15 mins (+ cooling) **COOK** 15 mins

155g (¾ cup) caster sugar
125g cream cheese, at room
    temperature, chopped
125g unsalted butter,
    at room temperature,
    chopped
2 tsp vanilla extract
250g (1²/₃ cups) plain flour,
    plus extra
155g (½ cup) raspberry jam
75g white chocolate, melted
2 tsp desiccated coconut

1 Preheat oven to 160°C/140°C fan forced. Line 2 baking trays with baking paper. Use electric beaters to beat the sugar, cream cheese and butter in a bowl until pale and creamy. Beat in the vanilla. Use a spatula to fold in the flour until just combined.

2 Roll level tablespoonfuls of the mixture into balls. Place on the prepared trays. Dip your thumb in flour and use to make a 2.5cm indent in each biscuit. Place a spoonful of jam into each indent. Bake for 15 minutes or until light golden underneath (biscuits will still be pale on top). Set aside on trays for 5 minutes to cool slightly before transferring to a wire rack to cool completely. Drizzle chocolate over cookies and sprinkle with coconut to serve.

COOK'S TIP

Swap out raspberry jam for apricot, strawberry or lemon curd, and drizzle with milk or dark chocolate.

Easy, delicious and quick. No complaints from anyone at home!
MMMICECREAMMM

● GLUTEN FREE ● MAKE AHEAD ● FREEZABLE ● EASY ● KID FRIENDLY

15
minutes
prep

Fairy bread melting MOMENTS

These rainbow melting moments are all dressed up for the party!

MAKES 15 **PREP** 30 mins (+ cooling) **COOK** 20 mins

250g butter, chopped,
   at room temperature
60g (⅓ cup) icing sugar
   mixture
1 tsp vanilla extract
225g (1½ cups) plain flour
70g (½ cup) custard powder,
   plus extra
120g (½ cup) hundreds and
   thousands, plus extra,
   to decorate

filling
100g butter, chopped,
   at room temperature
1 tsp vanilla extract
125g (¾ cup) icing sugar
   mixture

1 Preheat oven to 170°C/150°C fan forced.
Line 2 large baking trays with baking paper.
Use electric beaters to beat the butter, icing sugar
and vanilla in a bowl until pale and creamy.

2 Sift flour and custard powder over butter mixture.
Use a flat-bladed knife in a cutting motion to mix
until a soft dough comes together. Add hundreds
and thousands. Stir until well combined. Roll level
tablespoonfuls of dough into balls. Place on the
prepared trays, allowing room for spreading. Use
a fork dipped in extra custard powder to press balls
into 4cm discs (they should be about 1.5cm thick).

3 Bake, swapping trays halfway through, for
18 minutes. Set aside on trays for 5 minutes to cool
slightly. Transfer to a wire rack to cool completely.

4 To make the filling, use electric beaters to beat
the butter and vanilla in a bowl until pale and
creamy. Gradually add the icing sugar, beating
constantly, until well combined.

5 Spoon the filling into a piping bag fitted with
a 2cm plain nozzle. Pipe onto the base of half
the biscuits. Sandwich with the remaining biscuits,
base-side down. Place the extra hundreds and
thousands in a bowl and press the side of each
biscuit to coat the edge of the filling.

COOK'S TIP

Don't have a
piping bag? You
can spread the
filling onto the
biscuits instead.

● GLUTEN FREE ● MAKE AHEAD ● FREEZABLE ● EASY ● KID FRIENDLY

Rocky road cake mix
COOKIES

Thought cake mix was just for cake? Think again!

MAKES 16 **PREP** 20 mins (+ cooling & 15 mins resting) **COOK** 10 mins

440g pkt Green's Classic Chocolate Cake mix

70g (⅓ cup) dark choc chips, plus extra, to decorate

55g (⅓ cup) salted peanuts, coarsely chopped, plus extra, coarsely chopped, to decorate

25g (⅓ cup) shredded coconut, plus extra, to decorate

20g (⅓ cup) mini marshmallows, plus extra, to decorate

75g butter, melted, cooled

1 egg, lightly whisked

60ml (¼ cup) boiling water

1 Preheat oven to 180°C/160°C fan forced. Line 2 baking trays with baking paper.

2 Place cake mix in a large bowl. Add the choc chips, peanuts, coconut and marshmallows. Make a well in the centre. Add the butter and egg. Use a spatula to stir until well combined.

3 Roll heaped tablespoonfuls of the mixture into balls. Place on prepared trays, allowing room for spreading. Flatten slightly. Bake for 10 minutes. Set aside on trays for 5 minutes to cool slightly before transferring to a wire rack to cool completely.

4 Place the icing mix and boiling water in a bowl. Stir until smooth. Drizzle icing over the biscuits. Working quickly, sprinkle with the extra choc chips, peanuts, coconut and marshmallows. Set aside for 15 minutes or until icing is set then serve.

COOK'S TIP

Get creative with the mix-ins and toppings! Any nuts, soft lollies or dried fruit will work just as well.

● GLUTEN FREE ● MAKE AHEAD ● FREEZABLE ● EASY ● KID FRIENDLY

Cornflake BISCUITS

These classic ruffle biscuits will transport you back to Nanna's kitchen.

MAKES 14 **PREP** 20 mins (+ cooling) **COOK** 20 mins

125g butter, at room
   temperature
100g (½ cup) caster sugar
1 egg
150g (1 cup) self-raising flour
45g (¼ cup) currants
Pinch of salt
60g (2 cups) cornflakes,
   crushed slightly

1 Preheat the oven to 180°C/160°C fan forced.
Line 2 baking trays with baking paper.

2 Use electric beaters to beat butter and sugar in
a bowl until pale and creamy. Add egg and beat
until combined. Use a spatula to fold flour, currants
and salt into the butter mixture until just combined.

3 Place the cornflakes in a bowl. Spoon heaped
tablespoonfuls of butter mixture into cornflakes
and gently toss to coat. Shape into balls.

4 Place the balls 8cm apart on the prepared tray.
Bake for 15-18 minutes or until golden. Set aside
on the trays for 10 minutes to cool before transferring
to a wire rack to cool completely.

COOK'S TIP

Don't worry about crushing the cornflakes; they will crumble enough as you coat the biscuit dough.

★★★★★

*These are a childhood memory, did not disappoint.
Absolutely wonderful.*

HELENPAT

● GLUTEN FREE ● MAKE AHEAD ● FREEZABLE ● EASY ● KID FRIENDLY

Giant choc chip
COOKIE

Prep for this larger-than-life cookie takes just 10 minutes.

MAKES 2 **PREP** 10 mins (+ cooling) **COOK** 40 mins

300g (2 cups) plain flour
¾ tsp bicarbonate of soda
¾ tsp salt
125g unsalted butter,
  at room temperature
155g (¾ cup, firmly packed)
  brown sugar
70g (⅓ cup) caster sugar
1½ tsp vanilla extract
1 egg
1 egg yolk
80ml (⅓ cup) thickened
  cream
230g (1¼ cups) milk
  choc chips
Chocolate ganache and
  sprinkles, to decorate

1 Preheat oven to 180°C/160°C fan forced. Line a baking tray with baking paper. Whisk together flour, bicarb and salt in a bowl. Use electric beaters to beat butter, brown sugar and caster sugar in a separate bowl until pale and creamy. Add vanilla, egg and egg yolk and beat until well combined. With beaters on low speed, add flour mixture and cream in 2 alternating batches, beginning and ending with flour, until just combined. Add the choc chips and stir until combined.

2 Spoon half the batter into the centre of prepared tray and spread out to a 20cm-diameter circle. Bake for 15-20 minutes or until golden. Set aside on tray for 5 minutes to cool slightly. Transfer to a wire rack to cool completely. Repeat with remaining mixture.

3 Once cookies have cooled completely, decorate with piped chocolate ganache and sprinkles.

COOK'S TIP

To give your giant cookies a neat edge and even circle shape, gently press a spatula around the side of the biscuit while it is still warm.

● GLUTEN FREE ● MAKE AHEAD ● FREEZABLE ● EASY ● KID FRIENDLY

Mango margarita BITES

Take your taste buds on a trip to the tropics with these boozy bites.

MAKES 24 **PREP** 40 mins (+ cooling & 2 hours 30 mins chilling) **COOK** 30 mins

75g (½ cup) self-raising flour
75g (½ cup) plain flour
85g (1 cup) desiccated
    coconut
110g (½ cup) caster sugar
125g butter, melted, cooled
125ml (½ cup) coconut milk
2 eggs, lightly whisked
300ml ctn pouring
    cream, whipped
Pink rock salt, chilli powder
    and finely grated lime
    rind, to decorate
mango topping
500g mango flesh (about
    3-4 large mangoes)
60g (⅓ cup) icing sugar
80ml (⅓ cup) tequila
2 tbs fresh lime juice
1½ tbs triple sec liqueur
    or Cointreau
1 tbs gelatine powder

1 Preheat oven to 180°C/160°C fan forced. Grease a 20 x 30cm (base measurement) slice pan and line with baking paper.

2 Sift flours into a bowl. Add coconut and sugar and stir until combined. Make a well in the centre. Add butter, coconut milk and egg and stir until well combined. Transfer mixture to prepared pan and bake for 20-25 minutes or until light golden and firm to a gentle touch. Set aside in pan for 10 minutes to cool slightly. Turn onto a wire rack to cool completely.

3 To make the topping. place mango, icing sugar, tequila, juice and triple sec in a food processor. Process until smooth. Place 60ml (¼ cup) water in a small microwave-safe bowl. Sprinkle with the gelatine and stir until combined. Microwave for 10 seconds (do not overheat). Use a fork to whisk until gelatine dissolves. Set aside to cool slightly. Add to the mango mixture and process briefly until combined. Transfer to a bowl. Place in fridge, stirring occasionally, for 30 minutes, until thickened but not set.

4 Line slice pan again with baking paper, allowing paper to overhang the long sides. Place coconut cake, upside down, into the pan. Spread the mango mixture over the cake and smooth the surface. Place in the fridge for 2 hours or until set.

5 Place salt and a small pinch of chilli in a mortar and pound with a pestle until finely crushed. Transfer slice to a serving board. Cut into 24 squares. Pipe or spoon whipped cream onto each square. Sprinkle with chilli salt over. Scatter over lime rind.

COOK'S TIP

You can leave out the alcohol if you like. Simply substitute it with an equal amount of mango nectar.

● GLUTEN FREE ● MAKE AHEAD ● FREEZABLE ● EASY ● KID FRIENDLY

Red velvet crinkle
COOKIES

Make and freeze these blushing bikkies up to 1 month ahead.

MAKES 30 **PREP** 30 mins (+ 5 mins resting & cooling) **COOK** 10 mins

100g butter, at room
   temperature
100g (½ cup) caster sugar
100g (½ cup, firmly packed)
   brown sugar
2 tsp vanilla extract
2 eggs
Red food colouring, to tint
150g (1 cup) self-raising flour
150g (1 cup) plain flour
1 tbs cocoa
125g (¾ cup) icing sugar
   mixture

1 Preheat oven to 180°C/160°C fan forced. Line 3 baking trays with baking paper.

2 Use electric beaters to beat butter, caster sugar, brown sugar and vanilla in a bowl until pale and creamy. Add eggs, 1 at a time, beating well after each addition until combined. Add food colouring to tint mixture red. Beat until evenly coloured.

3 Sift the self-raising flour, plain flour and cocoa over butter mixture. Use a flat-bladed knife in a cutting motion to mix until just combined. Bring together in the bowl (the dough will be very soft). Set aside for 5 minutes to rest.

4 Place icing sugar on a plate. Roll tablespoonfuls of the mixture into balls. Roll balls in icing sugar until coated. Place on prepared trays, allowing room for spreading. Use back of a spoon to flatten slightly.

5 Bake for 8 minutes or until cracked and just firm. Set aside on trays for 5 minutes to cool slightly before transferring to a wire rack to cool completely.

COOK'S TIP

Although the cookie dough is soft and sticky at room temperature, don't be tempted to chill it before rolling as you won't get a good spread and crackle as they bake.

★ ★ ★ ★ ★

Great recipe, perfect every time.

PAGE.S.

● GLUTEN FREE ● MAKE AHEAD ● FREEZABLE ● EASY ● KID FRIENDLY

Giant lemon
MELTING MOMENT

This classic bake is really having a moment right now!

SERVES 8-10 **PREP** 30 mins (+ cooling) **COOK** 40 mins

250g butter, chopped,
    at room temperature
60g (⅓ cup) icing sugar
    mixture, plus extra, to dust
1 tsp vanilla extract
225g (1½ cups) plain flour
70g (½ cup) custard powder
buttercream filling
125g butter, chopped,
    at room temperature
210g (1⅓ cups) icing
    sugar mixture
1 tsp finely grated
    lemon rind

1 Preheat the oven to 150°C/130°C fan forced. Use electric beaters to beat the butter and icing sugar in a bowl until pale and creamy. Beat in the vanilla. Sift over the flour and custard powder. Use a flat-bladed knife in a cutting motion to mix until dough is just combined. Use your hands to divide dough into 2 portions.

2 Place 1 dough portion on a sheet of baking paper and gently press or roll out to a 16cm round. (If the dough is very soft, place in the fridge until chilled and easier to work with.) Transfer to a large baking tray. Repeat with the remaining dough, transferring to a separate baking tray. Press the top of 1 dough round gently with the side of a wooden spoon handle to create indents.

3 Bake for 40 minutes or until light golden. Set aside on trays for 10 minutes to cool slightly before transferring to a wire rack, carefully sliding off the paper, to cool completely.

4 To make filling, use electric beaters to beat butter and icing sugar in a bowl until pale and creamy. Beat in the lemon rind then spoon into a piping bag fitted with a fluted nozzle.

5 Transfer the biscuit without indents, top-side down, to a serving plate and pipe on the filling (if you don't have a piping bag, spread it). Top with the indented biscuit, top-side up, and dust lightly with extra icing sugar. Carefully cut into wedges to serve.

COOK'S TIP

Try not to overwork the biscuit dough as this will make it easier to cut the wedges cleanly and prevent cracks when baking.

● GLUTEN FREE ● MAKE AHEAD ● FREEZABLE ● EASY ● KID FRIENDLY

Oreo-stuffed COOKIES

These moreish peanut butter bikkies have a surprise inside!

MAKES 24 **PREP** 30 mins (+ 30 mins chilling & cooling) **COOK** 15 mins

200g butter, chopped, at room temperature

130g (½ cup) smooth peanut butter

1 tsp vanilla extract

100g (½ cup) caster sugar

155g (¾ cup, firmly packed) brown sugar

2 eggs

300g (2 cups) plain flour

150g (1 cup) self-raising flour

1 tsp bicarbonate of soda

80g (½ cup) unsalted peanuts, coarsely chopped

2 x 133g pkt Oreo Original cookies

100g dark chocolate, melted

1 Preheat oven to 180°C/160°C fan forced. Use electric beaters to beat the butter, peanut butter, vanilla, caster and brown sugars in a bowl until pale and creamy.

2 Add the eggs, 1 at a time, beating well after each addition. Sift in the plain and self-raising flours, and bicarb. Use a spatula to fold the flours into the butter mixture until combined. Stir in half the peanuts.

3 Lightly grease two 12-hole 80ml (⅓ cup) muffin pans (see tip). Roll level tablespoonfuls of dough into balls. Flatten slightly. Place an Oreo between 2 pieces of dough. Press edges to enclose Oreo. Place on a baking tray. Repeat with remaining Oreos and dough. Place tray in fridge for 30 minutes to chill.

4 Place the stuffed dough balls in prepared muffin pans. Bake for 12 minutes or until lightly browned. Set aside in the pans for 10 minutes to cool slightly before transferring to a sheet of baking paper to cool completely.

5 Drizzle melted chocolate over the cookies and scatter over remaining peanuts. Set aside until chocolate is set, then serve.

COOK'S TIP

If you don't have two 12-hole muffin pans, simply prepare and bake in 2 batches.

● GLUTEN FREE ● MAKE AHEAD ● FREEZABLE ● EASY ● KID FRIENDLY

SUPER SLICES

THE SLICE IS ALWAYS RIGHT WITH THIS COLLECTION
OF SOME OF OUR ALL TIME FAVOURITE
TREATS – ALL MADE TO SHARE!

Raspberry & rosewater
CHEESECAKE SLICE

Whip up this beautiful fruity-floral slice for special occasions.

MAKES 16 **PREP** 45 mins (+ cooling & overnight chilling) **COOK** 30 mins

155g (¾ cup) caster sugar

150g butter, chopped,
   at room temperature

1 tsp vanilla extract

2 eggs

150g (1 cup) self-raising
   flour, sifted

40g (¼ cup) plain flour, sifted

125g (½ cup) sour cream

2 tbs milk

Fresh raspberries, halved,
   meringue kisses and
   edible dried rose petals,
   to decorate

raspberry cheesecake

200g frozen raspberries,
   thawed

155g (¾ cup) caster sugar

500g cream cheese, at room
   temperature, chopped

3 tsp gelatine powder

500ml (2 cups) thickened
   cream

2-3 tsp rosewater, to taste

185g pistachio kernels,
   coarsely chopped

1 Preheat the oven to 180°C/160°C fan forced. Grease a 4.5cm-deep, 22.5 x 33cm (base size) slice pan and line with baking paper, allowing the paper to overhang the long sides. Use electric beaters to beat the sugar, butter and vanilla in a bowl until pale and creamy. Add eggs, 1 at a time, beating well after each addition until well combined. Stir in the flours, sour cream and milk in alternating batches until just combined.

2 Transfer the mixture to prepared pan. Bake for 20-25 minutes or until lightly browned and a skewer inserted into the centre comes out clean. Set aside in pan on a wire rack to cool.

3 Meanwhile, to make cheesecake. Place the frozen raspberries, 55g (¼ cup) sugar and 1 tbs water in a small saucepan over high heat. Bring to the boil. Reduce heat to low and simmer, stirring constantly, for 5 minutes. Strain through a fine sieve. Set aside to cool.

4 Use electric beaters to beat cream cheese and remaining sugar in a

bowl until smooth. Place 60ml (¼ cup) cold water in a small heatproof bowl. Sprinkle over the gelatine and stir until well combined. Place bowl inside a larger heatproof bowl. Pour boiling water into the larger bowl until it reaches halfway up the side of the smaller bowl. Set aside, stirring occasionally, for 5 minutes or until gelatine dissolves. Add to raspberry puree and stir until combined.

5 Use clean beaters to whisk cream in a large bowl until soft peaks form. Add raspberry mixture and stir until combined. Use a large metal spoon to fold the whipped cream and rosewater into cream mixture. Spread mixture over cooled cake. Smooth surface. Place in fridge for at least 4 hours or overnight to set.

6 Transfer the cake to a serving board and cut in half lengthways, then into slices. Press the pistachios into the edges of each slice. Top with the fresh raspberries, meringues and rose petals.

● GLUTEN FREE ● MAKE AHEAD ● FREEZABLE ● EASY ● KID FRIENDLY

Choc-strawberry OREO SLICE

We've packed 21 Oreos into this easy condensed milk slice!

MAKES 20-25 **PREP** 20 mins (+ cooling & 2 hours chilling) **COOK** 40 mins

270g (1¼ cups) caster sugar
200g butter, chopped
180g dark chocolate, chopped, plus extra, melted, to decorate
3 eggs, lightly whisked
200g (1⅓ cups) plain flour
30g (¼ cup) cocoa powder
21 Oreo Strawberry cookies, halved
Freeze-dried strawberries, crushed (see tip)

coconut ice
230g (1½ cups) icing sugar mixture
155g (1⅔ cups) desiccated coconut
395g can sweetened condensed milk
1 tsp vanilla extract
Pink food colouring, to tint

1 Preheat oven to 170°C/150°C fan forced. Grease a 16.5 x 26.5cm (base size) slice pan. Line with baking paper, allowing the paper to overhang the long sides.

2 Place the caster sugar, butter and chocolate in a saucepan over medium-low heat. Cook, stirring, until almost melted. Remove from heat and stir until smooth and well combined. Transfer to a heatproof bowl and set aside to cool slightly.

3 Add egg and whisk until combined. Sift over flour and cocoa then use a spatula to fold through until just combined. Pour into the prepared pan. Bake for 30-40 minutes or until set in the centre (it will still be a little bit soft). Set aside in pan to cool completely.

4 To make the coconut ice, place the icing sugar and coconut in a large bowl. Make a well in the centre. Add the condensed milk, vanilla and a few drops of food colouring to tint pink. Stir until well combined and evenly coloured.

5 Spread the coconut ice mixture over the brownie. Arrange the cookies, cut-side up, in rows on top, pressing slightly into the coconut ice. Place in the fridge for 2 hours or until set.

6 Drizzle over extra chocolate. Sprinkle with freeze-dried strawberries. Cut into squares to serve.

COOK'S TIP

Find freeze-dried strawberries at greengrocers, delis and online.

● GLUTEN FREE ● MAKE AHEAD ● FREEZABLE ● EASY ● KID FRIENDLY

Baklava vanilla
SLICE

All the best sweet, nutty goodness of baklava – with no fiddly filo!

MAKES 12-15 **PREP** 30 mins (+ overnight chilling) **COOK** 35 mins

85g (⅓ cup) walnuts

55g (⅓ cup) pistachio kernels

2 sheets frozen puff pastry, thawed

20g butter, melted

½ tsp ground cinnamon

375ml (1½ cups) pouring cream

1 tsp vanilla extract

375ml (1½ cups) milk

270g (1¼ cups) caster sugar

35g (¼ cup) cornflour

6 egg yolks

60ml (¼ cup) fresh lemon juice

2 tbs honey

6 whole cloves

1 cinnamon stick

1½ tbs rosewater

1 Preheat oven to 200°C/180°C fan forced. Grease a 7cm-deep, 9 x 19cm (base size) loaf pan. Line the base and sides with baking paper, allowing the paper to overhang the long sides. Line 2 large baking trays with baking paper. Coarsely chop half the walnuts and pistachio kernels. Transfer to a bowl and set aside. Finely chop remaining nuts and transfer to a separate bowl.

2 Place 1 sheet pastry on each tray. Brush sheets with butter. Sprinkle with the cinnamon then the finely chopped nuts. Drizzle over remaining butter. Bake for 8 minutes or until puffed and light golden. Use a metal skewer to pierce the pastry sheets 2-3 times. Use a baking tray to flatten sheets slightly until 1-1.5cm thick. Bake for 8 minutes. Set aside to completely.

3 Place the cream, vanilla, 250ml (1 cup) milk and 170g (¾ cup) sugar in a large saucepan over medium heat. Bring to a simmer. Remove from heat. Place cornflour, egg yolks and remaining milk in a jug Stir until combined. Gradually whisk

into cream mixture until combined. Place over medium-low heat. Cook, whisking constantly, for 5 minutes or until thickened.

4 Cut pastry sheets in half. Place 1 half, base-side up, over base of prepared pan, trimming to fit. Spread with one-third of the cream mixture. Top with another pastry half, base-side up. Top with half the remaining cream mixture. Repeat with remaining pastry half and cream mixture. Top with remaining pastry half. Place in fridge for 8 hours or overnight to set.

5 Place lemon juice, honey, cloves, cinnamon stick, remaining caster sugar and 80ml (⅓ cup) water in a small saucepan over medium heat. Cook, stirring, until sugar dissolves. Increase heat to medium-high. Simmer for 3 minutes or until thickened. Strain through a fine sieve. Discard cloves and cinnamon. Stir in rosewater. Set aside to cool completely.

6 Turn slice onto a serving plate. Sprinkle with coarsely chopped nuts. Drizzle over a little syrup. Slice and serve with remaining syrup.

● GLUTEN FREE ● MAKE AHEAD ● FREEZABLE ● EASY ● KID FRIENDLY

Passionfruit coconut
VANILLA SLICE

Vanilla slice gets a tropical island makeover.

MAKES 12 **PREP** 50 mins (+cooling & 4 hours chilling) **COOK** 25 mins

120g butter, chopped, at room temperature
100g (½ cup) caster sugar
2 egg yolks
150g (1 cup) plain flour
50g (⅓ cup) cornflour
35g (⅓ cup) desiccated coconut

vanilla custard
375ml (1½ cups) milk
3 egg yolks
70g (⅓ cup) caster sugar
1 tsp vanilla extract
35g (¼ cup) cornflour
150g unsalted butter, chopped, at room temperature
100g white chocolate, melted

passionfruit glaze
125ml (½ cup) passionfruit pulp (about 6 fresh passionfruit)
2 tsp cornflour
55g (¼ cup) caster sugar
½ tsp gelatine powder

1 Preheat oven to 180°C/160°C fan forced. Lightly grease a 4cm-deep, 23cm (base size) square cake pan. Line with baking paper, allowing paper to overhang sides. Use electric beaters to beat butter and sugar in a bowl until combined. Beat in egg yolks. Sift plain flour and cornflour over mixture. Add coconut and stir until combined. Transfer mixture to prepared pan. Gently press into base. Bake for 12-15 minutes or until lightly browned. Set aside in pan to cool.

2 Meanwhile, make custard. Place milk in a saucepan over medium heat. Bring to boil. Remove from heat. Use clean beaters to beat yolks, sugar and vanilla in a bowl until pale and creamy. Stir in cornflour. Gradually whisk in milk. Transfer the mixture to a clean saucepan. Whisk over medium-low heat for 3-5 minutes or until mixture boils and thickens. Transfer to a clean bowl and cover surface with plastic wrap. Set aside to cool.

3 Use electric beaters to beat the custard in a bowl until smooth. Add the butter and chocolate. Stir until well combined. Spread mixture evenly over biscuit base. Place in the fridge for 2-3 hours or until set.

4 Meanwhile, make the passionfruit glaze. Strain passionfruit pulp through a fine sieve. Return 1 tbs of the seeds to strained pulp. Place cornflour and 80ml (⅓ cup) water in a small saucepan. Stir until combined. Add the pulp and sugar. Cook, stirring, over medium heat until mixture boils and thickens slightly. Remove from heat. Whisk in gelatine until dissolved. Set aside to cool to room temperature. Pour over custard and smooth surface. Place in the fridge for 1 hour or until set. Cut into squares to serve.

★★★★★

Amazing. The custard mix is the best!!!
BUDGIE

● GLUTEN FREE ● MAKE AHEAD ● FREEZABLE ● EASY ● KID FRIENDLY

Old-fashioned chocolate SLICE

Need a last-minute treat? This chocolate slice is as easy as 1,2,3!

MAKES 12 **PREP** 10 mins (+ cooling) **COOK** 30 mins

150g (1 cup) plain flour
90g (1 cup) rolled oats
100g (½ cup) caster sugar
75g (¾ cup) desiccated
   coconut, plus extra,
   to serve
2 tbs cocoa powder
150g butter, melted
1 tsp vanilla essence
chocolate icing
210g (1⅓ cups) icing sugar
   mixture
2 tbs cocoa powder
15g butter
2-3 tbs boiling water

1 Preheat the oven to 180°C/160°C fan forced. Grease and line a 18 x 28cm (base size) slice pan with baking paper, allowing the paper to overhang the long sides.

2 Place the flour, oats, sugar, coconut and cocoa in a large bowl. Add the butter and vanilla and stir until combined. Press mixture over the base of the prepared pan. Bake for 30 minutes or until golden and cooked through. Set aside in the pan to cool.

3 Meanwhile, to make the icing, combine the icing sugar and cocoa powder in a large bowl. Place the butter in a heatproof bowl. Pour over 2 tbs of the boiling water. Stir until smooth. Stir into the icing sugar mixture, adding the remaining 1 tbs boiling water if necessary, until the icing is well combined and spreadable.

4 Top the slice with the chocolate icing and sprinkle with extra coconut. Set aside until icing sets. Trim edges and slice to serve.

COOK'S TIP

This slice will keep in an airtight container for up to 3 days.

Growing up, this super simple chocolate slice was mine and my brothers' favourite afternoon tea treat. I loved helping Mum make the icing and eventually it was one of the first recipes I baked on my own.

KATRINA WOODMAN, FOOD EDITOR

● GLUTEN FREE ● MAKE AHEAD ● FREEZABLE ● EASY ● KID FRIENDLY

Passionfruit melting MOMENT SLICE

It only takes six basic ingredients to create sweet passionfruit bliss.

MAKES 16 **PREP** 30 mins (+ cooling) **COOK** 20 mins

1 tsp vanilla extract

310g butter, chopped, at room temperature

210g (1⅓ cups) icing sugar mixture, plus 3 tbs, extra

225g (1½ cups) plain flour

70g (½ cup) custard powder, plus extra, to dust

3 passionfruit, plus extra, strained, to make icing

1 Preheat oven to 170°C/150°C fan forced. Grease a 19cm (base size) square cake pan. Line with baking paper, allowing the paper to overhang 2 sides. Line a baking tray with baking paper.

2 Use electric beaters to beat the vanilla, 250g butter and 60g (⅓ cup) sugar in a bowl until pale and creamy. Sift over flour and custard powder. Use a flat-bladed knife in a cutting motion to mix until evenly incorporated and a soft dough forms.

3 Press half the dough over base of prepared pan. Roll remaining dough into 16 balls. Place on the prepared tray 3cm apart. Lightly dust a fork with extra custard powder then use to press each ball to a 3.5cm disc. Bake, swapping tray and pan halfway through cooking, for 18 minutes or until light golden underneath. Set aside

biscuit base to cool completely. Set aside biscuits for 5 minutes to cool slightly before transferring to a wire rack to cool completely.

4 Use electric beaters to beat the remaining butter in a bowl until pale and creamy. Gradually add the remaining sugar, beating well after each addition until well combined. Scoop out the passionfruit pulp. Add to the butter mixture. Beat until combined.

5 Combine 2½ tbs of the extra sugar and a little of the extra strained passionfruit juice in a small bowl until icing is a drizzling consistency.

6 Use the baking paper to carefully lift the biscuit base out of the pan. Spread over the filling. Arrange the biscuits on top then dust with the remaining extra icing sugar. Drizzle over the icing. Cut into squares between biscuits to serve.

● GLUTEN FREE ● MAKE AHEAD ● FREEZABLE ● EASY ● KID FRIENDLY

Snickers tray bake SLICE

With a Snickers bar on every slice, everyone gets a fun-sized treat.

MAKES 24 **PREP** 15 mins (+ cooling & 30 mins chilling) **COOK** 30 mins

200g butter, chopped

200g (1 cup, firmly packed) brown sugar

180g white chocolate, coarsely chopped

160ml (⅔ cup) warm water

60ml (¼ cup) golden syrup

250g (1⅔ cups) plain flour

50g (⅓ cup) self-raising flour

2 eggs, at room temperature

3 x 180g pkt Snickers Fun Size chocolate bars

180g dark chocolate, finely chopped

125ml (½ cup) thickened cream

160g (⅔ cup) bought dulce de leche (see tip)

40g (¼ cup) crushed peanuts

1 Preheat oven to 160°C/140°C fan forced. Grease a 20 x 30cm (base size) slice pan. Line the base and sides with baking paper, allowing the paper to overhang the sides.

2 Place the butter, sugar, white chocolate, water and golden syrup in a large saucepan over low heat. Cook, stirring occasionally, for 5 minutes or until smooth and well combined. Remove from heat and set aside for 5 minutes to cool slightly.

3 Add plain and self-raising flours to the chocolate mixture. Stir until smooth. Add eggs, 1 at a time, stirring well after each addition, until well combined. Pour mixture into prepared pan.

4 Finely chop 4 Snickers. Scatter over mixture. Bake for 25 minutes or until a skewer inserted into the centre comes out clean. Set aside in pan to cool.

5 Meanwhile, combine the dark chocolate and cream in a microwave-safe bowl. Microwave on High, stirring every 30 seconds, until smooth. Place in the fridge, stirring occasionally, for 30 minutes or until chilled, thick and glossy.

6 Spread choc mixture over cake layer. Arrange remaining Snickers on top. Drizzle over caramel. Sprinkle with nuts. Set aside to set before slicing.

COOK'S TIP

You can find dulce de leche at selected supermarkets. Alternatively, you can use a thick caramel topping.

★★★★★

I love how the pieces in this slice are perfectly portion-controlled.

SHAWNTHEPRAWN

● GLUTEN FREE ● MAKE AHEAD ● FREEZABLE ● EASY ● KID FRIENDLY

Choc chip
COOKIE SLICE

One giant slab cookies means no measuring or rolling required!

MAKES 15-20 **PREP** 15 mins (+ cooling) **COOK** 25 mins

125g butter, chopped
155g (¾ cup, firmly packed) brown sugar
1 egg
1 tsp vanilla extract
190g (1¼ cups) plain flour
¾ tsp baking powder
100g (½ cup) milk choc chips
156g pkt Cadbury Cookies Choc Centre

1 Preheat oven to 160°C/140°C fan forced. Grease a 16.5 x 26.5cm (base size) slice pan and line with baking paper, allowing the paper to overhang the long sides.

2 Place the butter in a small saucepan over medium heat. Stir until melted. Add the sugar and stir until dissolved. Transfer to a bowl to cool slightly. Add the egg and vanilla to bowl. Whisk until combined. Sift over the flour and baking powder. Stir until combined. Add half the choc chips and stir until combined.

3 Spread half the mixture over the base of the prepared pan. Arrange the cookies on top. Spread over the remaining mixture. Sprinkle with the remaining choc chips, pressing slightly into the dough to secure. Bake for 20 minutes or until golden around the edges. Set aside in pan to cool completely. Cut into bars to serve.

COOK'S TIP

Don't over-mix the cookie dough as this can make the slice tough and dense instead of soft and chewy!

★★★★★

This was incred!

ALI C

● GLUTEN FREE ● MAKE AHEAD ● FREEZABLE ● EASY ● KID FRIENDLY

15
minutes
prep

Lemon butter
SHORTBREAD SLICE

This cheat's slice uses bought lemon butter to slash prep time.

MAKES 16 **PREP** 20 mins (+ cooling) **COOK** 25 mins

150g (1 cup) plain flour
50g (⅓ cup) cornflour
120g (⅔ cup) icing sugar
1 tsp vanilla bean paste
150g butter, chilled, chopped
55g (⅓ cup) unsalted pistachios kernels, coarsely chopped
1 tbs finely grated lemon rind
2 x 280g jars lemon butter
3 egg whites
155g (¾ cup) caster sugar

1 Preheat oven to 180°C/160°C fan forced. Grease a 3cm-deep, 16 x 25cm (base size) slice pan and line with baking paper, allowing the paper to overhang the long sides.

2 Place the plain flour, cornflour, icing sugar and vanilla in a food processor. Process until the mixture is well combined. Add the butter and process until the mixture just starts to come together. Stir in the pistachio and lemon rind. Press the mixture firmly over the base of the prepared pan. Bake for 20 minutes or until light golden then set aside to cool completely.

3 Place the lemon butter in a small bowl. Whisk until smooth then spread over the shortbread layer.

4 Use electric beaters to beat the egg whites in a small clean, dry bowl until soft peaks form. Gradually add the caster sugar, beating well after each addition, until the sugar dissolves and mixture is thick and glossy. Spoon the meringue into a piping bag fitted with a fluted nozzle and pipe on top of the lemon butter layer (see tip).

5 Bake for 3-5 minutes or until browned. Set aside in the pan for 15 minutes to cool before slicing.

COOK'S TIP

If you don't have a fluted nozzle or piping bag, use an offset palette knife to spread the meringue over the lemon layer, using the knife to make small peaks in the meringue.

★★★★★

Amazing delicious, my family loved it

CAPPS01

● GLUTEN FREE ● MAKE AHEAD ● FREEZABLE ● EASY ● KID FRIENDLY

Iced VoVo vanilla
CUSTARD SLICE

Pay homage to the classic bikkie with this pretty-in-pink treat.

MAKES 10 **PREP** 35 mins (+ overnight chilling & cooling) **COOKING** 1 hour 30 mins

250g caster sugar

105g (¾ cup) cornflour

70g (½ cup) custard powder

750ml (3 cups) milk

250ml (1 cup) thickened cream

2 tsp vanilla bean paste

2 tsp coconut essence (optional)

Pink gel food colouring, to tint

3 egg yolks

60g butter, chopped

3 sheets frozen puff pastry, just thawed

80g (¼ cup) raspberry jam

20g (¼ cup) desiccated coconut

6 Arnott's Iced VoVo biscuits, coarsely crushed

1 Place sugar, cornflour and custard powder in a saucepan. Add half the milk and whisk until smooth. Add cream, vanilla, coconut essence (if using) and remaining milk. Whisk until combined. Add food colouring to tint pink. Whisk until evenly coloured. Add egg yolks. Whisk until well combined. Place over medium-low heat. Cook, whisking constantly, for 5 minutes or until heated through. Increase heat to medium. Cook, whisking constantly, for 3-5 minutes or until thickened. Remove from heat. Whisk in butter. Pour mixture into a large bowl. Cover the surface with plastic wrap. Place in the fridge for 6 hours or overnight.

2 Preheat oven to 200°C/180°C fan forced. Line a baking tray with baking paper. Trim and discard a 6cm strip from 1 side of 1 pastry sheet to make a rectangle. Place on prepared tray. Cover with a sheet of baking paper. Top with another baking tray, then a heavy baking dish. Bake for 20-25 minutes or until golden and crisp. Set aside to cool completely. Repeat with remaining pastry sheets.

3 Use electric beaters to beat the custard in a bowl for 1-2 minutes or until smooth and creamy.

4 Spoon a little custard into centre of a serving plate. Place 1 pastry sheet on top gently press down to secure. Spoon remaining custard into a piping bag fitted with a large fluted nozzle. Pipe peaks of custard onto pastry. Drizzle 1 tbs raspberry jam over custard. Sprinkle with 1 tbs desiccated coconut and half the crushed biscuit. Repeat layering with another pastry sheet and half the remaining custard, jam and coconut. Sprinkle with remaining crushed biscuit. Top with the final layer of pastry. Spread the remaining jam down the centre of the pastry. Pipe peaks of custard along edges of pastry sheet. Sprinkle with remaining coconut. Place in the fridge until ready to serve.

● GLUTEN FREE ● MAKE AHEAD ● FREEZABLE ● EASY ● KID FRIENDLY

This slice was quite easy in the end! And absolutely delicious, of course.

F_BAKER_12

Classic chewy
BROWNIE

This is the ultimate no-fail recipe for chewy and indulgent brownies.

MAKES 16 **PREP** 10 mins **COOKING** 35 mins

125g unsalted butter, chopped
125g dark chocolate, chopped
3 eggs, lightly whisked
335g (1½ cups) white sugar
115g (¾ cup) plain flour
30g (¼ cup) cocoa powder
1 tsp vanilla extract
Pinch of salt

1 Preheat oven to 180°C/160°C fan forced. Grease a 20cm (base size) square cake pan and line with baking paper.

2 Place the butter and chocolate in a heatproof bowl over a saucepan of simmering water (don't let the bowl touch the water). Stir with a metal spoon until melted. Remove from heat. Quickly stir in egg, sugar, flour, cocoa powder, vanilla and salt until just combined. Pour into prepared pan. Bake for 30 minutes or until a skewer inserted in the centre comes out with moist crumbs clinging. Set aside to cool completely.

COOK'S TIP

Brownies freeze well due to their decadent, moist texture. Wrap the uncut brownie in 2 layers of foil and 1 layer of plastic wrap and freeze for up to 3 months.

★★★★★

I've made this many times – easy and always tastes absolutely luscious.

MILLIE99

● GLUTEN FREE ● MAKE AHEAD ● FREEZABLE ● EASY ● KID FRIENDLY

Carrot cake TRAY BAKE

Level up carrot cake as a crowd-pleasing bake with extra toppings.

MAKES 18 **PREP** 20 mins (+ cooling) **COOKING** 1 hour 10 mins

450g (3 cups) self-raising
    flour
300g (1½ cups, firmly
    packed) brown sugar
2 tsp ground cinnamon
1 tsp mixed spice
240g (3 cups) carrots,
    coarsely grated, plus
    3 small peeled carrots,
    extra, peeled into ribbons
4 eggs, lightly whisked
375ml (1½ cups) vegetable
    oil
215g (1 cup) caster sugar
90g (⅔ cup) pecans
375g cream cheese, at room
    temperature
150g (1 cup) pure icing
    sugar, sifted

1 Preheat oven to 180°C/160°C fan forced. Grease a 5cm-deep, 20 x 30cm (base size) slice pan and line base and sides with baking paper.

2 Combine flour, brown sugar, cinnamon and mixed spice in a large bowl. Add carrot, egg and oil. Stir until combined. Pour into prepared pan. Bake for 40-45 minutes or until a skewer inserted into centre comes out clean. Set aside for 5 minutes to cool slightly. Turn onto a wire rack to cool completely.

3 Increase oven to 200°C/180°C fan forced. Line 2 baking trays with baking paper. Stir caster sugar and 250ml (1 cup) water in a saucepan over medium heat until sugar dissolves. Increase heat to high and bring to the boil. Add extra carrot. Reduce heat to medium-low and simmer for 5-7 minutes or until the carrot ribbons are just tender (do not overcook). Use a slotted spoon or tongs to transfer carrot ribbons to 1 prepared tray. Add pecans to syrup mixture. Stir to coat. Use slotted spoon to transfer pecan mixture to the remaining prepared tray. Bake carrot ribbons for 10-15 minutes or until carrot looks translucent but still holds its shape, adding pecans in last 7 minutes of cooking. Set aside both trays to cool. Carefully use fingers to separate the carrot ribbons.

4 Chop cream cheese into a bowl. Add the icing sugar. Use electric beaters to beat until pale and creamy. Spread over the cooled cake. Scatter over the carrot ribbons and candied pecans to serve.

COOK'S TIP

Using oil rather than butter in this cake creates a different texture and increases moistness. This is because oil is liquid at room temperature and butter solid. As such, oil-based cake has more moisture.

● GLUTEN FREE ● MAKE AHEAD ● FREEZABLE ● EASY ● KID FRIENDLY

Added sultanas and chopped pecans, delicious! Moist and tasty!

EVIE

Neapolitan brownie
CHEESECAKE SLICE

Pipe the strawberry milkshake topping high on this retro mash-up!

MAKES 12 **PREP** 30 mins (+ cooling) **COOK** 1 hour 10 mins

130g unsalted butter,
   at room temperature
300g (2 cups) pure icing
   sugar, sifted
4 eggs
75g (½ cup) plain flour
30g (¼ cup) cocoa powder,
   sifted, plus extra, to serve
130g dark chocolate,
   melted, cooled slightly
400g cream cheese, at room
   temperature, chopped
2 tsp vanilla bean paste
strawberry cream
435ml (1¾ cups) thickened
   cream
140g (1 cup) Nestlé Nesquik
   Strawberry

1 Preheat oven to 170°C/150°C fan forced. Lightly grease a 5cm-deep, 20cm (base size) square cake pan. Line base and sides with baking paper, allowing the paper to overhang the sides.

2 Use electric beaters to beat the butter and 150g (1 cup) of icing sugar in a bowl until pale and creamy. Add 2 eggs, 1 at a time, beating well after each addition. Add the flour and cocoa powder and beat until just combined. Add the chocolate and beat until smooth and combined. Pour into prepared pan and smooth the surface.

3 Place the cream cheese, vanilla and remaining icing sugar in a bowl. Use clean electric beaters to beat until smooth and creamy. Add remaining eggs, 1 at a time, beating well after each addition. Pour over the brownie layer. Smooth the surface. Bake for 1 hour 10 minutes or until firm to the touch and golden around edges (the centre should still be pale). Place pan on a wire rack to cool completely.

4 To make the strawberry cream, use clean electric beaters to beat the cream and milk powder in a bowl until firm peaks form.

5 Transfer brownie to a serving plate. Use a flat-bladed knife to spread a little of the strawberry cream over the top of the cheesecake. Spoon remaining cream into a piping bag fitted with a large plain nozzle. Pipe peaks of cream over the top of cheesecake. Dust with cocoa to serve.

COOK'S TIP

To pipe the perfect peak, hold the piping bag upright and gently squeeze out the icing to form peaks, pulling the bag away at the end of each peak to form a point.

● GLUTEN FREE ● MAKE AHEAD ● FREEZABLE ● EASY ● KID FRIENDLY

Apple & ricotta SLICE

Nan would be proud of the classic flavours of this gooey custard slice.

MAKES 6-8 **PREP** 30 mins (+ 20 mins resting & 15 mins cooling) **COOK** 45 mins

200g (1⅓ cup) plain flour
3/4 tsp baking powder
70g (⅓ cup) caster sugar
90g butter, chilled, chopped
1 tsp vanilla extract
1-2 tsp iced water
2 eggs
385g can apple slices pie fruit
125g (½ cup) smooth ricotta
Pinch of ground cinnamon
Pure icing sugar, to dust

1 Place flour, baking powder and 55g (¼ cup) caster sugar in a food processor. Process for 30 seconds or until combined. Add butter and ½ tsp vanilla. Process until mixture resembles fine crumbs. Add water and 1 egg. Process again until just starts to come together. Gather dough together into a disc. Wrap in plastic wrap. Place in fridge for 20 minutes to rest.

2 Meanwhile, preheat oven to 180°C/160°C fan forced. Place the apple on a large plate and coarsely crush any large pieces. Place ricotta, cinnamon, and remaining caster sugar and egg in a large bowl. Whisk until combined.

3 Roll out three-quarters of the dough on a lightly floured surface until 5mm thick. Use to line base and sides of a 2.5cm-deep, 11 x 34cm rectangular fluted tart tin with removable base. Trim any excess. Prick the base. Pour ricotta mixture over base. Arrange apple on top.

4 Roll out remaining dough on a lightly floured surface until 5mm thick. Use a fluted ravioli wheel or small sharp knife to cut dough into 2.5cm-wide strips. Arrange at 2cm intervals in a diagonal pattern over the filling, trimming excess and re-rolling as necessary. Bake for 40-45 minutes or until golden. Set aside for 15 minutes. Dust with icing sugar then slice.

COOK'S TIP

Don't knead or overwork the pastry as this can make it difficult to roll and unpleasant (tough and dry) to eat.

★★★★★

Yum.

PELI13

● GLUTEN FREE ● MAKE AHEAD ● FREEZABLE ● EASY ● KID FRIENDLY

Crème caramel
CHOCOLATE SLICE

This decadent make-ahead slice is perfect for dinner parties.

MAKES 12 **PREP** 20 MINS (+ 2 HOURS COOLING) **COOK** 1 HOUR 15 MINS

370g (1¾ cup) caster sugar
115g (¾ cup) plain flour
35g (⅓ cup) cocoa powder
½ tsp baking power
½ tsp bicarbonate of soda
120g butter, at room temperature, plus extra, melted, to grease
5 eggs, at room temperature
2 tsp vanilla bean paste
185ml (¾ cup) buttermilk
395g sweetened condensed milk
385ml evaporated milk

1 Preheat oven to 180°C/160°C fan forced. Brush a straight-sided 20cm (base size) square cake pan with extra melted butter to grease.

2 Place 215g (1 cup) sugar and 60ml (¼ cup) water in a heavy-based saucepan over medium-high heat. Stir constantly until the sugar dissolves. Simmer, without stirring, brushing down the side of pan with a wet pastry brush to prevent sugar crystals forming, for 8 minutes or until just golden. Remove from heat and set aside until the bubbles subside. Pour into the prepared pan and tilt to evenly cover the base. Place the pan in a large roasting pan.

3 Sift the flour, cocoa, baking powder and bicarb into a bowl. Use electric beaters to beat the butter and remaining sugar in a large bowl until pale and creamy. Beat in 1 egg and half the vanilla until just combined. Beat in half the flour mixture and half the buttermilk until just combined. Repeat with the remaining flour mixture and buttermilk. Spread the cake mixture evenly over the caramel layer.

4 Whisk together the condensed milk, evaporated milk and remaining eggs and vanilla in a large jug or bowl. Pour over back of a wooden spoon over the cake mixture. Cover cake pan with foil. Pour enough boiling water into the roasting pan to come halfway up sides of the cake pan.

5 Bake for 1 hour or until the chocolate cake comes away from the sides of the pan. Remove cake pan from roasting pan and set aside for 2 hours to cool completely. Carefully run a flat-bladed palette knife around the sides of the pan. Turn onto a serving platter with a lip (to catch the dripping caramel sauce). Cut into slices to serve.

● GLUTEN FREE ● MAKE AHEAD ● FREEZABLE ● EASY ● KID FRIENDLY

Anzac caramel
SLICE

Go bananas for banoffee, choc and cheesecake in this epic dessert.

MAKES 12 **PREP** 1 hour (+ 4 hours chilling & cooling) **COOK** 15 mins

- 300g pkt Anzac biscuits, plus extra, chopped, to serve (optional)
- 125g butter, melted
- 2 x 250g pkt cream cheese, at room temperature
- 300ml sour cream
- 60ml (¼ cup) warm water
- 3 tsp gelatine powder
- 1 tsp finely grated lemon rind
- 1 tbs fresh lemon juice
- 125ml (½ cup) caramel topping, plus extra, to serve
- 3 bananas
- 250ml (1 cup) thickened cream
- 200g milk cooking chocolate, finely chopped
- 15g (¼ cup) salted toasted coconut flakes

1 Preheat oven to 180°C/160°C fan forced. Grease a 6cm-deep, 12 x 27cm (base size) loaf pan and line with baking paper, allowing the paper to overhang the long sides. Place the biscuits in a food processor. Process until finely crushed. Add the butter. Process until combined. Press mixture evenly over the base of prepared pan. Bake for 10 minutes. Set aside to cool.

2 Meanwhile, process the cream cheese and sour cream in a clean food processor until smooth. Place the water in a small heatproof bowl and sprinkle with the gelatine. Stir until well combined. Place the bowl inside a larger heatproof bowl. Pour boiling water into the larger bowl until it reaches halfway up the side of the smaller bowl. Set aside, stirring occasionally, for 5 minutes or until the gelatine dissolves. Add to the cream cheese mixture. Add the lemon rind and juice and pulse until mixture is well combined.

3 Spread caramel over biscuit base. Slice 2 bananas and arrange in a layer on top. Spoon over cream cheese mixture and use a spatula to smooth the surface. Place in the fridge for 1 hour to chill.

4 Meanwhile, place 125ml (½ cup) thickened cream in a small saucepan. Cook, stirring, until just comes to a simmer. Remove from heat. Add the chocolate and stir until smooth. Set aside to cool slightly. Spoon over the cream cheese layer and use a spatula to smooth the surface. Place in the fridge for 4 hours or overnight, until set.

5 Whisk the remaining cream in a bowl until soft peaks form. Spoon into a piping bag fitted with a fluted nozzle. Pipe the cream down the centre of the slice. Slice the remaining banana and arrange over top. Sprinkle with the coconut. Decorate with the extra biscuits. Drizzle with extra caramel.

● GLUTEN FREE ● MAKE AHEAD ● FREEZABLE ● EASY ● KID FRIENDLY

Rhubarb & coconut SLICE

This slice is free from gluten and dairy and perfect for lunch boxes.

MAKES 15 **PREP** 15 mins (+ cooling) **COOK** 35 mins

150g almond meal
60g coconut flour
60g shredded coconut
50g arrowroot (tapioca flour)
1 tsp ground cinnamon
2½ tbs coconut sugar
40g solidified coconut oil,
    plus extra, to grease
60ml (¼ cup) honey
1 egg
2 tsp finely grated fresh
    ginger
350g trimmed rhubarb,
    chopped (about
    1.5cm pieces)
topping
1 egg white
2 tbs honey
100g (1½ cups) shredded
    coconut

1 Preheat oven to 180°C/160°C fan forced. Grease a 16 x 26cm (base measurement) slice pan with the extra coconut oil and line with baking paper.

2 Process almond meal, flour, coconut, arrowroot, cinnamon and 1½ tbs sugar until well combined. Add the coconut oil. Process until well combined. Add the honey, egg and ginger. Process until a sticky mixture forms. Press into the prepared pan. Bake for 14-15 minutes or until golden. Set aside to cool.

3 Meanwhile, place the rhubarb in a baking dish. Sprinkle with the remaining sugar. Bake for 15 minutes or until the rhubarb is tender but still holds its shape. Set aside to cool.

4 For the topping, whisk the egg white and honey in a large bowl until frothy. Stir in the coconut until well combined.

5 Scatter the rhubarb over the base, leaving any juices behind in the baking dish. Sprinkle with the topping. Bake for 20 minutes or until golden. Set aside in pan to cool completely. Cut into 15 pieces.

COOK'S TIP

For a citrus twist, try replacing the ginger in the base with the finely grated rind of an orange.

● GLUTEN FREE ● MAKE AHEAD ● FREEZABLE ● EASY ● KID FRIENDLY

Choc berry coconut SLICE

Weet-Bix are the secret to this perfect gluten-free slice base.

MAKES 15 **PREP** 30 mins (+ cooling, 1 hour soaking & 2 hours freezing) **COOK** 10 mins

225g (1½ cups) raw cashews

10 Weet-Bix Gluten Free

125ml (½ cup) melted coconut oil, plus 80ml (⅓ cup), extra

1 tbs maple syrup

120g (¾ cup) frozen mixed berries

45g (½ cup) desiccated coconut

320g can sweet condensed coconut milk

1½ tbs white chia seeds

180g pkt Fry's Turkish Delight mini bars, sliced diagonally

80g fresh raspberries, torn

1½ tbs coconut flakes

1 tbs pistachio kernels, coarsely chopped

2 tsp edible dried rose petals (optional)

60g dark chocolate, melted

1 Place cashews in a heatproof bowl. Cover with boiling water. set aside for 1 hour to soak. Drain well.

2 Meanwhile, preheat oven to 180°C/160°C fan forced. Grease a 16 x 26cm (base size) slice pan and line the base and sides with baking paper. Process the Weet-Bix in a food processor until fine crumbs. Add coconut oil and maple syrup and process until combined. Transfer the mixture to the prepared pan. Use a glass with a flat base to press firmly and evenly over base of pan. Bake for 7 minutes or until light golden. Transfer to a wire rack to cool.

3 Blend the soaked cashews, berries, desiccated coconut, condensed coconut milk, extra coconut oil and 1 tbs chia seeds in a blender until smooth.

4 Pour the cashew mixture over the Weet-Bix base. Use a palette knife or the back of a metal spoon to smooth the surface. Place the slice in the freezer for 2 hours or until set.

5 Remove slice from the freezer 10 minutes before serving. Top with the Turkish Delight, raspberry, coconut flakes, pistachios and rose petals, if using. Sprinkle with remaining 2 tsp chia seeds. Drizzle with the melted dark chocolate. Cut into 15 pieces.

COOK'S TIP

If you don't want to serve the entire slice, you can leave a portion in the freezer, undecorated and well wrapped, where it'll keep for up to 1 week.

● GLUTEN FREE ● MAKE AHEAD ● FREEZABLE ● EASY ● KID FRIENDLY

Cacao & raspberry
QUINOA SLICE

For a nut-free version, swap almond meal for desiccated coconut.

MAKES 15 **PREP** 10 mins (+ cooling & setting) **COOK** 30 mins

225g (2¼ cups) quinoa
   flakes
70g (½ cup) buckwheat flour
45g (⅓ cup) almond meal
50g raw cacao nibs
1 tbs black chia seeds
185g (½ cup) rice malt syrup
80ml (⅓ cup) melted
   coconut oil
100g (⅓ cup) apple sauce
2 eggs, lightly whisked
1 tsp vanilla extract
125g fresh or frozen
   raspberries, plus extra,
   to decorate
45g bar Well, Naturally
   No Added Sugar Dark
   Chocolate, melted
Raw cacao nibs, extra,
   to decorate (optional)

1 Preheat the oven to 180°C/160°C fan forced. Grease the base and sides of a 16 x 26cm (base size) slice pan and line with baking paper, allowing the sides to overhang.

2 Place the quinoa flakes, buckwheat flour, almond meal, cacao nibs and chia seeds in a large bowl. Stir until combined and make a well in the centre.

3 Place the rice malt syrup and coconut oil in a heatproof bowl. Stir until combined. Microwave on High for 30 seconds or until smooth. Add the apple sauce, eggs, vanilla extract and rice malt syrup mixture to the flour well. Stir until combined. Gently fold through the raspberries. Spoon into prepared pan. Smooth the surface. Bake for 30 minutes or until browned and firm to touch. Set aside in pan to cool completely.

4 Use a sharp knife to cut the slice into 15 pieces. Drizzle over the melted chocolate and set aside until set. Decorate with the extra raspberries and extra cacao nibs, if using.

COOK'S TIP

Keep this slice
in an airtight
container lined
with baking paper
and store it in the
fridge for up to
1 week.

★★★★★

It's quite filling. I would make this again, I love the raspberries in it.
LOZBATEUP

● GLUTEN FREE ● MAKE AHEAD ● FREEZABLE ● EASY ● KID FRIENDLY

Gingerbread & salted
CARAMEL SLICE

Gingerbread isn't just for Christmas, it rocks the base of this slice.

MAKES 16 **PREP** 30 mins (+ 15 mins cooling & 1 hour 30 mins chilling) **COOK** 20 mins

170g (½ cup) white choc melts
215g (1 cup) caster sugar
160g butter, chopped
125ml (½ cup) thickened cream
Pinch of sea salt flakes
150g dark chocolate, chopped
125g salted pretzel twists
gingerbread
60ml (¼ cup) molasses (for stronger flavour) or golden syrup (for sweeter flavour)
55g (¼ cup) brown sugar
25g butter
1 egg
150g (1 cup) plain flour
40g (¼ cup) self-raising flour
1 tsp ground ginger
1 tsp ground cinnamon
¼ tsp ground cloves
¼ tsp bicarbonate of soda

1 To make gingerbread, stir molasses or golden syrup, brown sugar and butter in a small saucepan over medium heat until sugar dissolves. Transfer to a large bowl. Set aside for 15 minutes to cool.

2 Preheat oven to 180°C/160°C fan forced. Grease a 20cm (base size) square cake pan. Line the base and sides with baking paper.

3 Stir egg into butter mixture until combined. Sift in plain and self-raising flours, ginger, cinnamon, cloves and bicarb. Use a wooden spoon to mix until well combined and a dough forms. Wrap in plastic wrap. Place in the fridge for 20 minutes.

4 Roll out dough on a floured surface until large enough to line base of prepared pan. Transfer dough to pan base, spreading to edges. Bake for 20 minutes or until golden.

5 Meanwhile, place choc melts in a heatproof bowl. Place caster sugar and 60ml (¼ cup) water in a 20cm saucepan. Stir over medium heat until sugar dissolves. Increase heat to high.

Cook, brushing down side of pan with a wet pastry brush to prevent sugar crystals forming, for 6-8 minutes or until golden. Remove from heat. Carefully whisk in 100g butter until combined. Stir in the cream. Bring to a simmer over medium heat. Cook for 1 minute then pour over the choc. Whisk until smooth. Set aside for 10 minutes to cool. Place in fridge, stirring twice, for 1 hour 30 minutes-2 hours or until a spreadable consistency.

6 Spread caramel evenly over gingerbread. Place in fridge for 30 minutes or until firm.

7 Place the dark chocolate and remaining butter in a small heatproof bowl over a saucepan of simmering water (make sure the bowl doesn't touch the water). Stir until smooth and well combined. Use hands to coarsely break up three-quarters of the pretzels. Spread the chocolate evenly over caramel layer. Top with the broken and whole pretzels. Place in the fridge for 30 minutes. Cut into squares to serve.

★★★★★

Very delicious!

BAKERLOVER7

● GLUTEN FREE ● MAKE AHEAD ● FREEZABLE ● EASY ● KID FRIENDLY

Healthy lemon & coconut SLICE

Pucker up! You can make this slice ahead for an intense lemony hit!

MAKES 20 **PREP** 30 mins (+ cooling & overnight chilling) **COOK** 25 mins

200g (1¼ cups) wholemeal
   spelt flour
55g (⅓ cup) sunflower seeds
20g (¼ cup) desiccated
   coconut
60g (¼ cup) raw caster sugar
60g (⅓ cup) solidified
   coconut oil
2 eggs
2 tsp vanilla extract
1 tsp baking powder
Lemon slices, to serve
   (optional)
15g (¼ cup) flaked coconut,
   toasted

filling
160ml (⅔ cup) fresh
   lemon juice
110g (½ cup) raw caster
   sugar
5 tbs custard powder
4 eggs
800ml light coconut cream
1 tbs finely grated
   lemon rind

1 Preheat oven 180°C/160°C fan forced. Grease the base and sides of a 20 x 30cm (base size) slice pan. Line with baking paper, allowing the paper to overhang the 2 long sides.

2 Place the flour, sunflower seeds and desiccated coconut in a food processor. Process until almost finely ground. Add sugar, coconut oil, eggs, vanilla extract and baking powder. Process, scraping down side occasionally, until mixture sticks together. Use the back of a wet spoon to press the mixture evenly into the prepared pan. Prick the base with a fork. Bake for 10-15 minutes or until golden. Set aside in pan to cool.

3 For the filling, whisk the lemon juice, sugar and custard powder in a saucepan over low heat until smooth. Whisk in eggs, coconut cream and lemon rind until smooth. Continue whisking over medium-low heat until mixture just comes to the boil and thickens. Pour mixture over base, spreading evenly. Place in the fridge to chill overnight.

4 Remove the slice from the pan. Top with lemon slices, if using. Cut into 20 pieces and scatter over toasted coconut to serve.

COOK'S TIP

Store this slice in an airtight container in the fridge for up to 1 week.

★★★★★

The slice gets even more deliciously lemony after a few days. Yum!
WAFFLEISO

● GLUTEN FREE ● MAKE AHEAD ● FREEZABLE ● EASY ● KID FRIENDLY

Choc & blackberry
CRUMBLE SLICE

Traditional jam and coconut slice gets a superfood makeover!

MAKES 15 **PREP** 20 MINS (+ cooling) **COOK** 50 MINS

270g (3 cups) gluten-free rolled oats

30g (¼ cup) quinoa flakes

25g (⅓ cup) shredded coconut

75g (⅓ cup) coconut oil

125g (⅓ cup) organic coconut syrup, plus 3 tsp, extra

35g (⅓ cup) raw cacao powder

420g frozen blackberries

2 tsp lemon juice

¾ tsp finely grated lemon rind

1½ tbs black chia seeds

1 Preheat the oven to 180°C/160°C fan forced. Grease the base and sides of a 16 x 26cm (base size) slice pan and line with baking paper. Place 1 tbs oats, 1 tbs quinoa flakes, 2 tbs shredded coconut, 1 tsp coconut oil and 1 tsp coconut syrup in a small bowl. Stir until combined. Set aside.

2 Place the remaining oats, quinoa flakes, shredded coconut, coconut oil and coconut syrup in a food processor. Add the cacao powder and process until combined and a sticky mixture forms. Reserve ¼ cup of the cacao mixture. Press the remaining mixture into the prepared pan. Bake for 10 minutes or until firm. Set aside in the pan to cool completely.

3 Meanwhile, place blackberries, juice, extra syrup and rind in a saucepan over medium-low heat. Cook, stirring occasionally, for 6 minutes or until the berries release juices. Add chia seeds. Cook, gently stirring occasionally, for 6 minutes or until soft. Transfer to a heatproof bowl and set aside to cool completely.

4 Spread the cooled blackberry mixture over slice base. Add the reserved oat mixture to reserved cacao mixture. Toss until combined then sprinkle over top. Bake for 25 minutes or until golden. Set aside in pan to cool completely. Cut into 15 pieces.

COOK'S TIP

Find coconut syrup at select supermarkets and health food shops. You can also substitute it for maple syrup or honey.

★★★★★

I have eaten this twice with homegrown, frozen berries, delicious!

JACANDCHRIS

● GLUTEN FREE ● MAKE AHEAD ● FREEZABLE ● EASY ● KID FRIENDLY

Gooey loaded jam shortcake
BROWNIE

Raid the biscuit tin for the best brownie topping ever!

MAKES 12 **PREP** 20 MINS (+ cooling) **COOK** 50 MINS

200g butter, chopped
180g dark chocolate,
    chopped
215g (1 cup) caster sugar
60g (⅓ cup) brown sugar
3 eggs, lightly whisked
200g (1⅓ cups) plain flour
30g (¼ cup) cocoa powder
105g (⅓ cup) raspberry jam,
    strained, seeds discarded
180g milk chocolate,
    broken into pieces
250g pkt jam fancies
    biscuits

1 Preheat the oven to 170°C/150°C fan forced. Grease a 20cm x 30cm (base size) slice pan. Line the base and sides with baking paper, allowing the paper to overhang 2cm above sides.

2 Place butter and dark chocolate in a saucepan over medium heat. Cook, stirring, for 5 minutes or until melted and smooth. Remove from heat. Add the sugars and stir until combined. Set aside for 10 minutes to cool slightly.

3 Gradually whisk the egg into chocolate mixture until well combined. Add flour and cocoa and stir until combined. Spoon mixture into prepared pan. Spoon over the jam. Run a skewer through the jam to create a marbled effect. Gently push pieces of milk chocolate into the mixture. Spread mixture over chocolate slightly to cover. Arrange the biscuits in a single layer over the top of the mixture.

4 Bake for 40-45 minutes or until just firm. Set aside in the pan to cool completely. Cut into pieces, to serve.

COOK'S TIP

If you don't have raspberry jam, strawberry, blackberry, blueberry or cherry will taste delicious, too.

Really delicious. I like the crunch the biscuits added, think they would be nice chopped up and mixed through the batter too.

OONAGHDOONA

● GLUTEN FREE ● MAKE AHEAD ● FREEZABLE ● EASY ● KID FRIENDLY

Burnt sugar chocolate & VANILLA SLICE

Vanilla slice is twice as nice with a layer of decadent choc custard!

MAKES 6 **PREP** 20 MINS (+ 4 hours chilling) **COOK** 1 HOUR 10 MINS

3 sheets frozen puff pastry, just thawed
70g (½ cup) cornflour
4 egg yolks
80ml (⅓ cup) milk, plus 375ml (1½ cups), extra
300ml pouring cream
100g (½ cup) caster sugar
60g unsalted butter, chopped
1 tsp vanilla extract
60g dark chocolate, finely chopped
Icing sugar, to dust
Dark chocolate curls, to decorate

1 Preheat oven to 200°C/180°C fan forced. Line a baking tray with baking paper. Place 1 pastry sheet on tray. Prick all over with a fork. Top with a sheet of baking paper then a second baking tray. Bake for 15-20 minutes or until golden. Transfer to a wire rack to cool completely. Repeat with remaining pastry.

2 Line base and sides of a 23cm (base size) square cake pan with baking paper, allowing paper to overhang the sides.

3 Whisk cornflour, yolks and milk in a bowl. Place cream, sugar, butter, vanilla and extra milk in a saucepan over medium heat. Cook, stirring, until sugar dissolves and butter melts. Slowly add cream mixture to egg mixture, whisking constantly until smooth. Transfer mixture to saucepan. Place over medium heat and cook, whisking constantly, for 5 minutes or until mixture boils and thickens. Divide between 2 bowls. Add the chopped chocolate to 1 bowl and stir until combined.

4 Place 1 sheet pastry into prepared pan, trimming to fit. Spread the chocolate custard over the pastry. Top with another piece of pastry. Spread with vanilla custard. Top with remaining pastry, pressing down gently to secure. Cover. Place in fridge for 4 hours or until set.

5 Transfer slice to serving board. Use a large serrated knife to cut into 6 pieces. Dust with icing sugar. Heat a thick metal skewer over a flame until very hot and glowing red. Working quickly but carefully, hold ends of skewer with an oven glove and press onto icing sugar to caramelise the top in a crisscross pattern, reheating the skewer. Decorate with chocolate curls.

★★★★★

Everyone from my office said it was beautiful.

APANDACAITLIN

● GLUTEN FREE ● MAKE AHEAD ● FREEZABLE ● EASY ● KID FRIENDLY

Best-ever marbled cheesecake
BROWNIE SLICE

Have the best of both worlds with this epic dessert mash-up.

MAKES 15 **PREP** 15 mins (+ cooling) **COOK** 50 mins

300g dark chocolate,
   chopped
250g butter, chopped
140g (⅔ cup) caster sugar
3 eggs
190g (1¼ cups) plain flour
50g (⅓ cup) self-raising flour
2 x 143g pkt Baci Perugina
   Original Dark Chocolates,
   unwrapped
cheesecake swirl
250g cream cheese, at room
   temperature, chopped
70g (⅓ cup) caster sugar
1 tsp vanilla extract
1 egg

1 Preheat oven to 170°C/150°C fan forced. Grease an 18cm x 28cm (base size) slice pan. Line base and sides with baking paper, allowing paper to overhang 2cm above sides. Place dark chocolate and butter in a saucepan over medium heat. Cook, stirring occasionally, for 4-5 minutes or until mixture is melted and smooth. Remove from heat. Set aside for 10 minutes to cool slightly.

2 Meanwhile, to make the cheesecake swirl, use electric beaters to beat the cream cheese, sugar and vanilla in a bowl and until pale and creamy. Add the egg and beat until well combined.

3 Whisk sugar into chocolate mixture. Add eggs, 1 at a time, whisking well after each addition until well combined. Add flours and stir until combined. Spread half of the brownie mixture over the base of the prepared pan. Drop spoonfuls of remaining brownie and cheesecake mixtures, alternating, on top of brownie mixture in pan. Run a flat-bladed knife through the mixtures to create a marbled effect. Press Baci chocolates into the mixture. Bake for 45 minutes or until top is firm to touch. Set aside in the pan to cool completely. Cut into 15 pieces.

COOK'S TIP

This is a great recipe to make at Easter as you can use any kind of small, individual chocolates to top the slice.

★ ★ ★ ★ ★

I love the combination of flavours
HERBE-AUX-CHATS

● GLUTEN FREE ● MAKE AHEAD ● FREEZABLE ● EASY ● KID FRIENDLY

Vegan Vanilla SLICE

Bookmark this crispy, creamy slice for plant-based entertaining!

MAKES 20 **PREP** 30 mins (+ setting & chilling) **COOK** 35 minutes

2 sheets frozen puff pastry, just thawed (see notes)
1 vanilla bean, split
1L (4 cups) soy milk
100g (1 cup) caster sugar
180g (1⅓ cups) cornflour
100g Nuttelex original spread
¼ tsp ground turmeric
60g (⅓ cup) icing sugar mixture

1 Preheat oven to 200°C/180°C fan forced. Line 2 baking trays with baking paper. Place 1 pastry sheet on each tray. Bake pastry for 15 minutes or until golden, puffed and cooked through. Set aside for 5 minutes to cool slightly then gently flatten pastry. Set aside to cool completely.

2 Meanwhile, grease a 6cm-deep, 22cm (base size) square cake pan. Line base and sides with baking paper, allowing paper to overhang 2cm above sides.

3 Use a sharp knife to scrape seeds from vanilla bean. Place soy milk, vanilla bean and seeds in a saucepan over medium heat. Cook, stirring, for 10 minutes or until almost simmering (do not boil). Set aside for 10 minutes. Strain. Discard bean.

4 Place 1 sheet of pastry in prepared pan, trimming to fit. Place caster sugar and cornflour in a large, heavy-based saucepan. Gradually add the soy milk mixture, stirring constantly with a wooden spoon until smooth and well combined. Place over medium heat. Cook, stirring constantly, for 8-10 minutes or until mixture bubbles and thickens. Stir in Nuttelex and turmeric. Working quickly, remove from heat and spoon mixture over pastry. Top with remaining pastry sheet, trimming to fit. Set aside to cool for 30 minutes. Place in fridge for 4 hours or until cold and firm.

5 Transfer slice to serving board. Dust with icing sugar. Cut into squares. Serve.

COOK'S TIP

Most frozen puff pastry is naturally vegan, but remember to check the label carefully.

★★★★★

My vegan and non vegan family all loved it. Very easy to make.

LUTESS

● GLUTEN FREE ● MAKE AHEAD ● FREEZABLE ● EASY ● KID FRIENDLY

Peanut butter & choc chip COOKIE SQUARES

Need a quick sweet fix? These easy squares are ready in a flash!

MAKES 30 **PREP** 10 mins (+ cooling & setting) **COOK** 30 mins

150g butter, chopped,
at room temperature

100g (½ cup, firmly packed)
brown sugar

100g (½ cup) caster sugar

1 tsp vanilla extract

1 egg

130g (½ cup) smooth
peanut butter

150g (1 cup) plain flour

½ tsp baking powder

90g (1 cup) rolled oats

190g (1 cup) dark
choc chips

50g (1 cup) pretzels,
coarsely chopped, plus
30 extra, to decorate

300g dark chocolate,
melted

1 Preheat oven to 180°C/160°C fan forced. Grease a 20 x 30cm (base size) slice pan and line with baking paper, allowing paper to overhang long sides.

2 Use electric beaters to beat the butter, sugars and vanilla in a bowl until pale and creamy. Add egg and beat until well combined. Add peanut butter and beat until combined. Sift over flour and baking powder. Add oats, choc chips and chopped pretzels. Stir until combined. Press into prepared pan and smooth the surface. Bake for 25-30 minutes or until golden. Set aside in pan to cool completely.

3 Spread melted chocolate over cookie bar. Top with extra pretzels. Place in fridge for 20 minutes or until set. Cut into 30 squares.

COOK'S TIP

Feeling extra nutty? Swap the pretzels on top for roasted or chocolate coated peanuts.

★ ★ ★ ★ ★

A perfect slice, beautifully sweet and salty.

DR BEAKER

● GLUTEN FREE ● MAKE AHEAD ● FREEZABLE ● EASY ● KID FRIENDLY

Pumpkin pie
SLICE

This sweet and spiced tart is like Autumn on a plate!

MAKES 8 **PREP** 30 mins (+ freezing & cooling) **COOK** 1 hour 10 mins

300g (2 cups) plain flour
125g butter, chilled, chopped
70g (⅓ cup) caster sugar
3 eggs
395g can sweetened condensed milk
1½ tsp ground cinnamon
½ tsp ground ginger
½ tsp mixed spice
¼ tsp ground nutmeg
420g cooked kent pumpkin, pureed
Cinnamon sugar, to dust
Edible flowers, to decorate
meringue
100ml water
100g (½ cup) caster sugar
2 egg whites

1 Preheat oven to 200°C/180°C fan forced. Grease a 3cm-deep, 12 x 33cm (base size) fluted tart tin with removable base.

2 Place flour, butter and sugar in a food processor and process until fine crumbs. Add 1 egg. Process until dough just comes together. Transfer to prepared tin and use fingertips to press evenly over base and up sides. Place in freezer for 10 minutes to rest.

3 Place tin on a baking tray. Line the pastry with baking paper and fill with pastry weights or rice. Bake for 15 minutes. Remove the paper and pastry weights or rice and bake for a further 10 minutes or until pastry is light golden. Set aside to cool.

4 Reduce oven to 180°C/160°C fan forced. Place the condensed milk, cinnamon, ginger, mixed spice, nutmeg and remaining eggs in a bowl. Whisk until combined. Add the pumpkin and gently whisk until well combined. Pour into the pastry case. Bake for 45 minutes or until custard is just set. Transfer slice to a wire rack to cool completely.

5 For the meringue, stir water and sugar in a saucepan over medium heat, brushing down side of pan with a wet pastry brush to prevent sugar crystals forming, until sugar dissolves and mixture comes to the boil. Cook without stirring until mixture reaches 115°C (soft ball stage) on a sugar thermometer. While syrup continues to cook, use electric beaters to whisk the egg whites and a pinch of salt in a bowl until soft peaks form. When the syrup reaches 120°C (hard ball stage), and with the beaters on low speed, gradually add the syrup to the egg white mixture. Increase speed to medium and whisk for 10 minutes or until thick, glossy and cool.

6 Spoon the meringue into a piping bag fitted with a large plain nozzle. Pipe rows of meringue peaks onto the slice. Use a cook's blowtorch to caramelise. Sprinkle with cinnamon sugar and decorate with flowers.

● GLUTEN FREE ● MAKE AHEAD ● FREEZABLE ● EASY ● KID FRIENDLY

Loaded crunchy peanut
BRITTLE BROWNIE

Step up your brownie game with crunchy, salty peanut brittle!

MAKES 12 **PREP** 20 mins (+ cooling & setting) **COOK** 45 mins

215g (1 cup) caster sugar

180g dark chocolate, chopped, plus 100g extra, melted

150g butter, chopped

70g (1/3 cup, firmly packed) brown sugar

80ml (1/3 cup) milk

3 eggs, lightly whisked

30g (1/4 cup) cocoa powder

190g (1½ cups) plain flour

180g pkt Darrell Lea Peanut Brittle Milk Chocolate, chopped

70g (1/4 cup) smooth peanut butter

250g pkt chocolate cream biscuits

160g pkt Darrell Lea Peanut Brittle Balls, coarsely chopped

1 Preheat oven to 180°C/160°C fan forced. Grease a 20 x 30cm (base size) slice pan. Line the base and sides with baking paper, allowing the paper to overhang 2cm above the sides.

2 Place caster sugar, dark chocolate, butter, brown sugar and milk in a saucepan over medium heat. Cook, stirring, for 5 minutes or until melted and smooth. Set aside for 10 minutes to cool slightly.

3 Whisk eggs into chocolate mixture. Whisk in cocoa and flour. Fold in peanut brittle chocolate. Spoon batter into prepared pan. Dollop with peanut butter. Arrange biscuits over top of brownie.

4 Bake for 40 minutes or until top is just firm to touch. Cool in pan. Drizzle over extra dark chocolate. Sprinkle with peanut brittle balls. Set aside for 1 hour or until set. Cut into pieces to serve.

COOK'S TIP

Go for slightly under-baked rather than over-baked brownies, as they will continue to bake as they cool.

● GLUTEN FREE ● MAKE AHEAD ● FREEZABLE ● EASY ● KID FRIENDLY

Gingerbread choc-caramel SLICE

Caramel slice gets the festive treatment, and a dessert gold star!

SERVES 16 **PREP** 1 hour (+ cooling & 6 hours chilling time) **COOK** 1 hour

200g dark cooking chocolate, finely chopped
2 tsp vegetable oil
50g white cooking chocolate, finely chopped
gingerbread
50g butter, chopped
100g (½ cup) brown sugar
125ml (½ cup) honey
1 egg, lightly whisked
300g (2 cups) plain flour
75g (½ cup) self-raising flour
2 tsp ground cinnamon
2 tsp ground ginger
1 tsp ground cloves
½ tsp bicarbonate of soda
caramel
395g can sweetened condensed milk
45g (¼ cup, lightly packed) brown sugar
60g butter

1 Grease a square 20cm cake pan and line with baking paper, allowing it to overhang the sides.

2 To make the gingerbread. Place the butter, sugar and honey in a small saucepan over low heat. Cook, stirring, until melted. Pour into a large heatproof bowl then set aside to cool slightly. Whisk in the egg. Stir in flours, cinnamon, ginger, cloves and bicarb.

3 Turn the dough onto a lightly floured surface and knead until smooth. Cover with plastic wrap. Place in the fridge for 1 hour to rest.

4 Preheat the oven to 180°C/160°C fan forced. Divide gingerbread dough in half. Tear one portion of the dough into chunks and place in the base of the pan. Use the back of a spoon to press the dough evenly into the base. Prick the base all over with a fork. Bake for 15 minutes or until golden. Set aside.

5 Line a baking tray with baking paper. Use a floured rolling pin to roll out remaining portion of dough on baking paper until 4mm thick.

6 Use a 3cm star cutter to cut out 16 biscuits from dough. Place on the lined tray. Place in the fridge for 15 minutes. Bake for 8-10 minutes or until golden. Set aside to cool on the tray. Reduce the oven temperature to 160°C/140°C fan forced.

7 Make caramel. Place condensed milk, sugar and butter in a small saucepan over low heat. Cook, stirring, until sugar dissolves. Increase heat to medium and cook, stirring constantly, for 8-10 minutes or until the mixture thickens and starts to bubble. Pour over biscuit base. Smooth the surface.

8 Bake for 10-15 minutes or until set (there will be small bubbles on the surface). Set aside in pan to cool completely. Chill for 3 hours.

9 Place the dark chocolate and oil in a microwave-safe bowl. Microwave on Medium, stirring every minute, until the chocolate melts. Spread the melted chocolate over the caramel. Place stars on the top. Place in the fridge for 1 hour to set.

10 Place the white chocolate in a microwave-safe bowl. Microwave on Medium, stirring every minute, until melted and smooth. Drizzle over the slice. Place in the fridge for 2 hours or until set. Cut the slice into squares to serve.

● GLUTEN FREE ● MAKE AHEAD ● FREEZABLE ● EASY ● KID FRIENDLY

Pumpkin pecan pie
SLICE

Pecan and pumpkin pie collide in the ultimate diner-style slice!

MAKES 24 **PREP** 20 mins (+ cooling & overnight chilling) **COOK** 1 hour 15 mins

600g kent pumpkin, peeled, coarsely chopped
150g (1 cup) plain flour
70g (⅓ cup, firmly packed) brown sugar
50g (½ cup) rolled oats
125g butter, at room temperature
160ml (⅔ cup) milk
1 tbs cornflour
3 eggs, lightly whisked
140g (⅔ cup) caster sugar
1 tsp mixed spice
250g (2 cups) pecan halves, coarsely chopped
Icing sugar, to dust (optional)

1 Cook the pumpkin in a steamer basket over a saucepan of boiling for 20 minutes or until tender. Set aside to cool completely. Transfer to a food processor and process until smooth. Set aside.

2 Preheat oven to 200°C/180°C fan forced. Grease a 20cm x 30cm (base size) slice pan and line the base and sides with baking paper, allowing the paper to overhang 5cm above sides.

3 Place the flour, brown sugar and oats in a bowl and stir until combined. Add the butter and stir until a crumbly dough forms. Press mixture evenly over base of prepared pan. Bake for 15 minutes or until light golden. Set aside to cool slightly.

4 Meanwhile, whisk milk and cornflour in a bowl until combined. Add the egg, caster sugar, mixed spice and pumpkin and whisk until smooth and well combined. Pour mixture over pastry base. Top with pecans. Bake for 35-40 minutes or until set. Set aside in pan to cool. Place in fridge overnight or until set. Cut into pieces. Serve dusted with icing sugar, if using.

COOK'S TIP

If you can't find kent pumpkin, Queensland Blue or butternut pumpkin will work just as well.

● GLUTEN FREE ● MAKE AHEAD ● FREEZABLE ● EASY ● KID FRIENDLY

PASTRIES + PIES

IT'S CRISP, FLAKY PASTRY FOR THE WIN WITH THIS GOLDEN SELECTION OF PIES, TARTS AND PASTRY DELIGHTS.

Chocolate Kahlua CUSTARD PIE

It's custard pie, but not as you know it. It's better, and boozy to boot.

SERVES 10 **PREP** 20 mins (+ chilling) **COOK** 45 mins

150g (1 cup) plain flour

30g (¼ cup) cocoa powder, plus extra, to dust

60g (⅓ cup) pure icing sugar

125g unsalted butter, chopped, chilled

4 eggs

2 tsp vanilla extract

250ml (1 cup) milk

100g (½ cup) caster sugar

500ml (2 cups) thickened cream

100g milk chocolate, chopped

1 tbs cornflour

125ml (½ cup) Kahlua

1 Place flour, cocoa, icing sugar and a pinch of salt into bowl of a food processor. Process until well combined. Add butter and process until mixture resembles coarse crumbs. Lightly whisk 1 egg in a bowl. With the motor running, add egg and 1 tsp of vanilla and process until dough just comes together. Gather the dough together into a disc. Cover with plastic wrap. Place in the fridge for 2 hours to rest.

2 Preheat the oven to 200°C/180°C fan forced. Remove the dough from the fridge. Roll out between 2 sheets of baking paper until 4mm thick. Use to line the base and sides of a 23cm (base measurement) pie tin or fluted tart tin with removable base. Trim any excess dough. Place tin on a baking tray in the freezer for 15 minutes to chill.

3 Line the pastry with baking paper. Fill with pastry weights or rice. Bake for 15 minutes. Remove the paper and pastry weights or rice. Bake for a further 10 minutes or until golden. Set aside to cool slightly on the baking tray until required.

4 Meanwhile, place the milk, caster sugar and 250ml (1 cup) cream to a saucepan over medium heat. Bring to a simmer. Remove from heat. Add chocolate, cornflour and half the Kahlua. Stir until chocolate has melted. In a separate bowl whisk together remaining eggs and vanilla. Slowly pour in milk mixture, whisking constantly until thickened. Pour custard mixture into cooled tart tin. Bake for 20-25 minutes or until custard is just set. Set aside to cool completely. Place in fridge to chill.

5 Use electric beaters to beat the remaining cream and Kahlua in a large bowl until firm peaks form. Transfer to a piping bag fitted with a 1cm plain nozzle. Pipe peaks of cream on top of the pie. Lightly dust with cocoa powder.

COOK'S TIP

For easy dusting, use a small strainer to sift the cocoa powder over the cream.

You can make the pastry ahead of time. Follow step 1 and wrap in plastic wrap. Store pastry in the fridge for up to 3 days, or freeze for up to 2 months.

● GLUTEN FREE ● MAKE AHEAD ● FREEZABLE ● EASY ● KID FRIENDLY

Choc-mint PICNIC PIE

There's a Mint Slice hidden in every slice of this luxe chocolate pie.

MAKES 12 **PREP** 30 mins (+ 1 hour resting, 4 hours setting & cooling) **COOK** 35 mins

25g unsalted butter, chopped

150g dark cooking chocolate, finely chopped

250g Arnott's Mint Slice biscuits

1 tbs hot water

2 tsp gelatine powder

250g pkt cream cheese, at room temperature

70g (⅓ cup) caster sugar

125ml (½ cup) thickened cream

100g white chocolate, melted, cooled

1 tsp peppermint essence

Green liquid food colouring, to tint

Fresh mint leaves, to serve

chocolate pastry

225g (1½ cups) plain flour

45g (¼ cup) icing sugar mixture

2 tbs cocoa powder

150g butter, chilled, chopped

1 egg yolk

2 tbs milk

1 To make the pastry, process flour, icing sugar and cocoa in a food processor until combined. Add butter. Process until mixture resembles fine breadcrumbs. Add the yolk and milk. Process until the dough just comes together. Turn onto a floured surface. Knead until smooth. Shape into a disc and cover with plastic wrap. Place in the fridge for 30 minutes to rest.

2 Roll out the dough on a sheet of baking paper to a 4mm-thick disc. Line a 3cm-deep 24cm (base size) round fluted tart tin with removable base with dough. Trim excess. Place in the fridge for 30 minutes to rest.

3 Preheat oven to 200°C/180°C fan forced. Line pastry with baking paper. Fill with pastry weights or rice. Bake for 15 minutes. Remove pastry weights or rice and paper. Bake for a further 10-15 minutes or until cooked through and crisp. Set aside to cool.

4 Place the butter and 100g of the chocolate in a heatproof bowl. Microwave, stirring every 30 seconds, for 1-2 minutes or until melted and smooth. Spread over the pastry base. Press biscuits on top in a single layer. Place hot water in a heatproof bowl. Sprinkle with gelatine and stir until well combined. Place bowl in a larger heatproof bowl. Pour boiling water into the larger bowl until it reaches halfway up the side of the smaller bowl. Set aside, stirring occasionally, for 2-3 minutes or until the gelatine dissolves. Remove smaller bowl from water and set aside to cool slightly.

5 Meanwhile, use electric beaters to beat cream cheese in a bowl until smooth. Add sugar and cream. Beat until well combined. Beat in white chocolate and essence. Add food colouring to tint green and beat until evenly coloured. Beat in gelatine. Pour into the pastry case. Place in the fridge for 3-4 hours or until set.

6 Place the remaining chocolate in a heatproof bowl. Microwave, stirring every 30 seconds, for 1-2 minutes or until melted and smooth. Drizzle the melted chocolate over the pie to decorate. Top with mint leaves.

★★★★★

This is easy to make and tastes as good as it looks.

GOROSY

● GLUTEN FREE ● MAKE AHEAD ● FREEZABLE ● EASY ● KID FRIENDLY

Almond & raspberry
MERINGUE TARTS

Cheat's frangipane and raspberry jam make these tiny tarts sing!

MAKES 20 **PREP** 30 mins (+ chilling) **COOK** 15 mins

100g unsalted butter,
  chilled, finely chopped
150g (1 cup) plain flour
2 tbs caster sugar
1 egg yolk
2-3 tsp cold water
90g (¼ cup) raspberry jam
20 mini meringues
Icing sugar, to dust
filling
40g butter, at room
  temperature
2 tbs caster sugar
1 egg yolk
40g (⅓ cup) almond meal
1 tbs plain flour

1 Preheat oven to 180°C/160°C fan forced. Lightly grease 20 mini muffin pans. Process butter, flour and sugar in a food processor until mixture resembles fine breadcrumbs. Add egg yolk and a little water and process until dough just comes together, adding more water as needed. Turn onto a lightly floured surface. Knead until just smooth. Divide dough into 2 portions and shape each into a disc. Cover with plastic wrap. Place in the fridge for 15 minutes to rest.

2 Roll out 1 dough portion on a lightly floured surface to a 3mm-thick disc. Use a 7.5cm flower pastry cutter to cut out 10 flowers. Gently press into prepared pans. Repeat with remaining dough to make 20 tart shells. Place in the fridge.

3 For the filling, use a wooden spoon to beat butter and sugar in a small bowl until well combined. Add the egg yolk and stir until combined. Add the almond meal and flour and stir until just combined.

4 Spoon mixture among the pastry cases. Bake for 12 minutes or until golden brown. Cool in trays for 5 minutes. Transfer to a wire rack to cool completely.

5 Place a small spoonful of jam on top of each tart. Top with a mini meringue. Dust with icing sugar.

COOK'S TIP

If you can't find mini meringues, a small dollop of whipped cream on top will work in a pinch.

● GLUTEN FREE ● MAKE AHEAD ● FREEZABLE ● EASY ● KID FRIENDLY

Strawberry custard
MILLE-FEUILLE

This dazzling tart is secretly simple thanks to bought pastry and jam.

SERVES 12 **PREP** 40 mins (+ overnight chilling & cooling) **COOK** 1 hour 25 mins

750ml (3 cups) thickened cream

410ml (1²/₃ cups) milk

1 tbs vanilla bean paste

80g caster sugar

60g cornflour

2 egg yolks

50g unsalted butter, chopped

3 sheets frozen puff pastry, just thawed

150g (1 cup) pure icing sugar

500g fresh strawberries, hulled, halved

155g (½ cup) raspberry jam, warmed, strained

1 Bring 250ml (1 cup) cream, 250ml (1 cup) milk and 2 tsp vanilla to the boil in a saucepan over medium heat. Remove from heat. Whisk together the sugar, cornflour, yolks and remaining milk in a heatproof bowl until pale and creamy. Slowly pour milk mixture into the yolk mixture, whisking constantly, until mixture is smooth. Return to pan. Cook, whisking, over medium heat for 3-5 minutes or until thickened. Remove from heat. Whisk in butter. Transfer to heatproof bowl. Cover surface with plastic wrap. Place custard in fridge for 3 hours or overnight to set.

2 Preheat oven to 200°C/180°C fan forced. Place 1 pastry sheet on a baking tray lined with baking paper. Cover with another sheet of baking paper. Top with another baking tray then a heavy baking dish. Bake for 20-25 minutes or until golden and crisp. Set aside to cool completely. Use a small sharp knife to trim pastry to a 20 x 22cm rectangle. Repeat with the remaining pastry sheets.

3 Use electric beaters to whisk the remaining cream, vanilla and 80g (½ cup) icing sugar in a bowl until firm peaks form. Spoon into a piping bag fitted with a plain nozzle.

4 Use clean electric beaters to beat the custard for 1-2 minutes or until smooth. Spoon the custard into a separate piping bag fitted with a plain nozzle. Place the remaining icing sugar and 2 tsp water in a bowl. Stir until smooth and well combined. Spoon into a sealable plastic bag.

5 Pipe a little of the cream mixture into the centre of a serving plate. Top with a pastry sheet. Place the strawberries upright, cut-side out, around the edge of pastry sheet, then place remaining strawberries, cut-side down, over the base. Pipe the cream mixture over strawberries, filling gaps. Top with a pastry sheet. Pipe peaks of the custard over the pastry. Top with the final pastry sheet. Spread the jam over the top. Snip 1 corner from the end of the bag of icing. Pipe lines of icing crossways across the jam. Use a toothpick to gently drag the icing through the jam to create a feathered pattern.

● GLUTEN FREE ● MAKE AHEAD ● FREEZABLE ● EASY ● KID FRIENDLY

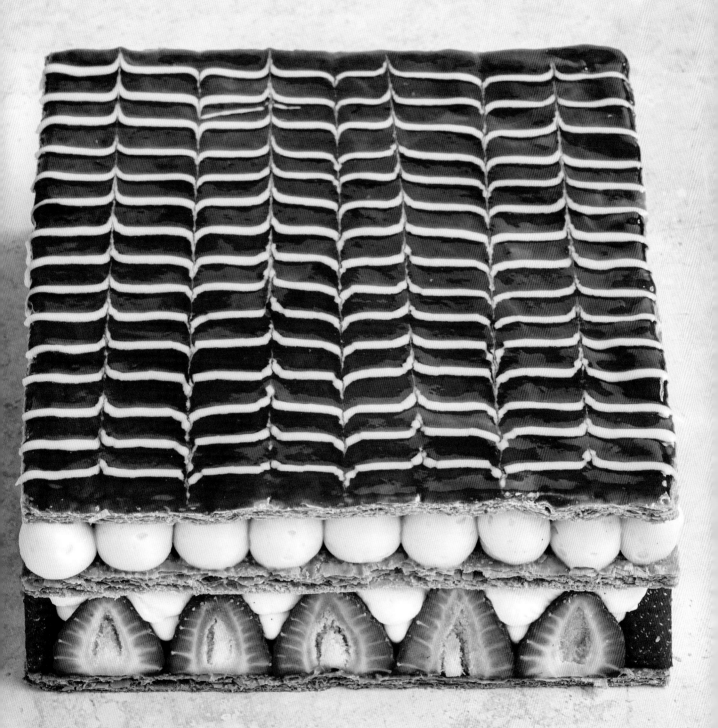

Lemon & earl grey TART

Earl grey tea adds a twist of floral bergamot, perfect with lemon!

SERVES 8-10 **PREP** 45 mins (+ resting & cooling) **COOK** 1 hour 5 mins

175ml pouring cream

1½ tbs loose leaf earl grey tea, plus extra, to decorate

5 eggs

215g (1 cup) caster sugar

160ml (²/₃ cup) fresh lemon juice, strained

1 tbs finely grated lemon rind

Whipped cream, to serve

pastry

265g (1¾ cups) plain flour

150g unsalted butter, chilled, chopped

55g (¼ cup) caster sugar

1 tsp finely grated lemon rind

¼ tsp vanilla bean paste

1 egg yolk, plus 1 egg, extra, whisked

1½ tbs chilled water

syrupy lemons

100g (½ cup) caster sugar

1 tsp loose leaf earl grey tea

1 lemon, thinly sliced

1 To make the pastry, process the flour, butter, sugar, lemon rind and vanilla in a food processor until fine crumbs form. Add the egg yolk and water. Process until dough just comes together. Turn onto a floured surface and knead until just smooth. Shape into a disc and cover with plastic wrap. Place in fridge for 1 hour to rest.

2 Roll out the dough on a sheet of lightly floured baking paper to a 4mm-thick disc. Line a round 3.5cm-deep, 23.5cm (base size) fluted tart tin with removable base with dough. Trim excess. Place in fridge for 1 hour to rest.

3 Preheat oven to 190°C/170°C fan forced. Line the pastry case with baking paper and fill with pastry weights or rice. Bake for 15 minutes. Remove paper and weights and bake for 10 minutes or until golden. Brush with the extra egg. Bake for 3 minutes or until sealed. Set aside to cool.

4 Meanwhile, place cream and tea in a saucepan over medium heat. Bring just to the boil. Remove from heat. Set aside for 20 minutes to infuse. Strain through a fine sieve into a bowl. Whisk together the eggs and sugar in a large jug. Whisk in the lemon juice and rind. Add the cream mixture and stir until just combined. Set aside for 15 minutes then skim off the foam.

5 Reduce oven to 150°C/130°C fan forced. Place the tin on a baking tray. Pour the egg mixture into the pastry case. Bake for 25-30 minutes or until just set. Set aside to cool.

6 Meanwhile, for the syrupy lemons, line a baking tray with baking paper. Heat the sugar, tea and 100ml water, in a frying pan over medium heat, stirring, for 2 minutes or until sugar dissolves. Add lemon. Cook, turning, for 5-6 minutes or until translucent. Transfer the lemon to the prepared tray. Set aside to cool.

7 Top the tart with cream and lemon. Drizzle over some syrup. Sprinkle with tea leaves to serve.

● GLUTEN FREE ● MAKE AHEAD ● FREEZABLE ● EASY ● KID FRIENDLY

Choc-orange
CANNONCINI

Petite pastry horns stuffed with a creamy choc-orange custard.

MAKES 20 **PREP** 30 mins (+ cooling & 2 hours chilling) **COOK** 40 mins

125ml (½ cup) thickened
   cream
125ml (½ cup) milk
2 wide strips orange rind,
   plus finely grated rind,
   to serve
2 egg yolks
55g (¼ cup) caster sugar
2 tbs cornflour
50g dark chocolate,
   chopped, plus extra,
   grated, to serve
2 sheets frozen butter puff
   pastry, just thawed
1 egg, lightly whisked
Icing sugar, to dust

1 Place the cream, milk and orange rind strips in a small saucepan over medium-low heat. Cook, stirring, until the mixture comes to a simmer. Remove from heat and set aside.

2 Whisk together the egg yolks and sugar in a heatproof bowl until pale and creamy. Add the cornflour and whisk until well combined.

3 Remove and discard the orange rind from milk mixture. Slowly pour the milk mixture into the egg mixture, whisking constantly, until combined. Return the mixture to the saucepan. Cook, stirring constantly, over low heat, for 3 minutes or until thickened (do not boil). Add the chocolate and stir until smooth and well combined. Transfer to a heatproof bowl and set aside for 5 minutes, stirring occasionally, to cool slightly. Cover the surface with plastic wrap. Place in fridge for 2 hours to chill.

4 Preheat the oven to 200°C/180°C fan forced. Line 2 large baking trays with baking paper. Spray

10 metal pastry horn moulds (or ice-cream cones wrapped in foil) with oil. Cut each pastry sheet into ten 2cm-wide strips. Transfer strips to 1 prepared tray. Wrap the pastry strips, overlapping slightly, around the moulds. Brush with egg. Place, seam side down, on remaining prepared tray. Cover remaining pastry and place in fridge.

5 Bake for 10 minutes or until light golden. Set aside on the tray to cool slightly. Carefully slide pastry off moulds. Return to tray. Bake for 3-4 minutes or until crisp. Transfer to a wire rack to cool completely. Repeat with remaining pastry and egg to make 20 pastry cones.

6 Spoon the chocolate custard into a piping bag fitted with a small fluted nozzle. Pipe the chocolate custard into the pastry cones. Dust with icing sugar and sprinkle with grated orange rind and extra chocolate. Serve immediately.

● GLUTEN FREE ● MAKE AHEAD ● FREEZABLE ● EASY ● KID FRIENDLY

Caramel drizzle CHURRO CAKE

This epic churro stack is baked, not fried, so prep is fuss-free.

SERVES 10 **PREP** 30 mins (+ cooling) **COOK** 1 hour 5 mins

120g unsalted butter, chopped
2 tbs caster sugar
½ tsp salt
150g (1 cup) plain flour
4 eggs
750ml (3 cups) thickened cream
2 tsp ground cinnamon
310ml (1¼ cup) caramel spread

cinnamon sugar
155g (¾ cup) caster sugar
3 tsp ground cinnamon

1 Preheat oven to 180°C/160°C fan forced. Place the butter, sugar, salt and 250ml (1 cup) water in a saucepan over medium heat. Cook, stirring constantly, until mixture just comes to the boil. Add the flour and stir for 1 minute or until dough comes away from side of pan. Remove from heat. Set aside for 10 minutes to cool.

2 Transfer the dough to a large bowl. Use electric beaters to beat the eggs, 1 at a time, beating well after each addition, into dough. Spoon the dough into a large piping bag fitted with a 1.5cm fluted nozzle.

3 To make the cinnamon sugar, place the sugar and cinnamon in a small bowl and stir until combined.

4 Line 3 large baking trays with baking paper. Trace around the base of a 15cm-diameter plate to make 5 circles on the paper. Turn the paper ink-side down. Pipe a ring of dough around the edge of 1 circle. Pipe rings of dough inside the larger ring, leaving a small gap between each ring, until disc is full. Sprinkle with 1 tbs of cinnamon sugar. Repeat piping with the remaining dough and cinnamon sugar to make 5 discs.

5 Bake for 35 minutes or until golden brown. Flip churro discs. Bake for a further 30 minutes or until golden and cooked through. Lightly spray top of each churro disc with oil then sprinkle with the cinnamon sugar. Set aside to cool completely.

6 Use clean electric beaters to beat cream and cinnamon in a bowl until firm peaks form. Place 1 disc on a serving plate. Top with one-fifth of the cinnamon cream then drizzle with 60ml (¼ cup) caramel. Repeat with remaining discs, cream and caramel.

★ ★ ★ ★ ★

Easy to make, and yummy. Everyone enjoyed it.

BJT

● GLUTEN FREE ● MAKE AHEAD ● FREEZABLE ● EASY ● KID FRIENDLY

Vegan pumpkin
PIE

Get ahead and make this plant-based pie up to 3 days in advance.

SERVES 10 **PREP** 1 hour (+ cooling & overnight chilling) **COOK** 50 mins

1.5kg kent pumpkin, peeled, coarsely chopped

2½ tbs coconut oil, melted

115g (1¼ cups) gluten-free rolled oats

80g (½ cup) pepitas

170g (about 9) fresh dates, pitted, chopped

1 tsp cold water

35g (¼ cup) gluten-free cornflour

200ml coconut milk

60ml (¼ cup) maple syrup, plus extra, to serve

1¼ tsp ground cinnamon, plus extra, to dust

1¼ tsp mixed spice

Pinch of salt

Whipped coconut cream, to serve

1 Preheat oven to 180°C/160°C fan forced. Line 2 baking trays with baking paper. Arrange the pumpkin in a single layer on 1 tray. Drizzle with 2 tsp of the oil and toss until coated. Roast, turning halfway through cooking, for 40 minutes or until very tender but not browned. Set aside to cool.

2 Meanwhile, grease a 1.4L, 19cm (base size) pie dish. Spread oats and pepitas over remaining prepared tray. Bake, stirring once, for 7-8 minutes or until golden. Set aside to cool slightly. Process cooled oats and pepitas in a food processor until coarsely chopped. Add the dates, water and remaining oil. Process until well combined. Transfer the mixture to the prepared dish. Press evenly over the base and side. Place in the fridge for 1 hour or until firm.

3 Place pumpkin in a clean food processor and process until smooth. Place the cornflour and coconut milk in a large saucepan and whisk until smooth. Add the pumpkin, maple syrup, cinnamon, mixed spice and salt. Cook, stirring, over medium-low heat for 8-10 minutes or until boiling and thickened. Set aside, stirring occasionally, for 30 minutes to cool. Pour into crust. Smooth surface. Place in the fridge for 8 hours to set. Top with coconut cream, sprinkle with cinnamon and drizzle over extra maple syrup.

COOK'S TIP

You can make this tart up to 3 days ahead. Store in an airtight container in the fridge. Top with the coconut cream, cinnamon and extra syrup on day of serving,

★★★★★

Easy to make, not too many ingredients.

TRUHOW

● GLUTEN FREE ● MAKE AHEAD ● FREEZABLE ● EASY ● KID FRIENDLY

Funfetti whoopie PIES

Get the party started with these buttercream-filled whoopie pies!

MAKES 26 **PREP** 30 mins (+ cooling) **COOK** 30 mins

125g butter, chopped,
at room temperature
100g (½ cup) caster sugar
80g (½ cup, lightly packed)
brown sugar
1 tsp vanilla extract
1 egg
1 tsp bicarbonate of soda
375g (2½ cups) plain flour
330ml (1⅓ cups) buttermilk
90g (⅓ cup) hundreds and
thousands
buttercream filling
125g butter, chopped,
at room temperature
230g (1½ cups) icing
sugar mixture
1½ tbs milk
Pink food colouring, to tint

1 Preheat oven to 190°C/170°C fan forced. Line 2 baking trays with baking paper. Beat the butter, sugars and vanilla in a bowl until pale and creamy. Add the egg and beat until well combined.

2 Stir in the bicarb. Use a large metal spoon to fold in the flour and buttermilk, in alternating batches, until just smooth (the mixture should be a little stiff).

3 Use a 3cm-diameter ice-cream scoop to place scoops of mixture on prepared trays, leaving 5cm between each to allow room for spreading. Use your finger to gently smooth the mixture around the edges. Sprinkle with hundreds and thousands.

4 Bake, swapping trays halfway through cooking, for 10 minutes or until firm. Set aside to cool slightly before transferring to a wire rack to cool completely. Repeat with the remaining mixture.

5 To make the filling, beat the butter and icing sugar in a bowl until well combined. Add the milk and beat until combined. Divide the buttercream between 2 bowls. Add food colouring to 1 bowl to tint pale-pink. Beat until evenly coloured. Add more food colouring to second bowl to tint dark-pink. Beat until evenly coloured. Spread the pale-pink icing on one side of a piping bag fitted with a 1cm fluted nozzle. Spread the dark-pink icing on the other side.

6 Pipe buttercream onto half the whoopie pies. Sandwich together with remaining whoopie pies.

COOK'S TIP

These whoopie pies can be frozen, un-iced, and defrosted and filled on the day of use. Defrost on a wire rack.

● GLUTEN FREE ● MAKE AHEAD ● FREEZABLE ● EASY ● KID FRIENDLY

Lemon tart with
CANDIED LEMON

When life gives you lemons, make candied lemon tart!

SERVES 8 **PREP** 20 mins (+ resting & cooling) **COOK** 1 hour 5 mins

4 eggs
185ml (¾ cup) double cream
125ml (½ cup) lemon juice
100g (½ cup) caster sugar
1 tbs finely grated
   lemon rind
Cream or crème fraîche,
   to serve
sweet shortcrust pastry
225g (1½ cups) plain flour
2 tbs icing sugar mixture
150g unsalted butter,
   chilled, chopped
1 egg yolk
2 tbs cold water
candied lemon
60ml (¼ cup) water
55g (¼ cup) caster sugar
1 lemon, thinly sliced

1 To make the pastry, process the flour, sugar and butter in a food processor until fine crumbs form. Add the yolk and water. Process until dough just comes together. Knead on a floured surface until smooth. Cover. Place in fridge for 30 minutes to rest.

2 Roll out pastry on a sheet of baking paper to a 3mm-thick disc. Line a round 23cm (base size) fluted tart tin, with removable base, with the pastry. Trim any excess. Place in fridge for 30 minutes to rest.

3 Preheat oven to 200°C/180°C fan forced. Line the pastry case with baking paper. Fill with pastry weights and bake for 15 minutes. Remove paper and weights. Cook for a further 10 minutes or until golden.

4 Meanwhile, to make the candied lemon, place water and sugar in a small saucepan over low heat. Cook, stirring, for 2-3 minutes or until sugar dissolves. Bring to the boil. Add the lemon slices and cook, turning, for 10 minutes or until translucent.

5 Whisk together eggs, cream, lemon juice and caster sugar in a large bowl until combined. Strain through a fine sieve into a large jug. Stir in lemon rind.

6 Reduce oven to 160°C/140°C fan forced. Place the tart tin on a baking tray. Pour egg mixture into the pastry case. Bake for 40 minutes or until just set (the middle may wobble). Set aside to cool. Top with the candied lemon slices and serve with cream.

COOK'S TIP

Candied lemon can be made in advance. Keep in an airtight container for up to 3 days.

★★★★★

LOVE the tang, base is amazing and all round hit!!

SMELLIRAQUELLI

● GLUTEN FREE ● MAKE AHEAD ● FREEZABLE ● EASY ● KID FRIENDLY

Greek condensed milk
FILO PIE

10 minutes prep is all it takes to make this jaw-dropping custard pie.

SERVES 8 **PREP** 10 mins (+ 10 mins cooling) **COOK** 40 mins

100g butter, melted
10 sheets filo pastry
395g can sweetened
   condensed milk
250ml (1 cup) milk
2 eggs
1 tsp vanilla extract
Icing sugar, to dust

1 Preheat oven to 180°C/160°C fan forced. Lightly grease a 4.5cm-deep, 1.5L (6 cup) baking dish with melted butter.

2 Place 1 pastry sheet on a clean work surface. Cover the remaining sheets with a clean, dry tea towel and then a damp tea towel (to prevent pastry from drying out). Brush the pastry sheet with a little melted butter. From 1 short end, drag the pastry until it forms an accordion-like strip about 2cm wide. Place around edge of prepared dish. Repeat with remaining pastry sheets, working towards the centre and scrunching slightly to fit as necessary, until base of dish is covered. Place the dish on a baking tray and bake for 20 minutes or until golden and crisp.

3 Whisk together the condensed milk, milk, eggs and vanilla in a jug until well combined. Carefully pour the mixture over the pastry. Bake for 20 minutes or until set. Set aside for 10 minutes to cool slightly. Dust with icing sugar and serve warm.

COOK'S TIP

This simple dessert is extra delicious when served with stewed fruit or fresh berries and cream.

★ ★ ★ ★ ★

Loved this, super quick and easy and it was a HUGE hit!

DAWN CLEAVES

● GLUTEN FREE ● MAKE AHEAD ● FREEZABLE ● EASY ● KID FRIENDLY

Spiced peach & CHERRY PIE

Make this festive pie a day ahead for the picture perfect slice!

SERVES 12 **PREP** 45 mins (+ 1 hour 30 mins chilling & overnight cooling) **COOK** 1 hour 15 mins

300g unsalted butter, chilled, chopped
45g (¼ cup) pure icing sugar, sifted
½ tsp salt
450g (3 cups) plain flour
125ml (½ cup) iced water
2 tbs apple cider vinegar
600g ripe firm peaches, cut into 2cm pieces
300g fresh or frozen cherries, pitted
155g (¾ cup) caster sugar, plus 2 tbs, extra
45g (⅓ cup) arrowroot (tapioca) flour
2 tsp mixed spice
1 egg, lightly whisked
Vanilla custard, to serve

1 Place the butter, icing sugar, salt and 2 cups (300g) flour until in a food processor and process until the mixture resembles breadcrumbs. Add the remaining flour and pulse until combined. Add the water and vinegar and process until the dough just comes together. Bring the dough together on a lightly floured surface. Wrap two-thirds of the dough in plastic wrap. Wrap the remaining dough portion in plastic wrap. Place in the fridge for 1 hour to chill.

2 Grease a 4cm-deep, 19cm (base size) fluted tart tin with removable base. Roll out the larger dough portion on a lightly floured surface to a 3mm-thick disc. Use dough to line tin and trim excess. Reserve pastry scraps. Roll out the smaller dough portion on a sheet of baking paper to a 3mm-thick disc. Use a 3.5cm star pastry cutter to cut stars out of centre of pastry. Reserve stars. Place all pastry in fridge for 30 minutes to chill.

3 Preheat oven to 200°C/180°C fan forced. Place peaches, cherries, sugar, arrowroot and mixed spice in a bowl and stir until combined. Spoon mixture into the pie shell. Cover with pastry lid. Press edges to seal. Trim excess. Reroll pastry scraps and use a small star pastry cutter to cut out stars to decorate edges. Brush with egg. Sprinkle with extra sugar. Place on a baking tray. Loosely cover edge with foil. Bake for 30 minutes.

4 Reduce the oven to 180°C/160°C fan forced. Remove and discard the foil. Bake for 45 minutes or until golden. Cool in the tin for 4 hours or overnight. Serve with vanilla custard.

This is so delicious. Will 100% do again

16ALLYCAT16

● GLUTEN FREE ● MAKE AHEAD ● FREEZABLE ● EASY ● KID FRIENDLY

Choc-banoffee
FILO STACK

Stack these breezy banana stacks high with lashings of creamy filling.

SERVES 6 **PREP** 20 mins (+ cooling) **COOK** 10 mins

45g (¼ cup) hazelnuts,
  finely chopped,
  plus extra, to serve
2 tsp coconut or
  brown sugar
½ tsp ground cinnamon
8 sheets filo pastry
375g tub smooth ricotta
300g vanilla-flavoured
  Greek-style yoghurt
2 tsp vanilla extract
1 lemon, rind finely grated
2 tsp cocoa powder
3 large bananas,
  thinly sliced
Cacao nibs and coconut
  syrup, to serve

1 Preheat oven to 190°C/170°C fan forced. Place nuts, sugar and cinnamon in a bowl and stir until combined. Line 3 baking trays with baking paper.

2 Place 1 sheet of filo on a clean work surface and spray with oil. Sprinkle with a little nut mixture. Place another filo sheet on top. Continue layering with oil, nut mixture and filo until you have 4 layers. Repeat with the remaining filo, oil and nut mixture to make another stack of 4 layers. Cut each stack into 12 squares. Place on prepared trays. Bake for 10 minutes or until golden. Set aside to cool.

3 Place the ricotta, yoghurt, vanilla and lemon rind in a bowl. Divide mixture between 2 bowls. Add the cocoa to 1 bowl and stir until combined. Swirl mixtures together slightly. Top 4 squares with some ricotta mixture, banana, cacao nibs and extra nuts. Stack the topped squares on top of each other. Repeat with the remaining ingredients to make 6 stacks in total. Drizzle with a little coconut syrup. Serve immediately.

COOK'S TIP

Find coconut syrup at select supermarkets and health food shops. You can also substitute it with maple syrup or honey.

● GLUTEN FREE ● MAKE AHEAD ● FREEZABLE ● EASY ● KID FRIENDLY

No-fuss cherry
CRUMBLE GALETTE

Cherry pie gets an easy-peasy makeover as a free-form galette.

SERVES 4 **PREP** 15 mins (+ thawing) **COOK** 30 mins

400g frozen cherries, pitted

1 sheet shortcrust pastry, just thawed

30g (¼ cup) macadamia meal (see tip)

2 tsp custard powder

1 egg, lightly whisked

2 tbs raw sugar

2 Anzac biscuits, coarsely crushed

Berry-flavoured frozen yoghurt, to serve

1 Place the cherries on a plate lined with paper towel to thaw and drain well. Preheat oven to 200°C/180°C fan forced. Line a baking tray with baking paper. Cut pastry into a 23cm round disc. Place on the prepared tray.

2 Sprinkle the pastry with the macadamia meal and custard powder, leaving a 4cm border. Top with the cherries. Fold in the pastry edge over the fruit to slightly enclose the filling, pinching to seal. Brush the edges of the pastry with egg then sprinkle with sugar. Bake for 15 minutes. Sprinkle with the crushed biscuit. Bake for a further 15 minutes or until pastry is golden. Serve with frozen yoghurt.

COOK'S TIP

Find macadamia meal at health food stores and independent grocers. You can also substitute it for almond or hazelnut meal.

● GLUTEN FREE ● MAKE AHEAD ● FREEZABLE ● EASY ● KID FRIENDLY

15
minutes
prep

Lemon
MERINGUE PIE

Our smart swaps can make lemon meringue pie better-for-you!

SERVES 10 **PREP** 45 mins (+ resting, cooling & 30 mins chilling) **COOK** 55 mins

2 tbs finely grated lemon rind
2 tbs honey
1 tbs raw sugar
2 tsp cornflour
3 eggs
3 egg yolks
250ml (1 cup) fresh lemon juice
60ml (¼ cup) coconut milk

almond quinoa pastry
60g (⅓ cup) raw or roasted almonds, skins on
25g (¼ cup) quinoa flakes
80g (½ cup) wholemeal plain flour
75g (½ cup) plain flour
100g chilled butter, chopped
1 egg
3 tsp chilled water

meringue
3 egg whites
Pinch of cream of tartar
100g (½ cup) caster sugar
1 tsp vanilla extract

1 For the pastry, process almonds and quinoa flakes in a food processor until very finely chopped. Add the flours and butter and process until the mixture resembles coarse breadcrumbs. Add egg and water and process until mixture just comes together. Turn onto a lightly floured surface and gently knead until just smooth (don't overwork). Cover and place in fridge for 15 minutes to rest.

2 Grease a 3cm-deep, 22cm (base size) fluted tart tin with removable base. Roll out pastry on a sheet of lightly floured baking paper to a 2-3mm-thick disc. Carefully drape over a rolling pin (gently remove baking paper) and line prepared tin with pastry. Trim excess and discard. Place in fridge for 15 minutes to rest.

3 Preheat oven to 180°C/160°C fan forced. Place the tin on a large baking tray. Line the pastry case with baking paper. Fill with pastry weights or rice. Bake for 10 minutes. Remove paper and pastry weights or rice and bake for a further 8-10 minutes or until golden. Set aside to cool completely.

4 Whisk together lemon rind, honey, sugar, cornflour, egg and yolks in a large jug. Whisk in lemon juice and coconut milk. Pour into pastry case. Bake for 20-25 minutes or until just set (mixture should still wobble slightly in centre). Set aside to cool completely.

5 For the meringue, increase oven temperature to 210°C/190°C fan forced. Use electric beaters to beat egg whites and cream of tartar in a clean, dry bowl until soft peaks form. Gradually add sugar, 1 tbs at a time, beating well after each addition until thick and glossy. Beat in vanilla.

6 Spread meringue over filling. Use back of a spoon to create peaks. Bake for 10 minutes or until golden.

● GLUTEN FREE ● MAKE AHEAD ● FREEZABLE ● EASY ● KID FRIENDLY

Strawberry & orange galette
WITH OAT PASTRY

Tuck into a big helping of this healthier, low-sugar galette.

SERVES 8 **PREP** 30 mins (+ 1 hour resting) **COOK** 30 mins

1 orange, peeled,
   thinly sliced
250g strawberries,
   hulled, sliced
2 tbs coconut sugar
1 tbs arrowroot
   (tapioca flour),
   plus extra, to dust

oat pastry

75g (¾ cup) gluten-free
   rolled oats
100g (1 cup) almond meal
55g (⅓ cup) buckwheat flour
35g (¼ cup) coconut sugar,
   plus 2 tsp extra
30g (¼ cup) arrowroot
   (tapioca flour)
1 tbs desiccated coconut
1 small orange, rind
   finely grated
60ml (¼ cup) solidified
   coconut oil, chilled,
   chopped, plus 1½ tsp,
   extra, melted
2 tsp honey or rice
   malt syrup
1 tsp vanilla extract
   with seeds
3 tsp-1 tbs chilled water

1 Make the oat pastry. Reserve 1 tbs oats. Process the remaining oats in a food processor until almost finely ground. Add the almond meal, buckwheat flour, sugar, arrowroot, coconut and rind. Pulse until just combined. Add the oil, honey or syrup, vanilla and 3 tsp water. Process until dough just comes together. Add the remaining water, if necessary. Gently bring the dough together. Shape into a disc. Cover and place in fridge for 1 hour to rest.

2 Preheat oven to 200°C/180°C fan forced. Place the reserved oats, extra sugar and extra oil in a small bowl and stir until combined. Set aside. Roll out the pastry on a sheet of baking paper lightly dusted with arrowroot to a 30cm disc and press any cracks together with fingers. Carefully transfer the dough and paper to a large baking tray.

3 Place orange, strawberries, sugar and arrowroot in a bowl. Toss until sugar dissolves. Transfer the mixture to centre of pastry. Fold the edge over filling and use fingers to press together any cracks. Sprinkle with the oat mixture. Bake for 30 minutes or until dark golden. Set aside to cool before serving.

COOK'S TIP

Serve this vibrant galette with cream, vanilla ice-cream, or crème fraîche

● GLUTEN FREE ● MAKE AHEAD ● FREEZABLE ● EASY ● KID FRIENDLY

Condensed milk
CHOC-RIPPLE PIE

Spiked with coffee liqueur, this decadent dessert is for adults only!

SERVES 6 **PREP** 25 mins (+ cooling) **COOK** 40 mins

395g can sweetened condensed milk
30g (¼ cup) cocoa powder
2 tbs plain flour
125ml (½ cup) milk
60ml (⅓ cup) Kahlúa Coffee Liqueur
2 eggs
2 tsp vanilla extract
2 x 250g pkt Arnott's Choc Ripple biscuits
100g (⅓ cup) Nutella
Chocolate sauce (see tip) and crumbled Cadbury Flake chocolate bar, to serve

marshmallow cream
100g (1 cup) vanilla marshmallows
300ml ctn thickened cream
1 tsp vanilla extract

1 Preheat oven to 180°C/160°C fan forced. Place the condensed milk in a large bowl. Sift over the cocoa and flour. Whisk until combined. Add the milk, liqueur, egg and vanilla and whisk until combined.

2 Arrange half of the biscuits, in 2 layers, over base of a 5cm-deep, 21cm round (base size) ceramic pie dish, trimming biscuits to fill any gaps. Drizzle over half of the Nutella. Pour over half of the milk mixture. Repeat layering with remaining biscuits, Nutella and milk mixture. Bake for 35-40 minutes or until just set.

3 Meanwhile, to make the marshmallow cream, place the marshmallows in a small microwave-safe bowl. Microwave on High, stirring halfway, for 30-40 seconds or until melted and smooth. Set aside to cool completely.

4 Using electric beaters to the beat cream and vanilla in a large bowl until firm peaks form. Add a tablespoonful of the whipped cream to the marshmallow and stir until combined. Use a large metal spoon to fold the marshmallow mixture into the remaining cream until just combined.

5 Working quickly, spoon the cream mixture onto the pie then drizzle with chocolate sauce, swirling gently to create a marbled effect. Sprinkle with the crumbled chocolate and serve immediately.

COOK'S TIP

We used Hershey's Syrup Chocolate Flavour, but any chocolate sauce or syrup would work just as well.

★★★★★

Dangerously good. Turned out perfectly.

KIRSTENK

● GLUTEN FREE ● MAKE AHEAD ● FREEZABLE ● EASY ● KID FRIENDLY

French apple TART

Our easy puff pastry makes this rustic apple tart taste magnifique!

SERVES 8 **PREP** 30 mins (+ 1 hour resting & chilling) **COOK** 30 mins

60g butter, chopped,
    at room temperature
55g (¼ cup) caster sugar
1 tsp vanilla extract
1 egg
55g (½ cup) almond meal
2 tbs plain flour
2 large red apples, cored,
    halved
20g butter, melted
2 tbs apricot jam, warmed
rough puff pastry
200g (1⅓ cups) plain flour
2 tbs icing sugar mixture
140g butter, frozen, coarsely
    grated (see tip)
80ml (⅓ cup) iced water

1 To make the puff pastry, sift the flour and icing sugar into a large bowl. Add the butter and toss until coated. Add the water. Use a flat-bladed knife in a cutting motion to mix until evenly incorporated and the mixture just begins to hold together. Turn the dough onto a lightly floured surface and shape into a disc. Place on a sheet of baking paper and use a lightly floured rolling pin to roll out to a 12 x 14cm rectangle. Fold the paper over the dough. Place in the fridge for 1 hour to rest.

2 Preheat oven to 190°C/170°C fan forced. Line a large baking tray with baking paper. Use a lightly floured rolling pin to roll out dough on a lightly floured surface to a 26 x 30cm rectangle. Transfer to the prepared tray. Place in the fridge until required.

3 Use electric beaters to beat the butter and sugar in a bowl until pale and creamy. Beat in vanilla and egg until combined. Add the almond meal and flour and stir until combined.

4 Use a mandoline or very sharp knife to thinly slice the apple. Spread the butter mixture over pastry, leaving a 1.5cm border. Arrange apple slices in rows, overlapping slightly, over the mixture. Brush with the melted butter. Bake for 30 minutes or until pastry is golden and apple is tender. Brush the jam over the apple and serve immediately.

COOK'S TIP

To make the pastry prep easy, freeze an entire block of butter ahead of time, then coarsely grate 140g straight into the bowl.

● GLUTEN FREE ● MAKE AHEAD ● FREEZABLE ● **EASY** ● KID FRIENDLY

Roast grape
PASTRIES

Under 100 cals per serve, you can enjoy these little pastries guilt-free.

MAKES 16 **PREP** 30 mins **COOK** 35 mins

16 sheets filo pastry

30g (¼ cup) almond meal

2 tbs brown sugar

½ tsp ground cinnamon

¼ tsp ground cloves

150g seedless red grapes, halved

150g seedless green grapes, halved

Maple syrup, to serve

Natural yoghurt or whipped cream, to serve (optional)

1 Preheat oven to 200°C/180°C fan forced. Line 2 large baking trays with baking paper. Cover the filo with a damp tea towel.

2 Place 1 sheet of filo on a clean work surface and spray with oil. Fold in half lengthways. Starting at 1 long side, roll up pastry about three-quarters of the way along then fold into a circle, tucking under the extra pastry and sealing the edges, to make a small tart case. Place on 1 prepared tray. Repeat with the remaining pastry to make 16 cases in total.

3 Place the almond meal, sugar, cinnamon and cloves in a bowl. Sprinkle over the base of each pastry case. Fill with the grapes then spray with oil. Bake for 30-35 minutes or until golden and crisp.

4 Drizzle over maple syrup. Serve with yoghurt or cream, if using.

COOK'S TIP

Grapes out of season? Try canned apricot halves or pear wedges instead for a delicious last-minute dessert.

● GLUTEN FREE ● MAKE AHEAD ● FREEZABLE ● EASY ● KID FRIENDLY

Nectarine pastry DOME

An easy golden lattice is the crowning glory of this impressive treat.

MAKES 6 **PREP** 1 hour (+ 4 hours setting) **COOK** 45 mins

165g (¾ cup) caster sugar
175ml (¾ cup) water
700g ripe nectarine, cut into wedges, plus extra, to serve
2 tsp lemon juice
1 tbs gelatine powder
300ml thickened cream
pastry domes
6 sheets frozen puff pastry, just thawed
1 egg yolk, whisked
1 tbs caster sugar
1 tsp gelatine powder

1 Heat sugar and water in a frying pan over medium heat. Cook, stirring, until sugar dissolves. Add the nectarine. Reduce heat to low. Cover. Cook for 5 minutes or until softened slightly. Use a slotted spoon to transfer the nectarine to a heatproof plate. Set aside to cool. Simmer syrup for 5 minutes until thickened slightly.

2 Grease six 185ml (¾ cup) capacity dariole moulds. Remove and discard skin from 12 of the nectarine wedges. Place 2 peeled wedges in the base of each mould. Reserve 80ml (⅓ cup) syrup and set aside. Use a stick blender to blend the remaining syrup and nectarine until smooth. Strain through a fine mesh sieve. Discard solids. Add the lemon juice and stir until combined.

3 Place 2 tbs water in a small heatproof bowl. Sprinkle with the gelatine and stir until well combined. Place bowl inside a larger heatproof bowl. Pour boiling water into the larger bowl until it reaches halfway up the side of the smaller bowl. Set aside, stirring occasionally, for 5 minutes or until the gelatine

dissolves. Add to nectarine puree and stir until well combined.

4 Use electric beaters to beat the cream in a bowl until soft peaks form. Use a spatula to fold cream into nectarine mixture, in 2 separate batches, until combined. Divide among moulds. Place in the fridge for 4 hours or overnight to set.

5 To make the domes, preheat oven to 200°C/180°C fan forced. Brush the pastry sheets with egg yolk then set aside to dry out slightly. Cut the pastry with a lattice pastry roller. Cut a 22cm-diameter disc from each sheet. Cover six 14cm (top size) ovenproof ceramic bowls with foil to form a dome. Grease the foil well. Place the pastry over foil. Trim excess. Press edges together. Place bowls on a baking tray. Bake for 20-25 minutes until golden. Remove from moulds. Heat sugar, gelatine and 1 tbs water in a saucepan over low heat. Cook, stirring, until dissolves. Brush mixture over warm pastry to glaze. Turn the creams onto serving plates. Drizzle over reserved syrup. Top with a pastry dome. Serve with extra nectarine.

● GLUTEN FREE ● MAKE AHEAD ● FREEZABLE ● EASY ● KID FRIENDLY

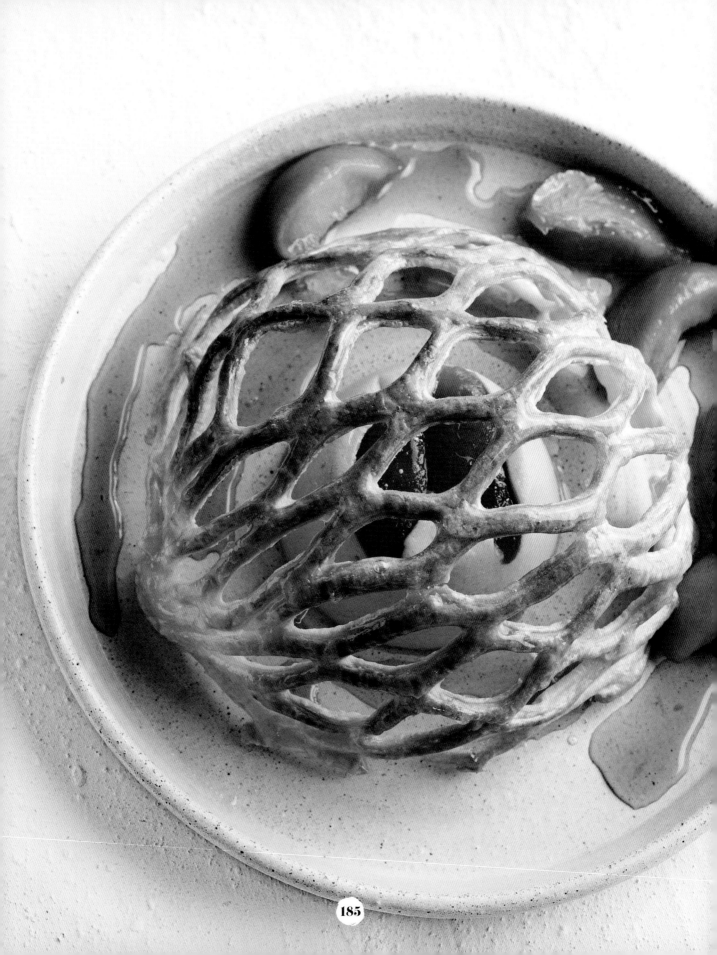

Fairy bread meringue
CUSTARD PIE

Nothing says party time like a custard-filled fairy bread pie!

SERVES 12 **PREP** 30 mins (+ 1 hour chilling & cooling) **COOK** 1 hour 15 mins

340g (2¼ cups) plain flour
70g (⅓ cup) caster sugar
Pinch of salt
180g butter, chilled, chopped
1 egg
1 tbs iced water
60g (½ cup) hundreds and thousands
12 mini meringues
custard
625ml (2½ cups) milk
125ml (½ cup) thickened cream
2 tsp vanilla bean paste
4 egg yolks
155g (¾ cup) caster sugar
70g (½ cup) cornflour
50g unsalted butter, chopped

1 Place flour, sugar and salt in a food processor. Process until combined. Add butter. Process until mixture resembles fine crumbs. Add egg and water. Process until dough just comes together. Turn onto a lightly floured surface. Gather dough together. Divide dough into 2 portions. Shape into discs. Cover with plastic wrap. Place in fridge for 30 minutes to rest.

2 Meanwhile, line a baking tray with baking paper. Grease a 3.5cm-deep, 24cm (top size) round pie dish. Use a lightly floured rolling pin to roll out 1 dough portion on a lightly floured until 4mm thick. Sprinkle dough with hundreds and thousands. Use a rolling pin to gently press into surface. Use pie tin, top-side down, as a guide to cut a 24cm disc from dough. Cut disc into 12 wedges. Remove and discard excess dough. Place wedges on prepared tray then place in fridge. Roll out remaining dough portion on a lightly floured surface until 4mm thick. Use dough to line prepared dish. Trim and discard excess. Use a fork to prick base. Place in the fridge for 30 minutes to chill.

3 Preheat oven to 180°C/160°C fan forced. Place dish on a baking tray. Line pastry case with baking paper and fill with pastry weights or rice. Bake for 15 minutes. Remove paper and pastry weights or rice. Bake for a further 10 minutes or until golden. Set aside to cool completely.

4 To make the custard, place milk, cream and vanilla in a saucepan over medium heat. Cook, stirring, until mixture comes to the boil. Remove from heat. Use electric beaters to beat egg yolks and sugar in a large heatproof bowl until pale and creamy. Add cornflour and whisk until combined. Slowly pour milk mixture into egg mixture, whisking constantly, until smooth. Return mixture to saucepan. Cook, whisking constantly, over medium heat for 3-5 minutes or until mixture boils and thickens. Remove from heat. Add the butter and whisk until well combined.

5 Pour the custard into pastry case and smooth surface. Secure foil around edge of pastry to prevent burning. Bake for 20 minutes or until the custard is just set. Set aside to cool completely. Bake the pastry wedges for 15 minutes or until golden and crisp. Set aside to cool completely.

6 Arrange the meringues on top of the pie. Top with pastry wedges, slightly overlapping, to serve.

● GLUTEN FREE ● MAKE AHEAD ● FREEZABLE ● EASY ● KID FRIENDLY

Custard tarts with coconut
CHIA PASTRY

Follow our simple steps to nail this nourishing and creamy tart.

SERVES 6 **PREP** 25 mins (+ chilling & cooling) **COOK** 45 mins

250ml (1 cup) milk
3 eggs
2 tsp cornflour
2 tbs maple syrup
1 tsp vanilla extract or seeds
60ml (¼ cup) pouring cream
Finely grated fresh nutmeg,
  to serve

coconut chia pastry
155g (1 cup) wholemeal
  spelt flour
40g (¼ cup) sesame seeds
1 tbs white chia seeds
20g (¼ cup) shredded
  coconut
60g butter, chilled, chopped
2 tsp maple syrup
2 tbs cold water

1 To make the pastry, grease six 3cm-deep, 8cm (base size) fluted tart tins with removable bases. Place the flour, sesame seeds, chia seeds, shredded coconut and butter in a food processor and process until the mixture resembles fine crumbs. Add the maple syrup and water. Process again until dough comes together.

2 Turn onto a lightly floured surface and knead until just smooth. Divide the dough into 6 portions. Roll each portion out on a sheet of baking paper to a circle large enough to line base and side of each prepared tin.

3 Line tins with dough, pressing into fluted edges. Trim excess. Place on a baking tray. Place in the fridge for 10-15 minutes or until chilled.

4 Preheat the oven to 180°C/160°C fan forced. Line the pastry cases with baking paper. Fill with pastry weights or rice. Bake for 10 minutes. Remove the paper and pastry weights or rice. Bake for a further 10-15 minutes or until light golden. Set aside to cool.

5 Meanwhile, whisk together the milk, eggs and cornflour in a large bowl until smooth. Whisk in the maple syrup, vanilla and cream until combined.

6 Pour the custard mixture into the cooled pastry cases. Sprinkle with nutmeg. Bake for 15-20 minutes or until the custard is just set. Set aside in the tins to cool slightly. Serve the custard tarts warm or chilled.

● GLUTEN FREE ● MAKE AHEAD ● FREEZABLE ● EASY ● KID FRIENDLY

Plum & white chocolate
CUSTARD PIES

Start the crumble rumble with these petite individual fruit pies.

MAKES 6 **PREP** 25 mins (+ chilling & cooling) **COOK** 45 mins

185g butter, chilled,
  chopped
340g (2¼ cups) plain flour
100g (½ cup) caster sugar
1 egg yolk
1-2 tsp iced water
700g can whole plums
  in juice, drained
Ice-cream, to serve

white chocolate custard
1 tbs custard powder
1 tbs caster sugar
250ml (1 cup) milk
60g white chocolate,
  coarsely chopped

streusel topping
75g (½ cup) plain flour
½ tsp mixed spice
55g (¼ cup, firmly packed)
  brown sugar
2 tsp finely grated
  orange rind
70g (½ cup) pecans,
  coarsely chopped
60g butter, chilled, chopped

1 Place the butter, flour and sugar in a food processor and process until the mixture resembles fine crumbs. Add the yolk and iced water and process until the dough just comes together, adding an extra 1 tsp iced water if needed. Shape dough into a disc. Cover with plastic wrap. Place in the fridge for 30 minutes or until firm.

2 To make the custard. Place the custard powder, sugar and 2 tbs milk in a saucepan. Stir until smooth. Gradually stir in the remaining milk. Place over medium-high heat and cook, stirring, until the mixture just starts to thicken. Add the chocolate and stir until combined. Continue stirring until the mixture just simmers and the custard thickens and coats the back of a spoon. Transfer to a heatproof bowl. Cover the surface with plastic wrap and set aside for 20 minutes to cool slightly. Place in the fridge for 3 hours or until chilled.

3 Meanwhile, preheat oven to 200°C/180°C fan forced. Grease six 2cm-deep, 9.5cm (base size) round fluted tart tins with removable bases. Divide dough in half. Roll out 1 portion between 2 sheets of baking paper until 5mm thick. Line the bases and sides of 3 prepared pans with pastry. Trim edges. Place on a baking tray. Repeat with remaining pastry and pans. Line the pastry cases with baking paper and fill with pastry weights or rice. Bake for 15 minutes. Remove weights or rice and paper. Bake for a further 5-10 minutes until base is just firm. Set aside in pans to cool completely.

4 Cut plums in half. Discard pits. Place on paper towel to drain.

5 To make the streusel topping, place the flour, mixed spice, sugar, rind and pecans in a large bowl and stir until combined. Use your fingertips to rub the butter into the flour mixture until well combined.

6 Divide the plum among the pastry cases. Top with the custard and sprinkle with the streusel. Bake for 20 minutes or until golden. Set aside to cool slightly. Serve with ice-cream.

● GLUTEN FREE ● MAKE AHEAD ● FREEZABLE ● EASY ● KID FRIENDLY

Christmas chocolate
PASTRY TREE

Only four ingredients required to make this clever festive treat.

MAKES 1 **PREP** 30 mins (+ chilling) **COOK** 20 mins

2 x 375g pkt Carême Puff
   Pastry
100g (⅓ cup) choc-hazelnut
   spread
1 egg
Sesame seeds, to sprinkle

1 Preheat oven to 210°C/190°C fan forced. Roll out each sheet of pastry to a 28 x 36cm rectangle. Place 1 rectangle on a large sheet of baking paper. With the short side facing you, gently score a large triangle on the pastry.

2 Spread the choc-hazelnut spread over triangle, keeping within the lines. Top with the remaining rectangle of pastry. Press the pastry around the choc -hazelnut spread to seal. Place in the fridge for 15 minutes or until firm.

3 With the shortest side of the triangle shape facing you, cut around sealed edges of pastry to form a triangle filled with choc spread. Reserve pastry scraps. Cut two strips from base of triangle to create a tree trunk. Leaving a 2cm-wide strip down the middle of the triangle, cut lines running outwards from the strip at 2cm intervals to create branches.

4 Beginning at the base, twist the pastry branches away from you. Brush with whisked egg. Cut out a star from the pastry scraps. Attach the star to the top of the tree. Brush the tree and star with egg then sprinkle with sesame seeds. Bake for 15-20 minutes or until golden and cooked through.

COOK'S TIP

For a complete step-by-step guide including pictures, visit taste.com.au/ xmaspastrytree

● GLUTEN FREE ● MAKE AHEAD ● FREEZABLE ● EASY ● KID FRIENDLY

Apple & golden syrup
DUMPLING PIE

This is the ultimate in comfort baking, for those cold winter's nights.

SERVES 6 **PREP** 15 mins **COOK** 35 mins

45g unsalted butter
6-7 large (1kg) Granny Smith
   apples, peeled,
   cored, sliced
160ml (⅔ cup) golden syrup
55g (¼ cup) brown sugar
1 tbs cornflour
2 tsp cold water
1 tsp ground cinnamon
Bought ready-made custard,
   to serve
dumplings
190g (1¼ cups) self-raising
   flour
55g (¼ cup) brown sugar
60ml (¼ cup) milk
50g unsalted butter,
   melted, cooled
1 egg, lightly whisked

1 Preheat oven to 180°C/160°C fan forced. Melt 25g of the butter in a large, deep frying pan over medium heat. Add the apple, golden syrup, 1 tbs of sugar and a pinch of salt. Cook, stirring occasionally, for 4-5 minutes or until apples are just tender.

2 Place the cornflour in a small jug. Add water and stir until smooth. Add cornflour mixture and cinnamon to apple mixture. Stir to combine. Cook for 1 minute or until mixture thickens and coats the apples. Spoon into a 4.5cm-deep, 24cm round ovenproof dish.

3 To make the dumplings, combine flour, sugar and a pinch of salt in a bowl. Add milk, butter and egg. Stir until combined.

4 Melt remaining butter in a small saucepan over low heat. Top apple mixture with tablespoonfuls of the dumpling mixture. Sprinkle with remaining sugar. Drizzle the melted butter over the top. Place pie dish on a baking tray and bake for 30 minutes or until the dumpling top is golden brown. Drizzle over custard to serve.

COOK'S TIP

For a berry flavour twist, throw in a handful of frozen blueberries or raspberries at the end of Step 1.

● GLUTEN FREE ● MAKE AHEAD ● FREEZABLE ● EASY ● KID FRIENDLY

Golden staircase
PIE

Dig into layers of dreamy citrus custard in this retro Aussie dessert.

SERVES 10 **PREP** 40 mins (+ 4 hours chilling & cooling) **COOK** 30 mins

225g (1½ cups) plain flour

125g unsalted butter, chilled, chopped

2 tbs caster sugar

1 egg yolk

1-1½ tbs iced water

Whipped cream, to serve

lemon custard

70g (⅓ cup) caster sugar

2 tbs cornflour

1½ tbs custard powder

250ml (1 cup) milk

165ml (⅔ cup) thickened cream

20g butter, chopped

1 tbs finely grated lemon rind

2 tbs fresh lemon juice

orange custard

100g (½ cup) caster sugar

35g (¼ cup) custard powder

2 tbs cornflour

310ml (1¼ cups) fresh orange juice

30g butter, chopped

1 tbs finely grated orange rind

Red and yellow liquid food colouring, to tint

1 Place the flour, butter and sugar in a food processor and process until mixture resembles fine crumbs. Add egg yolk and 1 tbs iced water. Process until dough just starts to come together, adding ½ tbs more water, if necessary. Turn dough onto a lightly floured surface. Knead until smooth. Use a lightly floured rolling pin to roll out the dough to a disc about 2cm thick. Wrap in plastic wrap. Place in the fridge for 30 minutes or until firm.

2 Grease a 3cm-deep, 20cm (base size) round glass or ceramic dish. Roll out dough between 2 sheets of baking paper to a 4mm-thick disc. Use the dough to line the prepared dish. Trim excess. Use your fingertips to crimp pastry edge. Place in the fridge for 30 minutes to chill.

3 Preheat oven to 200°C/180°C fan forced. Line pastry case with baking paper and fill with pastry weights or rice. Bake for 15 minutes. Remove paper and pastry weights or rice and bake for a further 10 minutes or until golden. Set aside to cool.

4 Meanwhile, to make the lemon custard, place the sugar, cornflour and custard powder in a saucepan.

Gradually whisk in the milk and cream until smooth. Cook, stirring, over medium heat until mixture thickens and comes to the boil. Cook, stirring, for a further 2 minutes. Remove from heat. Add the butter, lemon rind and juice and stir until combined.

5 Pour the lemon custard into the pastry case and place in the fridge for 1 hour or until firm.

6 Make the orange custard, place the sugar, custard powder and cornflour in a saucepan and stir until combined. Gradually whisk in the juice and 160ml (⅔ cup) water until smooth. Cook, stirring, over medium heat until mixture thickens and comes to boil. Cook, stirring, for 2 minutes. Remove from heat. Stir in the butter and rind. Tint orange with colouring.

7 Pour half of the orange custard mixture over lemon custard layer. Place in the fridge for 2 hours or until set. Pour remaining mixture into a small plastic container and place in fridge for 2 hours or until set.

8 Turn container of orange custard onto a clean work surface and cut into cubes. Top pie with cream and orange custard cubes to serve.

● GLUTEN FREE ● MAKE AHEAD ● FREEZABLE ● EASY ● KID FRIENDLY

Wagon wheel
PARIS-BREST

The classic French pastry gets a retro choc-berry twist.

SERVES 10 **PREP** 40 mins (+ cooling & 1 hour setting) **COOK** 45 mins

100g butter, chopped
Pinch of salt
150g (1 cup) plain flour,
  sifted
5 eggs, lightly whisked
90g (¼ cup) raspberry jam,
  warmed
180g dark chocolate,
  melted, cooled slightly
Arnott's Wagon Wheels
  Original Minis, assorted
  marshmallows and fresh
  raspberries, to decorate
marshmallow
300g (1½ cups) caster sugar
160ml (⅔ cup) boiling water
2 tbs gelatine powder
1 tsp vanilla extract
Pink food colouring

1 Preheat oven to 200°C/180°C fan forced. Draw a 20cm circle on baking paper. Place, ink-side down, on a baking tray.

2 Heat the butter, salt and 250ml (1 cup) water in a saucepan over high heat. Cook, stirring, until butter melts and mixture comes to the boil. Add the flour. Use a wooden spoon to beat for 1 minute or until mixture comes away from the side of the pan. Set aside for 10 minutes to cool.

3 Use electric beaters to gradually beat in the egg, 1 tbs at a time, beating well after each addition. The mixture should be stiff enough to hold a wooden spoon upright, but soft enough to pipe (you may not need to add all of the egg). Spoon the mixture into a piping bag fitted with a 1.5cm plain nozzle. Pipe a ring of pastry over the circle marked on the baking paper, then pipe another ring of pastry mixture directly inside it. Pipe a third ring directly over seam where the 2 circles meet. Splash the dough lightly with a little cold water.

4 Bake for 35-40 minutes or until golden. Turn off oven. Leave pastry in oven for 30 minutes or until cooled slightly. Transfer to a wire rack to cool completely. Use a large serrated knife to carefully cut the pastry ring in half horizontally. Remove and discard any uncooked dough from centre.

5 Meanwhile, make marshmallow. Place sugar and 160ml (⅔ cup) cold water in a saucepan. Cook, stirring, until the sugar dissolves and mixture comes to the boil. Remove from heat. Pour the boiling water into a jug. Add the gelatine and whisk to dissolve. Pour the gelatine mixture into the saucepan and stir for 2 minutes. Transfer the mixture to a bowl and set aside for 15 minutes to cool.

6 Place the pastry ring base on a serving plate. Use electric beaters to beat the gelatine mixture on high for 10-12 minutes or until cooled to room temperature and very thick. Add the vanilla and beat for a further 1 minute. Add a few drops of pink food colouring to marshmallow and fold through. Spoon into pastry ring. Set aside for 30 minutes or until set.

7 Spoon the jam into a sealable plastic bag and snip 1 corner. Drizzle the jam over the marshmallow. Cover with the top pastry ring.

8 Drizzle the melted chocolate over the pastry ring. Decorate with the Wagon Wheels, marshmallows and raspberries. Use a cook's blowtorch to lightly toast the marshmallows. Allow to set before serving.

● GLUTEN FREE ● MAKE AHEAD ● FREEZABLE ● EASY ● KID FRIENDLY

Apple pie with
CHEDDAR CRUST

This sweet and savoury flavour combo is pie perfection!

SERVES 10 **PREP** 30 mins (+ 30 mins chilling & 30 mins cooling) **COOK** 1 hour 10 mins

2kg Granny Smith apples,
   peeled, cored, cut into
   2cm-thick slices
100g (½ cup) caster sugar,
   plus 2 tbs, extra
2 cinnamon sticks
2 wide lemon rind strips
60ml (¼ cup) fresh lemon
   juice
1 tbs cornflour
1 egg, lightly whisked
Vanilla ice-cream, to serve
cheddar pastry
450g (3 cups) plain flour
200g unsalted chilled butter,
   chopped
40g (½ cup) coarsely grated
   vintage cheddar
2 tbs icing sugar mixture
2 egg yolks
80ml (⅓ cup) cold milk

1 Grease a 5cm-deep, 24cm (top size) fluted tart tin with removable base with butter.

2 To make the cheddar pastry, place flour and butter in a food processor and process until mixture resembles fine crumbs. Add cheddar and icing sugar. Process until just combined. Add egg yolks and milk. Process until dough just starts to come together.

3 Use a lightly floured rolling pin to roll out two-thirds of dough on a lightly floured surface to a disc about 4mm thick. Use to line prepared tin. Place in fridge for 30 minutes or until firm. Shape remaining dough into a ball. Wrap in plastic wrap and place in the fridge until needed.

4 Preheat oven to 200°C/180°C fan forced. Heat a baking tray in the oven. Place the apple, caster sugar, cinnamon, lemon rind and juice, and 60ml (¼ cup) water in a saucepan. Stir until combined. Cover and bring to a simmer over medium-low heat. Cook, stirring, for 8-10 minutes or until apple is tender but holding shape. Place cornflour and 1 tbs water in a small jug. Stir until smooth. Pour over apple mixture and stir until combined. Remove and discard the cinnamon and lemon rind. Set aside, uncovered, for 30 minutes to cool.

5 Brush pastry case with some of the egg. Spoon the apple mixture into the pastry case. Use a lightly floured rolling pin to roll out remaining dough into a disc large enough to cover the top of pie. Place over apple mixture. Press edge to seal. Trim excess. Brush the pastry with egg and sprinkle with extra caster sugar. Cut 3 slits in the pastry top to allow steam to escape. Place pie on the heated tray and bake for 20 minutes. Reduce oven to 180°C/160°C fan forced and bake for a further 30-40 minutes or until crisp and golden. Serve with ice-cream.

● GLUTEN FREE ● MAKE AHEAD ● FREEZABLE ● EASY ● KID FRIENDLY

Golden syrup & jam
ROLY-POLIES

Let the sweet times roll with jammy pastries baked in apple caramel.

SERVES 6 **PREP** 25 mins **COOK** 35 mins

- 225g (1½ cups) self-raising flour
- 115g (¾ cup) plain flour
- 1 tbs caster sugar
- 100g butter, chilled, finely chopped
- 125ml (½ cup) milk
- 1 egg yolk
- 90g (⅓ cup) raspberry jam
- 160ml (⅔ cup) apple juice
- 3 tbs golden syrup
- 60g (⅓ cup, lightly packed) brown sugar
- Vanilla custard, to serve

1 Preheat oven to 180°C/160°C fan forced. Grease a 1.5L (6 cup) rectangular ovenproof dish.

2 Place the flours and caster sugar in a large bowl and stir until combined. Use your fingertips to rub 75g butter into the flour mixture until resembles fine crumbs. Make a well in the centre. Whisk milk and egg yolk in a jug. Add to flour mixture. Gently stir until a soft, sticky dough forms. (Do not over-mix.)

3 Turn the dough onto a lightly floured surface. Gently knead for 30 seconds. Roll dough into a 40 x 30cm rectangle. Spread the jam over the dough. Roll dough firmly from 1 long end to form a log. Use a serrated knife to cut log into 12 equal slices. Arrange the slices in prepared dish (see tip).

4 Place apple juice, 80ml (⅓ cup) water, golden syrup, brown sugar and remaining butter in a saucepan. Stir over medium heat until melted and heated through. Pour mixture into dish around dough slices. Bake for 25-30 minutes or until golden and cooked through. Drizzled over custard to serve.

COOK'S TIP

The roly-poly dough will puff quite a bit during cooking, so allow for a little spreading when arranging in the dish.

● GLUTEN FREE ● MAKE AHEAD ● FREEZABLE ● EASY ● KID FRIENDLY

Chocolate & beetroot tart with
BRANDY JELLY

The boozy cherry jelly tops off this gorgeous ganache tart.

SERVES 8-10 **PREP** 1 hour (+ cooling, chilling & setting) **COOK** 1 hour 20 mins

125g beetroot

300g fresh cherries, pitted

55g (¼ cup) caster sugar

60ml (¼ cup) brandy

60ml (¼ cup) water

1 tbs lemon juice

Egg white, to brush

400g dark chocolate,
  finely chopped

330ml (1⅓ cups) thickened
  cream

3 gelatine leaves

Micro herbs, to serve

chocolate pastry

250g (1⅔ cups) plain flour

150g unsalted butter,
  chilled, chopped

45g (¼ cup) icing sugar
  mixture

2 tbs cocoa powder

2 egg yolks

1 Preheat oven to 180°C/160°C fan forced. Grease a 3cm-deep, 24.5cm (base size) fluted tart tin with removable base.

2 To make the pastry, place the flour, butter, icing sugar and cocoa in a food processor. Process until mixture resembles breadcrumbs. Add the egg yolks. Process until dough just comes together. Turn onto a floured surface and knead until smooth. Shape the dough into a disc. Cover. Place in the fridge for 30 minutes to chill.

3 Roll dough out between 2 sheets of baking paper until 4mm thick. Use the dough to line tin. Trim excess. Place in fridge for 30 minutes to chill.

4 Wrap the beetroot in foil. Roast for 40 minutes or until tender. Set aside to cool slightly. Peel then coarsely chop. Place beetroot and cherries in a clean food processor and process until finely chopped.

5 Place the sugar and brandy in a saucepan over medium-low heat. Cook, stirring, for 1-2 minutes or until sugar dissolves. Bring to boil. Simmer for 1 minute or until thickened. Add the sugar syrup, water and lemon juice to the beetroot mixture and process until smooth. Strain through a sieve set over a bowl, pressing to

extract liquid. Discard solids. Strain. (You should have 250ml (1 cupful) of liquid. If short, top with water).

6 Place the tin on baking tray. Line the pastry case with baking paper and fill with pastry weights or rice. Bake for 15 minutes. Remove paper and pastry weights or rice and bake for a further 12-15 minutes or until cooked through. Brush base and any cracks with egg white. Place in the oven for 2 minutes. Set aside to cool.

7 Place the chocolate in heatproof bowl. Place cream in saucepan over medium-low heat. Bring to the boil. Pour over the chocolate. Set aside for 2 minutes. Stir until melted and smooth. Set aside, stirring occasionally, for 5 minutes or until cooled slightly. Pour into the pastry case. Place in the fridge for 1 hour.

8 Soak the gelatine in cold water for 5 minutes. Squeeze to remove excess liquid. Place in a saucepan over low heat. Stir for 30 seconds or until dissolved. Remove from heat. Whisk in the beetroot mixture. Strain into jug. Skim foam from surface. Pour over the chocolate. Place in the fridge for 2 hours or until set. Set aside at room temperature for 15 minutes before serving. Sprinkle with herbs.

● GLUTEN FREE ● MAKE AHEAD ● FREEZABLE ● EASY ● KID FRIENDLY

Fig tart with almond crumble
ICE-CREAM

Wow the crowd with this sticky tart wrapped in zesty pastry.

SERVES 8 **PREP** 40 mins (+ 6 hours freezing) **COOK** 1 hour 10 mins

45g unsalted butter,
   at room temperature
45g raw caster sugar
45g almond meal, toasted
1 egg, lightly whisked
8 fresh figs, quartered
2 tbs fig jam, warmed
orange pastry
225g (1½ cups) plain flour
1 tbs raw caster sugar
½ tsp sea salt
1 orange, rind finely grated
140g unsalted butter,
   chilled, chopped
2½ tbs iced water
almond crumble ice-cream
50g (½ cup) rolled oats
75g (½ cup) plain flour
55g (¼ cup, firmly packed)
   brown sugar
2 tsp ground cinnamon
60g butter, chilled, chopped
50g (½ cup) flaked almonds
2L ctn vanilla ice-cream

1 To make the crumble ice-cream, preheat oven to 160°C/140°C fan forced. Line a baking tray with baking paper. Place oats, flour, sugar and cinnamon in a bowl and stir until well combined. Add the butter. Use your fingertips to rub the butter into the flour mixture until mixture resembles breadcrumbs. Add almonds and stir until combined. Spread mixture over prepared tray. Bake, stirring twice, for 15 minutes or until golden and crisp. Set aside to cool completely. Reserve ¼ cupful crumble. Transfer ice-cream to a large bowl. Fold the remaining crumble mixture into the ice-cream. Return to carton. Place in the freezer for 6 hours or until firm.

2 Meanwhile, to make the pastry, place the flour, sugar, salt and rind in a food processor and process until combined. Add the butter and pulse until just combined. Add the water and process until dough just comes together. Turn onto a lightly floured surface. Shape into a disc. Cover with plastic wrap. Place in the fridge for 30 minutes to rest.

3 Use electric beaters to beat butter and sugar in a bowl until pale and creamy. Beat in almond meal. Beat in 1½ tbs of the egg until just combined.

4 Turn dough onto a piece of baking paper. Use a lightly floured rolling pin to roll out to a 28cm disc. Transfer the dough and paper to a baking tray. Spread with the almond mixture, leaving a 3-4cm border. Arrange the figs over the mixture. Fold dough over to form a pleated rim. Brush rim with remaining egg. Place in the fridge for 15 minutes to rest.

5 Preheat oven to 190°C/170°C fan forced. Bake tart for 50-55 minutes or until golden. Brush with the jam. Set aside for 15 minutes to cool slightly. Top with reserved crumble and serve with the ice-cream.

● GLUTEN FREE ● MAKE AHEAD ● FREEZABLE ● EASY ● KID FRIENDLY

Rocky road meringue
PIE

Rock their world with this fully-loaded chocolate pie!

SERVES 12 **PREP** 40 mins (+ 1 hour 30 mins chilling & cooling) **COOK** 30 mins

3 egg whites
155g (¾ cup) caster sugar
40g dark chocolate, melted
1 tbs shredded coconut
Maraschino cherries,
    to serve
chocolate shortcrust pastry
225g (1½ cups) plain flour
2 tbs Dutch processed
    cocoa powder
2 tbs caster sugar
150g butter, chilled,
    chopped
2½ tbs iced water
chocolate custard
100g (⅔ cup) custard
    powder
2 tsp Dutch processed
    cocoa powder
500ml (2 cups) milk
150g dark chocolate,
    chopped
50g (¼ cup) red glacé
    cherries
40g (⅔ cup) mini
    marshmallows, plus
    extra, to decorate
40g (¼ cup) roasted salted
    peanuts, plus extra,
    chopped, to decorate

1 To make the pastry, place the flour, cocoa and sugar in a food processor. Process until combined. Add butter and process until mixture resembles fine crumbs. Add the iced water and process until the dough just comes together. Shape into a disc. Cover with plastic wrap and place in the fridge for 30 minutes.

2 Preheat oven to 180°C/160°C fan forced. Grease a 3cm-deep, 22.5cm round fluted tart tin with removable base. Place the tin on a baking tray. Roll the dough between 2 sheets of baking paper until about 5mm thick and big enough to line the tin. Place the dough in the tin, folding the excess over the edge. Use a fork to prick the base. Place in the fridge for 15 minutes. Line the dough with baking paper and fill with pastry weights or rice. Bake for 15 minutes. Remove the paper and weights. Bake for a further 15 minutes or until light golden. Set aside to cool.

3 Meanwhile, to make the custard, place the custard powder and cocoa in a saucepan and stir until combined. Whisk in one-third of the milk until smooth. Whisk in remaining milk. Cook, stirring, over medium-high heat for 5 minutes or until thickened. Remove from heat. Stir in chocolate. Set aside for 5 minutes. Stir until smooth. Cover surface with plastic wrap. Set aside for 30 minutes.

4 Stir glacé cherries, marshmallows and nuts through custard mixture. Trim excess pastry. Transfer tart shell to a plate. Fill with custard. Level top. Place in the fridge for 1 hour to set.

5 Use electric beaters to beat the egg whites and sugar in a clean, dry bowl for 8-10 minutes or until the sugar dissolves. Dollop the meringue over the custard layer. Use a cook's blowtorch to lightly brown meringue. Decorate with melted chocolate, coconut, maraschino cherries, extra marshmallows and peanuts.

● GLUTEN FREE ● MAKE AHEAD ● FREEZABLE ● EASY ● KID FRIENDLY

Oaty golden
SYRUP TART

Syrupy macadamia filling and brown sugar pastry? Sweet as!

SERVES 8 **PREP** 40 mins (+ chilling & cooling) **COOK** 50 mins

150g (1 cup) plain flour

100g butter, chilled, chopped

45g (¼ cup, lightly packed) brown sugar

35g (⅓ cup) rolled oats, plus extra 2 tsp

1 egg yolk

3 tsp iced water

Vanilla ice-cream, to serve

filling

150g raw macadamias

60g (⅓ cup, lightly packed) brown sugar

125g butter, chopped, at room temperature

125ml (½ cup) golden syrup, plus extra, to serve

2 eggs

40g (¼ cup) plain flour

20g (¼ cup) desiccated coconut

1 Preheat oven to 200°C/180°C fan forced. Grease a 3cm-deep, 23cm (top size) fluted tart tin with removable base. Place the flour, butter and sugar in a food processor and process until the mixture resembles fine crumbs. Add the oats, egg yolk and water and process until mixture just comes together. Turn onto a lightly floured surface and gently knead until just smooth. Shape into a disc. Cover with plastic wrap and place in the fridge for 15 minutes.

2 Use a lightly floured rolling pin to roll dough on a lightly floured surface until large enough to cover base and side of tin. Line the tin with dough and trim excess. Line with baking paper and fill with pastry weights or rice. Bake for 10 minutes. Remove paper and weights and bake for a further 10 minutes or until golden. Set aside in tin to cool.

3 To make filling, reduce oven to 180°C/160°C fan forced. Place the nuts in food processor and process until coarsely chopped. Add the sugar and process until fine crumbs form (do not over-process).

4 Use electric beaters to beat the butter in a bowl until pale and creamy. Add the syrup and beat until combined. Add the eggs, 1 at a time, beating well after each addition. Add the nut mixture, flour and coconut and beat until well combined. Spoon mixture into tart shell. Sprinkle with extra oats and bake for 30 minutes or until golden (see tip). Set aside in pan to cool slightly. Serve with ice-cream and extra golden syrup.

COOK'S TIP

If the pastry is starting to get too dark or burnt, cover it with foil and continue baking until it's just firm to a gentle touch.

● GLUTEN FREE ● MAKE AHEAD ● FREEZABLE ● EASY ● KID FRIENDLY

Bittersweet chocolate
RASPBERRY PIE

Decadent dark chocolate and pops of tangy berry. Yum!

SERVES 8 **PREP** 45 mins (+ 45 mins resting) **COOK** 55 mins

225g (1½ cups) plain flour

2 tbs caster sugar

35g (⅓ cup) dark cocoa powder

150g butter, chilled, chopped

1½ tbs water

Icing sugar, to dust

Ice-cream or cream, to serve (optional)

filling

140g dark chocolate, chopped

30g (¼ cup) almond or hazelnut meal

375g fresh raspberries

1 tbs caster sugar

1 Preheat the oven to 180°C/160°C fan forced. Grease a 2.5cm-deep, 19 x 29.5cm (base size) rectangular, fluted tart tin with removable base. Place the flour, sugar, cocoa and butter in a food processor. Process until mixture resembles breadcrumbs. Add the water and process until the dough just comes together. Turn onto a lightly floured surface. Knead gently until just smooth. Shape into a disc. Wrap in plastic wrap. Place in the fridge for 30 minutes to rest.

2 Roll dough out on a lightly floured sheet of baking paper until 3mm thick. Line prepared pan with dough. Trim excess, reserving scraps. Place in the fridge for 15 minutes to rest.

3 Meanwhile, re-roll the dough scraps on a sheet of lightly floured baking paper until 3mm thick. Use a 3cm-diameter heart-shaped pastry cutter to cut out shapes. Place in the fridge for 15 minutes to rest.

4 Place the tin on a baking tray. Line the pastry with baking paper and fill with pastry weights or rice. Bake for 15 minutes. Remove paper and pastry weights or rice. Bake for a further 10 minutes or until golden and crisp. Set aside to cool.

5 To make the filling, place half the chocolate in a heatproof bowl. Microwave, stirring every minute, until melted. Spread over pastry. Sprinkle with almond meal, berries and sugar. Scatter over the remaining chocolate. Top with hearts. Bake for 25-30 minutes or until the raspberries have softened and chocolate has melted. Dust with icing sugar. Serve tart with ice-cream or cream, if using.

● GLUTEN FREE ● MAKE AHEAD ● FREEZABLE ● EASY ● KID FRIENDLY

Roasted white chocolate
CARAMEL TART

This retro revival treat is inspired by the iconic chocolate bar.

MAKES 6 **PREP** 20 mins (+ 1 hour chilling & 3 hours setting**) COOK** 1 hour 5 mins

**200g white chocolate,
    chopped**
60g butter
**Pinch sea salt flakes, plus
    extra, to serve**
**185ml (¾ cup) pouring
    cream**
Crème fraîche, to serve
**Shaved white chocolate,
    to serve**
sweet shortcrust pastry
225g (1½ cups) plain flour
**150g butter, chilled,
    chopped**
2 tbs icing sugar mixture
1 egg yolk
1 tbs chilled water

1 To make the shortcrust pastry, place the flour, butter and icing sugar in a food processor and process until mixture resembles breadcrumbs. Add egg yolk and water. Process until dough just comes together. Turn onto a lightly floured surface and knead until just smooth. Shape into a disc. Cover with plastic wrap. Place in the fridge for 30 minutes to rest.

2 Grease six round 2.5cm-deep, 8.5cm (base size) fluted tart tins with removable base. Divide dough into 6 portions. Gently roll each portion out on a sheet of baking paper until about 3mm thick. Ease into prepared tins and press the dough into the sides. Trim the excess. Place the tarts in the fridge for 30 minutes to chill.

3 Preheat oven to 200°C/180°C fan forced. Line the pastry cases with baking paper. Place on baking tray and fill with pastry weights or rice. Bake for 15 minutes. Remove paper

and pastry weights or rice. Bake for a further 10 minutes or until golden and crisp. Set aside to cool.

4 Reduce oven to 140°C/ 120°C fan forced. Place chocolate in a shallow baking dish. Bake, stirring every 10 minutes with a spatula to spread and melt on the tray, for 25-35 minutes or until a rich caramel colour. (Chocolate may look grainy but continue to stir and it will melt and eventually become smooth.) Spoon into a heatproof bowl. Add the butter and salt. Stir until combined.

5 Place the cream in a saucepan over medium heat. Cook, stirring until almost to the boil. Pour cream over chocolate mixture and set aside for 5 minutes. Whisk together until smooth and well combined. Pour into pastry cases. Place in the fridge for 2-3 hours or until set. Top with crème fraîche. Sprinkle with the chocolate shavings and extra salt to serve.

★ ★ ★ ★ ★

I cheated and bought pastry cases. Definitely a recipe to keep.

EDP73

● GLUTEN FREE ● MAKE AHEAD ● FREEZABLE ● EASY ● KID FRIENDLY

Maple pecan pie with spiced
RUM ICE-CREAM

Tried and tested, this extra-special pecan pie recipe is our go-to.

SERVES 8 **PREP** 20 mins (+ 6 hours freezing & chilling) **COOK** 50 mins

3 eggs, lightly whisked
125ml (½ cup) maple syrup
100g (½ cup, firmly packed)
   brown sugar
50g butter, melted
½ tsp vanilla bean paste
300g pecan halves
spiced rum ice-cream
1.5L vanilla ice-cream,
   softened slightly
40ml (¼ cup) spiced rum
½ tsp ground cinnamon
pastry
225g (1½ cups) plain flour
2 tbs icing sugar mixture
150g butter, chilled,
   chopped
1 egg yolk
2 tbs chilled water

1 To make the spiced rum ice-cream. Place the ice-cream, rum and cinnamon in a large bowl and stir until well combined. Transfer to a shallow metal container. Cover with foil. Place in the freezer for 6 hours or until firm.

2 To make the pastry, place the flour, icing sugar and butter in a food processor and process until mixture resembles breadcrumbs. Add yolk and water. Process until the dough just comes together. Knead on lightly floured surface until smooth. Cover with plastic wrap. Place in fridge for 30 minutes to chill.

3 Preheat oven to 200°C/180°C fan forced. Grease a 3cm-deep, 26cm (top size) fluted tart tin with removable base. Roll out dough between 2 sheets of baking paper to a 4mm-thick disc. Line the tin with the dough. Trim and reserve excess. Place in the fridge for 15 minutes, to chill.

4 Line the pastry case with baking paper and fill with pastry weights or rice. Bake for 15 minutes. Remove the paper and pastry weights or rice. Bake for a further 10 minutes or until crisp and golden.

5 Reduce oven temperature to 180°C/160°C fan forced. Place the egg, syrup, sugar, butter and vanilla in a bowl and whisk until combined. Add the pecan. Pour into pastry base. Bake for 25 minutes or until set. Set aside for 1 hour to cool. Decorate with pastry leaves (see tip). Top with ice-cream to serve.

COOK'S TIP

To make the pastry leaves, cut leaf shapes from the pastry scraps. Brush with egg wash and bake on a lined tray until golden.

● GLUTEN FREE ● MAKE AHEAD ● FREEZABLE ● EASY ● KID FRIENDLY

Strawberry heart TART

Saying 'I love you' is easy with this cheat's blushing berry pastry.

MAKES 2 **PREP** 15 mins **COOKING** 20 mins

100g butter, at room
   temperature
100g (½ cup) caster sugar
1 egg
100g (1 cup) almond meal
40g (¼ cup) plain flour
1 tsp vanilla extract
2 sheets frozen puff pastry,
   just thawed
500g strawberries, hulled,
   thinly sliced
115g (⅓ cup) strawberry
   jam, warmed, strained
Crème fraîche, to serve
Small fresh mint leaves,
   to serve

1 Preheat oven to 200°C/180°C fan forced. Place 2 baking trays in the oven. Place strawberries on a paper towel-lined plate to drain.

2 Use electric beaters to beat the butter, sugar and egg in a bowl until pale and creamy. Add almond meal, flour and vanilla and stir until combined.

3 Place each sheet of pastry on a sheet of baking paper. Use a small, sharp knife to cut out a large heart shape from each pastry sheet. Score a border 1cm from the edge. Use a fork to prick pastry all over. Divide the mixture between pastry hearts and spread to the border. Arrange the strawberry slices on top. Carefully slide pastries and baking paper onto the hot trays. Bake, swapping trays halfway through, for 20 minutes or until pastry is crisp. Brush with jam and serve with a dollop of crème fraîche.

COOK'S TIP

Switch up strawberries for fresh blueberries, or thinly sliced blackberries or raspberries.

● GLUTEN FREE ● MAKE AHEAD ● FREEZABLE ● EASY ● KID FRIENDLY

15
minutes
prep

CUPCAKES + CAKES

WHETHER YOU'RE AFTER A BAKE SALE BEAUTY, SIMPLE AFTERNOON TEA TREAT, OR SOMETHING IN BETWEEN, WE'VE GOT THE PERFECT RECIPE YOU.

Round tip

Large flower-drop tip

Star tip

Open star tip

How to ice
A CUPCAKE

Love piped cupcakes but not sure how to replicate the look? Food director Michelle Southan guides us on getting those swirls, twirls and flourishes. You'll need a piping bag and set of these decorating nozzles to start.

ROUND TIP

Choose this tip to get that smooth, plump buttercream look on your baked beauties. Works equally well on cupcakes as when making a border on a larger cake.

OPEN STAR TIP

This tip gives instant star appeal to your cupcakes and cakes. The defined lines and swirls it creates can help make you look like a professional decorator.

STAR TIP

Probably the most used of all the tips, the star tip gives you that classic cupcake swirl as well as a more intricate petal pattern. It can take some practice to get right.

LARGE FLOWER-DROP TIP

If you're wanting a looser more freestyle vibe with your decorations, then this is the tip for you. May take some getting used to but practice makes perfect.

ROUND TIP

Starting at the edge of the cake, swirl the icing into the centre in one smooth circular motion, slightly overlapping as you go. Gently pull the bag away in the centre to form a peak.

ROUND TIP

Starting in the centre, hold the piping bag upright and gently squeeze out the icing to form small peaks, pulling the bag away at the end of each peak to form a point.

STAR TIP

Starting at the edge of the cake, swirl the icing into the centre in one smooth circular motion, slightly overlapping as you go. Gradually pull bag away towards the centre to form a peak.

STAR TIP

Starting at the edge of the cake, move the piping bag in a 'C' shape (rotating your wrist) to form swirls around the edge and into the centre, slightly overlapping, to cover the cake.

OPEN STAR TIP

Starting in the centre, hold the piping bag upright and gently squeeze out the icing to form small peaks, pulling the bag away at the end of each peak to form a point.

OPEN STAR TIP

Working around the edge of the cake, move the piping bag in a small circular motion to form swirls with peaks, pulling the bag away at the end of each peak to form a point.

LARGE FLOWER-DROP TIP

Starting at the edge of the cake, move the piping bag in a 'C' shape (rotating your wrist) to form swirls around the edge. Finish in the centre with a swirl that fills the gap.

LARGE FLOWER-DROP TIP

Starting in the centre of the cake, swirl the icing in a smooth circular motion towards the edge, slightly overlapping as you go, to cover the cake and form a rose shape.

Giant flower CUPCAKE

Say it with flowers, and cake, with this stunning baked bouquet.

SERVES 30 **PREP** 1hour 30mins **COOK** 1hour

675g (4½ cups) self-raising flour

645g (3 cups) caster sugar, plus 100g (½ cup), extra

375g unsalted butter, chopped, at room temperature

6 eggs

300g ctn sour cream

125ml (½ cup) milk

3 tsp vanilla extract

125ml (½ cup) boiling water

Edible flowers, to decorate

buttercream

750g unsalted butter, chopped, at room temperature

900g (6 cups) icing sugar mixture

1 tbs vanilla extract

Pink, blue, orange, yellow and green food colouring, to tint

1 Preheat oven to 170°C/150°C fan forced. Lightly grease 2 deep 18cm (base size) round cake pans. Line bases with baking paper. Lightly grease a 2L (8 cup) pudding basin and dust with flour. Line base with a round of baking paper.

2 Use electric beaters to beat 450g (3 cups) flour, 430g (2 cups) caster sugar, 250g butter, 4 eggs, 200g sour cream, 80ml (⅓ cup) milk and 2 tsp vanilla in a large bowl on low speed until combined. Increase speed to medium-high and beat for 1 minute or until mixture is pale. Divide the mixture between prepared cake pans. Smooth the surface. Bake for 55 minutes or until a skewer inserted into the centres comes out clean. Set aside in pans for 5 minutes before turning onto a wire rack to cool completely.

3 Repeat step 2 with the remaining flour, caster sugar, butter, eggs, sour cream, milk and vanilla, spooning mixture into prepared pudding basin. Bake for 1 hour. Set aside in basin for 5 minutes before turning onto a wire rack to cool completely.

4 Meanwhile, place extra caster sugar and boiling water in a bowl. Stir until sugar dissolves. Cool slightly.

5 To make buttercream, use electric beaters on medium-high speed to beat butter in a bowl for 6-8 minutes or until pale and creamy. Add icing sugar, vanilla and a pinch of salt. Reduce speed to low. Mix until combined. Increase speed to medium. Beat for 6-8 minutes or until pale and creamy.

6 Trim top of each cake, to level. Cut each in half horizontally. Use a little buttercream to secure a basin cake half to a cake board. Brush with some sugar syrup. Spread over ½ cupful buttercream to cover. Repeat layering with final basin cake, more syrup and buttercream to create cupcake base. Finish with a layer of buttercream. Stack 4 round cake halves on a tray, layering with syrup and buttercream, finishing with final cake. Use a large serrated knife to cut cake stack from top to bottom, sloping inwards, to create the rounded cupcake top.

7 Spread a thin layer of buttercream over side and top of cupcake base and cupcake top (this is called a crumb coat). Place both cakes in fridge for 30 minutes or until firm.

8 Divide remaining buttercream between 4 bowls. Use food colourings to tint 1 bowl pale pink, 1 pale blue, 1 peach and 1 green.

9 Cover side of cupcake base with green buttercream. Use a palette knife to make vertical lines in buttercream. Top with cupcake top.

10 Spoon remaining coloured buttercream into piping bags fitted with various sized fluted nozzles. Use picture as a guide to pipe flowers onto cupcake top. Top with flowers.

● GLUTEN FREE ● MAKE AHEAD ● FREEZABLE ● EASY ● KID FRIENDLY

Neapolitan zebra CAKE

People go wild for neapolitan flavours and this marble-ous cake.

SERVES 8-10 **PREP** 30 mins (+ cooling & setting) **COOKING** 1 hour 15 mins

300g (2 cups) plain flour, plus 1 tbs extra
½ tsp baking powder
¼ tsp bicarbonate of soda
190g unsalted butter, at room temperature
355g (1⅔ cups) caster sugar
5 eggs
235g (1 cup) sour cream
2 tsp vanilla extract
1½ tbs cocoa powder, sifted
1 tbs Queen Strawb'ry & Cream flavouring
Pink liquid food colouring, to tint
80g (⅓ cup) white chocolate melts

chocolate glaze
180g block dark chocolate, chopped
125ml (½ cup) thickened cream
1 tbs glucose syrup, or light corn syrup

1 Preheat oven to 160°C/140°C fan forced. Lightly grease a 7cm-deep, 14 x 24cm (base size) loaf pan. Line with baking paper, allowing the 2 long sides to overhang.

2 Sift the flour, baking powder and bicarb into a bowl. Use electric beaters to beat the butter and sugar in a bowl until pale and creamy. Add the eggs, 1 at a time, beating well after each addition. Gently fold the flour mixture into the butter mixture, alternating with the sour cream, until just combined.

3 Divide cake mixture among 3 bowls. To the first bowl, add the vanilla and fold gently to combine. To the second bowl, add the cocoa powder and fold gently to combine. To the remaining bowl, add the strawberry flavouring and a few drops of the food colouring. Fold gently to combine. Place 2 tablespoons of strawberry mixture in the centre of the prepared pan. Place 2 tablespoons of the vanilla mixture directly on top. Place 2 tablespoons of chocolate mixture on top of the vanilla mixture. Continue alternating strawberry, vanilla and chocolate mixtures, gently tapping the pan every so often to help the mixture spread. Cover pan

with foil. Bake for 1 hour 10 minutes, or until a skewer inserted into the centre comes out clean. Set aside in the pan for 15 minutes to cool slightly. Transfer to a wire rack to cool completely.

4 Meanwhile, line a large baking tray with baking paper. Place chocolate melts in a microwave-safe bowl. Microwave in 30-second bursts, stirring between each burst, until melted and smooth. Pour over the prepared tray and use a palette knife, or back of a metal spoon, to spread thinly. Working quickly, roll up the baking paper from the shortest end to form a large cylinder. Place in the fridge for 30 minutes to set. Unroll the paper to crack and create pieces of chocolate bark.

5 To make the chocolate glaze, heat the chocolate, cream and glucose in a small saucepan over medium-low heat, stirring, for 2-3 minutes or until the chocolate begins to melt. Remove from heat and stir until smooth. Set aside for 10-15 minutes to thicken slightly.

6 Transfer the cake to a serving plate. Drizzle over the warm chocolate glaze, allowing it to drip down the sides of the cake. Decorate the top with chocolate bark to serve.

● GLUTEN FREE ● MAKE AHEAD ● FREEZABLE ● EASY ● **KID FRIENDLY**

Pumpkin & walnut CUPCAKES

These gourd-geous treats are packed with goodness.

MAKES 12 **PREP** 30 mins (+ cooling) **COOKING** 20 mins

2 eggs
60ml (¼ cup) milk
100g (½ cup, firmly packed) brown sugar or rapadura sugar
125ml (½ cup) extra virgin olive oil (or walnut oil)
125g (1 cup) coarsely grated pumpkin
55g (½ cup) almond meal
45g (⅓ cup) chopped walnuts (optional)
160g (1 cup) wholemeal self-raising flour
½ tsp ground cinnamon or ground cardamom, or a mixture of both
1 lemon, zested

lemon cream cheese icing

150g cream cheese, chopped, at room temperature
60g (⅓ cup) icing sugar, sifted
2-4 tsp lemon juice

1 Preheat the oven to 180°C/160°C fan forced. Line twelve 80ml (⅓ cup) muffin pans with paper cases.

2 Whisk together the eggs, milk, sugar and oil in a large bowl. Stir in the grated pumpkin, almond meal and chopped walnuts, if using. Add the wholemeal flour and cinnamon or cardamom and stir until just combined.

3 Divide the mixture among the prepared pans and bake for 20 minutes or until a skewer inserted into the centre comes out clean. Set aside for 5 minutes, then transfer to a wire rack to cool completely.

4 For the icing, use electric beaters to beat the cream cheese, icing sugar and 2 tsp of the lemon juice in a bowl until well combined and smooth. Add the remaining lemon juice until smooth and to taste.

5 Use a piping bag fitted with a 1cm plain piping nozzle to pipe the icing over the cupcakes. Sprinkle with lemon zest.

COOK'S TIP

For a nut-free version, omit the walnuts (the mixture will make 11 cupcakes) and replace the almonds with a ground seed mix, such as a mix of ground pepitas, sunflower seeds and sesame seeds.

★★★★★

So easy to make and absolute delicious – light and fluffy.

JANICEWEINSTOCK

● GLUTEN FREE ● MAKE AHEAD ● FREEZABLE ● EASY ● KID FRIENDLY

Best-ever gluten-free
CHOCOLATE CAKE

Here's a super-easy recipe for that allergy-friendly cake you need.

SERVES 10 **PREP** 30 mins (+ cooling) **COOKING** 40 mins

70g (⅔ cup) cocoa powder
250ml (1 cup) boiling water
400g (2⅔ cups) gluten-free
   self-raising flour
250g butter, chopped, at
   room temperature
335g (1½ cups) caster sugar
4 eggs

chocolate buttercream
125g butter, chopped, at
   room temperature
200g (1½ cups) icing sugar
   mixture
30g (¼ cup) cocoa powder
100g gluten-free dark
   chocolate, melted,
   cooled
1 tbs milk

1 Preheat oven to 180°C/160°C fan forced. Grease two 20cm (base size) round cake pans and line the bases with baking paper.

2 Sift the cocoa into a bowl and stir in the boiling water until smooth. Set aside to cool completely. Place the flour into a separate bowl.

3 Use electric beaters to beat the butter and sugar in a bowl until pale and creamy. Add the eggs, 1 at a time, beating well after each addition. Fold in half the flour, then the cocoa mixture, then the remaining flour until just combined.

4 Divide the batter evenly between the prepared pans. Bake for 40 minutes or until a skewer inserted into the centre comes out clean. Set aside in the pan for 10 minutes to cool slightly before turning onto a wire rack to cool completely.

5 To make the buttercream icing, use electric beaters to beat the butter in a bowl for 3 minutes or until pale and creamy. Sift the icing sugar and cocoa powder together. Add to the butter, a large spoonful at a time, beating constantly, until combined. Add the chocolate and beat to combine. Beat in the milk.

6 Place 1 cake on a plate and spread with half the buttercream. Place the remaining cake on top and spread with remaining buttercream.

COOK'S TIP

Please note, some brands of cocoa powder can contain small amounts of gluten. Check the packet carefully before purchasing.

● GLUTEN FREE ● MAKE AHEAD ● FREEZABLE ● EASY ● KID FRIENDLY

Literally is the BEST EVER (and I've tried a lot of GF choc cakes).

DANI.BROUGHAM

Coconut ice
CUPCAKES

We heart sweet memories of coconut ice, now in cupcake form.

MAKES 12 **PREP** 20 mins (+ cooling & setting) **COOKING** 25 mins

125g butter, chopped, at
  room temperature
155g (¾ cup) caster sugar
½ tsp vanilla extract
2 eggs, at room temperature
190g (1¼ cups) self-raising
  flour
45g (¾ cup) moist coconut
  flakes
270ml can coconut cream
Mini pearl sprinkles, to serve
chocolate hearts
100g white chocolate melts,
  melted
buttercream
375g unsalted butter,
  chopped, at room
  temperature
380g (2½ cups) icing sugar
  mixture, sifted
60ml (¼ cup) milk
Pink and orange food
  colouring, to tint

1 Preheat oven to 180°C/160°C fan forced. Line twelve 80ml (⅓ cup) muffin pans with paper cases. Use electric beaters to beat butter, sugar and vanilla in a bowl until pale and creamy. Add eggs, 1 at a time, beating well after each addition, until combined. In 2 alternating batches, stir in the flour, coconut flakes and coconut cream.

2 Divide the mixture evenly among the prepared pans. Bake for 20-25 minutes or until a skewer inserted into the centres comes out clean. Turn onto a wire rack to cool.

3 For the chocolate hearts, line a baking tray with baking paper. Dip the back of a teaspoon in the melted chocolate and gently drag the spoon across the paper to create a teardrop shape. Dip the spoon in chocolate again and repeat next to this, making sure the teardrops join at the tip to create a rustic heart shape. Repeat to make 24 hearts. Allow to set.

4 To make the buttercream, use electric beaters to beat the butter in a bowl until pale and creamy. Gradually add icing sugar and milk, in alternating batches, beating until combined. Divide the buttercream between 2 bowls. Add a few drops of pink food colouring to 1 bowl. Stir to combine. Add a few of drops of orange food colouring to the other bowl. Stir to combine.

5 Spoon the pink icing down one side of a piping bag with a 1cm fluted nozzle. Spoon the orange icing down the other side of the piping bag. Pipe the icing onto the cooled cupcakes. Scatter the pearl sprinkles over the top and decorate with chocolate hearts.

★ ★ ★ ★ ★

*Theses cupcakes are so easy to make, light, moist and delicious.
This is my go-to cupcake recipe, love it.* **CHEZ.COOPER**

● GLUTEN FREE ● MAKE AHEAD ● FREEZABLE ● EASY ● KID FRIENDLY

Maltesers CUPCAKES

Nothing pleases like Maltesers, and these liqueur-spiked treats.

MAKES 12 **PREP** 30 mins (+ cooling) **COOKING** 30 mins

125g butter, chopped

100g dark chocolate
(70% cocoa), chopped

125ml (½ cup) hot water

2 tsp instant coffee

60ml (¼ cup) chocolate
or coffee liqueur

200g (1 cup, firmly packed)
brown sugar

100g (⅔ cup) plain flour

40g (¼ cup) self-raising flour

2 tbs cocoa powder

1 egg

Maltesers, to decorate

maltesers buttercream

250g unsalted butter,
chopped, at room
temperature

500g icing sugar mixture

1½ tbs milk

100g Maltesers, finely
crushed

chocolate ganache

100g dark chocolate
(70% cocoa), chopped

125ml (½ cup) pouring
cream

1 Preheat oven to 160°C/140°C fan forced, then line twelve 125ml (½ cup) muffin pans with paper cases.

2 Combine butter, chocolate, water, coffee and liqueur in a saucepan over low heat. Cook, stirring, for 5 minutes or until melted. Remove from heat. Add the sugar. Stir to combine. Set aside for 5 minutes to cool slightly.

3 Add flours and cocoa. Use a balloon whisk to stir to combine. Add egg and stir to combine. Divide among prepared pans. Bake for 20 minutes or until a skewer inserted into the centre comes out clean. Set aside to cool completely.

4 For the buttercream, use electric beaters to beat the butter in a bowl until very pale. Gradually add the icing sugar and milk, in alternating batches, whisking well between each batch. Add the crushed Maltesers and beat until well combined.

5 For the ganache, combine the chocolate and cream in a saucepan over low heat. Cook, stirring with a metal spoon, for 5 minutes or until chocolate melts and mixture is smooth. Remove from heat.

6 Use a piping bag with a 1.5cm plain nozzle to pipe buttercream peaks onto the cupcakes. Drizzle the warm ganache over the cupcakes and decorate with Maltesers.

COOK'S TIP

To turn these cupcakes into an even more indulgent treat, swap the milk in the frosting for Kahlua.

★★★★★

These were divine. The cake was rich and moist, and the icing was yummy. Sweet tooths will love this one.

JASPER 2017

● GLUTEN FREE ● MAKE AHEAD ● FREEZABLE ● EASY ● KID FRIENDLY

Coconut & strawberry
SPONGE CAKE

No one has to miss out with this gluten- and dairy-free cake.

SERVES 8 **PREP** 30 mins (+ cooling & 6 hours 30 mins chilling) **COOK** 35 mins

270ml can coconut milk
3 eggs, separated
2½ tbs caster sugar
40g (¼ cup) coconut sugar
½ tsp vanilla extract
70g (½ cup) gluten-free cornflour
45g (¼ cup) brown rice flour
¾ tsp cream of tartar
½ tsp bicarbonate of soda
1 tbs fine desiccated coconut
250g strawberries, hulled, chopped
1 tbs lemon juice
1½ tsp chia seeds
½ tsp vanilla bean paste
Pure icing sugar, to dust

1 Chill the can of coconut milk for 6 hours or until firm. Preheat oven to 180°C/160°C fan forced. Grease and line base and side of a 6cm-deep, 20cm (base size) round cake pan.

2 Use electric beaters to beat egg whites in a bowl for 1 minute or until frothy. Combine caster sugar and 2 tbs of the coconut sugar in a bowl. Add sugar mixture to egg whites, 1 tbs at a time, beating well after each addition. Beat for 2 minutes or until tripled in volume. Add yolks, 1 at a time, beating well after each addition. Beat in vanilla until just combined. Sift flours, cream of tartar and bicarb into a bowl. Sift flour mixture over egg mixture. Add desiccated coconut. Gently fold in dry ingredients until just combined. Spoon into prepared pan. Smooth surface. Bake for 20-22 minutes or until cake is firm and springs back when lightly touched. Cover with a tea towel. Cool in pan for 5 minutes.

Turn onto a wire rack. Cover with tea towel. Cool completely.

3 Meanwhile, combine the strawberry, lemon juice and remaining coconut sugar in a saucepan. Stand for 5 minutes. Cook, stirring, over low heat for 2 minutes or until the sugar dissolves. Cook, stirring occasionally, for 5 minutes or until the strawberry breaks down. Stir in the chia seeds and cook for 2 minutes or until thickened. Transfer to a bowl. Cool for 30 minutes. Chill for 30 minutes until cooled completely.

4 Remove coconut milk from fridge. Carefully open. Spoon solidified coconut milk from surface into a glass bowl. Reserve liquid for another use. Use a balloon whisk to whisk solidified coconut milk and vanilla until thick.

5 Slice cake in half horizontally. Spread with coconut cream. Top with strawberry mixture. Sandwich with cake top. Dust with icing sugar and serve immediately.

● GLUTEN FREE ● MAKE AHEAD ● FREEZABLE ● EASY ● KID FRIENDLY

Choc-centre
CUPCAKES

Talk about a hidden gem, each cake has a salted caramel secret.

MAKES 12 **PREP** 30 mins (+ cooling time) **COOK** 20 mins

120g almond meal
75g (½ cup) plain flour
50g (½ cup) dark cocoa powder
2 tsp baking powder
140g (½ cup) Nutella
80g butter, melted
2 tsp vanilla extract
2 eggs
125ml (½ cup) buttermilk
60ml (¼ cup) maple syrup
12 Lindt Lindor Sea Salt Caramel balls
50g Nestlé Bakers' Choice Dark Chocolate Chunks, melted, cooled

buttercream
125g butter, chopped, at room temperature
155g (¾ cup firmly packed) dark brown sugar

1 Preheat the oven to 180°C/160°C fan forced. Line twelve 80ml (⅓ cup) muffin pans with paper cases.

2 Combine the almond meal, flour, cocoa powder, baking powder, Nutella, butter, vanilla, eggs, buttermilk and maple syrup in a food processor. Process, scraping down the sides halfway, for 20-30 seconds or until the mixture is just smooth. Divide the mixture among prepared pans. Bake for 20 minutes or until just firm to the touch. Set aside to cool completely in the pan.

3 Use a small sharp knife to cut a small cone-shaped piece from the top of each cake, leaving a 1cm-wide border. Reserve the cone. Insert a Lindor ball into hole. Trim the pointed end of cone and insert the top over the Lindor ball to sit level.

4 For the buttercream, use electric beaters to beat the butter and sugar in a bowl until pale and creamy. Spoon into a piping bag fitted with a 1cm nozzle.

5 Pipe the buttercream onto the cakes, covering the cut marks on the top, and drizzle with the melted chocolate.

COOK'S TIP

To give these cupcakes a crunchy, nutty centre, replace the whole Lindt Lindor balls with chocolate-covered almonds or hazelnuts.

● GLUTEN FREE ● MAKE AHEAD ● FREEZABLE ● EASY ● KID FRIENDLY

Neapolitan muffin
PAN SCROLLS

Sticky and cinnamony, these scrolls deliver on taste and texture.

MAKES 14 **PREP** 40 mins (+ proving & cooling) **COOK** 20 mins

500g (3⅓ cups) plain flour,
  plus extra, to dust
70g (⅓ cup) caster sugar
2 tsp (7g sachet) dried yeast
½ tsp salt
250ml (1 cup) milk
60g unsalted butter, chopped
1 tsp vanilla bean paste
1 egg
choc-cinnamon filling
60g unsalted butter, at room
  temperature
100g (½ cup, firmly packed)
  brown sugar
2 tbs cocoa powder
1 tsp ground cinnamon
strawberry icing
100g cream cheese, at room
  temperature
90g unsalted butter,
  chopped, at room
  temperature
195g (1¼ cups) icing sugar,
  sifted
1 tbs Queen Strawb'ry
  & Cream flavouring
Pink liquid food colouring,
  to tint

1 Combine the flour, caster sugar, yeast and salt in a stand mixer fitted with a dough hook. Place the milk, butter and vanilla in a small saucepan over low heat. Cook, stirring, for 1-2 minutes or until the butter is just melted. Set aside to cool for 2-3 minutes. Add egg and whisk to combine. Mix the milk mixture into the flour mixture until dough starts to come together. Use hands to knead dough in bowl for 8-10 minutes or until smooth and pulls away from sides of the bowl. Transfer to a lightly greased bowl. Cover with a clean tea towel. Set aside in a warm, draught-free place for 1 hour to prove or until dough doubles in size.

2 Meanwhile, to make the choc-cinnamon filling, place the butter, brown sugar, cocoa and cinnamon in a bowl and stir until mixture is a thick paste. Set aside.

3 Preheat oven to 190°C/170°C fan forced. Lightly grease fourteen 80ml (⅓ cup) muffin pans (you will need two 12-hole muffin pans). Roll out the dough on a lightly floured surface to form a 30 x 45cm rectangle. Top the dough with the filling and use the back of a spoon to evenly spread all over. With 1 long side facing you, tightly roll dough to enclose the filling. Use a sharp knife to trim ends then slice roll into 2.5cm-wide pieces. Place pieces, cut side up, in the prepared pan holes. Cover. Set aside for 15 minutes or until slightly risen.

4 Bake scrolls for 10-15 minutes or until golden. Transfer to a wire rack to cool slightly.

5 Meanwhile, to make the icing, use electric beaters to beat the cream cheese and butter in a bowl until smooth and creamy. Add the icing sugar, strawberry flavouring and a few drops of food colouring. Beat for 2-3 minutes or until well combined.

6 Drizzle strawberry icing over the warm scrolls. Serve warm or at room temperature.

● GLUTEN FREE ● MAKE AHEAD ● FREEZABLE ● EASY ● KID FRIENDLY

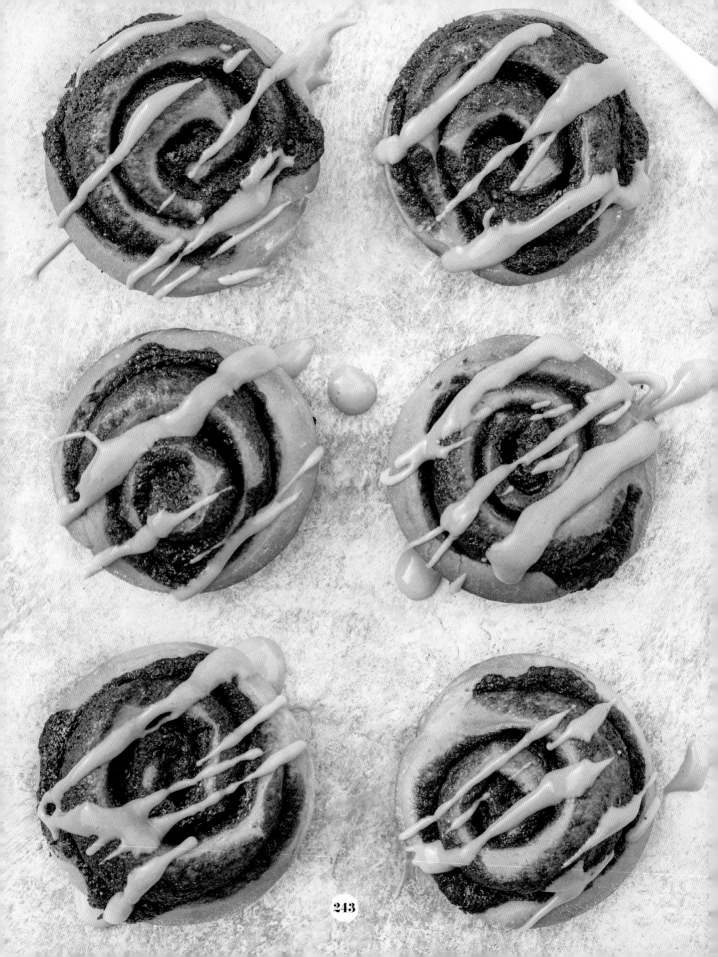

Strawberries & cream
OREO CUPCAKES

This is the sweet result of combining classic flavours.

MAKES 12 **PREP** 20 mins (+ cooling) **COOK** 25 mins

190g (1¼ cups) self-raising
flour
30g (¼ cup) cocoa powder
1 tbs cornflour
230g caster sugar
125g butter, chopped, at
room temperature
2 eggs
125ml (½ cup) milk
18 Oreo biscuits
Sliced fresh strawberries and
crushed freeze dried
strawberry, to decorate
strawberries & cream icing
250g pkt cream cheese,
chopped, at room
temperature
250g butter, chopped, at
room temperature
2 tsp vanilla bean paste
300g (2 cups) icing sugar
mixture, sifted

1 Preheat oven to 180°C/160°C fan forced. Line twelve 100ml muffin pans with large paper cases.

2 Sift flour, cocoa and cornflour into a large bowl. Add sugar, butter, eggs and milk. Use electric beaters to beat for 4-5 minutes or until mixture is smooth and well combined. Place a heaped teaspoonful of mixture into each patty case. Place 1 Oreo on top into each case. Divide remaining mixture among prepared pans. Smooth surface. Bake for 20-25 minutes or until a skewer inserted into the centre comes out clean. Transfer to a wire rack to cool completely.

3 Meanwhile, to make the icing, use electric beaters to beat the cream cheese, butter and vanilla in a large bowl until pale and creamy. Add the icing sugar in batches, beating well after each addition, until well combined. Spoon into a piping bag fitted with a 1.5cm star nozzle.

4 Pipe icing onto cupcakes. Cut remaining Oreos in half. Decorate cupcakes with Oreo halves and fresh strawberry. Sprinkle with the freeze-dried strawberry to serve.

COOK'S TIP

We used Oreo
Strawberry
cookies for
this recipe.
If unavailable
substitute with
Oreo Double Stuff
Neopolitan or
Oreo Original.

★★★★★

Kids loved it. They couldn't get enough of it.

I DU

● GLUTEN FREE ● MAKE AHEAD ● FREEZABLE ● EASY ● KID FRIENDLY

Condensed milk choc
RIPPLE LOG

This 'too easy' ripple log makes for a cheeky midweek dessert.

SERVES 8 **PREP** 10 mins (+ 15 mins cooling) **COOK** 35 mins

395g can sweetened
  condensed milk
125ml (½ cup) milk
1 egg
1 tsp vanilla extract
2 tbs dark cocoa powder,
  plus extra, to dust
1 tbs plain flour
250g pkt Arnott's Choc
  Ripple biscuits
biscuits
100g dark chocolate,
  chopped, plus 50g,
  extra, melted
Vanilla ice-cream, to serve
  (optional)

1 Preheat oven to 180°C/160°C fan forced. Grease a 10 x 20cm (base measurement) loaf pan. Line pan with baking paper, allowing the paper to overhang the 2 long sides.

2 Whisk together the condensed milk, milk, egg, vanilla, cocoa and flour in a jug until well combined. Place one-third of the biscuits in the prepared pan, layering to cover the base. Pour one-third of the condensed milk mixture over biscuits. Sprinkle with one-third of the chopped chocolate.

3 Repeat layering 2 more times with the remaining biscuits, condensed milk mixture and chocolate. Gently press down so top layer absorbs some of the condensed milk mixture. Bake for 35 minutes or until just set but still a little wobbly in the centre. Set aside for 15 minutes to cool.

4 Use the paper to carefully lift the log out of the pan and transfer to a serving board. (The log will still be a bit gooey in the centre.) Drizzle the extra chocolate over the top of the log. Dust with the extra cocoa and serve with ice-cream.

COOK'S TIP

Make this gluten free by using Arnott's Gluten Free Choc Ripple Original biscuits and gluten-free plain flour.

★★★★★

Quick and easy! Very rich – who knew you could make chocolate ripple biscuits taste like this?!

POSSUM00

● GLUTEN FREE ● MAKE AHEAD ● FREEZABLE ● EASY ● KID FRIENDLY

Cupcake BOUQUET

Special occasion baking just got sweeter with this flower bouquet.

MAKES 12 regular cupcakes & 15 mini cupcakes **PREP** 45 mins (+ cooling) **COOK** 40 mins

200g unsalted butter, chopped, at room temperature
315g (1½ cups) caster sugar
2 tsp vanilla extract
3 eggs
300g (2 cups) self raising flour, sifted
185ml (¾ cup) milk
buttercream
560g unsalted butter, chopped, at room temperature
600g (4 cups) pure icing sugar, sifted
1 tbs vanilla extract
Assorted gel food colourings, to tint

COOK'S TIP

Russian piping tips can be found at cake decorating stores or online. You can find 2D nozzles at BIG W, Spotlight, cake-decorating stores or online.

1 Preheat the oven to 180°C/160°C fan forced. Line 12 holes of an 80ml (⅓ cup) muffin pan with paper cases. Line 15 holes of a 20ml (1 tbs) mini muffin pan with paper cases.

2 Use electric beaters to beat the butter, sugar and vanilla in a large bowl until pale and creamy. Add eggs, 1 at a time, beating well after each addition. In 2 batches, stir in flour and milk, until combined.

3 Divide mixture evenly between prepared pans. Bake mini muffin pans for 15 minutes or until cakes spring back when lightly pressed. Bake the muffin pans for 25 minutes or until cakes spring back when lightly pressed. Set aside in pans for 2 minutes to cool slightly before transferring to a wire rack to cool completely.

4 To make the buttercream, use electric beaters on medium-high speed to beat butter in a large bowl for 8 minutes or until pale and creamy. Add icing sugar, vanilla and a pinch of salt. Reduce speed to low. Beat until combined. Increase speed to medium-high. Beat for 6-8 minutes or until pale and creamy. Divide between 6 bowls. Tint each with a different gel colour to create 6 varying shades (we've used a purple and pink colour palette, but you could use any colours you like).

5 To make the large rose cupcake, spoon some of one shade of the buttercream into one side of a piping bag fitted with a 2D closed star tip nozzle. Spoon some of another shade of buttercream down the other side of the piping bag. Twist top of bag to seal. Pipe from the centre of the cupcake outwards in a spiral pattern to form a rose shape.

6 To make the hydrangea cupcake, spoon some of one shade of buttercream into one side of a piping bag fitted with a 2D closed star tip nozzle. Spoon some of another shade of buttercream down other side of piping bag. Twist top of bag to seal. Starting in the centre, hold piping bag upright and gently squeeze out icing to form small stars.

7 To make the small rosette cupcake, spoon buttercream into a piping bag fitted with a rose-shaped Russian piping tip. Starting in the centre, hold piping bag upright and gently squeeze out icing to form small rosettes.

8 Use remaining buttercream to pipe solid flowers onto cupcakes.

9 To make a bouquet of flower cupcakes, place the larger cupcakes in the centre of a serving platter. Place the smaller cupcakes around the outside.

● GLUTEN FREE ● MAKE AHEAD ● FREEZABLE ● EASY ● KID FRIENDLY

Lemon & yoghurt SYRUP CAKES

Zesty and sticky lemon syrup cakes are a crowd-pleasing dessert.

SERVES 6 **PREP** 20 mins (+ cooling time) **COOKING** 30 mins

60ml (¼ cup) solid
   coconut oil
2½ tbs coconut sugar
150g (1 cup) white spelt
   flour, sifted
2 eggs, separated
½ tsp baking powder
¼ tsp bicarbonate of soda
2 tsp finely grated
   lemon rind
150ml low-fat Greek yoghurt,
   plus extra, to serve
2 tbs lemon juice
lemon syrup
60ml (¼ cup) lemon juice
2 tbs coconut sugar
1 lemon, zested

1 Preheat oven to 180°C/160°C fan forced. Grease six 125ml (½ cup) dariole moulds and line the bases with baking paper. Use electric beaters to beat the oil and sugar in a bowl until pale and creamy. Add 2 tbs of the flour and beat until combined. Add yolks, 1 at a time, beating well after each addition. Stir in baking powder, bicarb, lemon rind and half the remaining flour. Stir in half the yoghurt and half the lemon juice. Repeat with the remaining flour, yoghurt and lemon juice, stirring until a stiff batter forms.

2 Use clean electric beaters to beat the egg whites in a clean dry bowl until soft peaks form. Fold half the egg white mixture into the batter. Fold in the remaining egg whites and spoon into the prepared moulds.

Place on a baking tray and bake for 20-22 minutes or until a skewer inserted into the centre comes out clean. Cool in moulds for 5 minutes. Transfer to a wire rack set over a baking tray. Use a skewer to poke 3 holes in each cake.

3 Meanwhile, for the lemon syrup, combine the juice and sugar in a saucepan over low heat. Cook, stirring, for 2 minutes or until sugar dissolves. Bring to a simmer. Simmer, without stirring, for 2 minutes. Add lemon zest. Simmer for a further 1 minute or until thick.

4 Pour half the syrup over the warm cakes. Set aside to cool completely.

5 Serve the cakes topped with a spoonful of yoghurt and drizzled with the remaining syrup.

● GLUTEN FREE ● MAKE AHEAD ● FREEZABLE ● EASY ● KID FRIENDLY

Choc-Guinness MUD CAKE

This grown up version of mud cake has a lick of Irish stout.

SERVES 12 **PREP** 30 mins (+ cooling) **COOKING** 1 hour 30mins

250g butter, chopped, at
    room temperature
200g dark chocolate
    (50% cocoa), chopped
100g dark chocolate
    (70% cocoa), chopped
215g (1 cup) caster sugar
100g (½ cup firmly packed)
    dark brown sugar
250ml (1 cup) Guinness
    Extra Stout
1 tbs golden syrup
2 tsp vanilla extract
3 eggs
85g (⅓ cup) sour cream
225g (1½ cups) plain flour
2 tbs dark cocoa powder
1 tsp baking powder
beer ganache
200g dark chocolate
    (50% cocoa), chopped
190g (¾ cup) sour cream
2 tbs Guinness Extra Stout
1½ tbs golden syrup

1 Preheat oven to 160°C/140°C fan forced. Grease a 22cm (base size) springform pan and line with baking paper.

2 Place the butter, dark chocolates, sugars, Guinness, golden syrup and vanilla in a saucepan over low heat. Cook, stirring, for 6-8 minutes or until melted and smooth. Transfer to a large bowl and set aside for 15 minutes to cool.

3 Place the eggs and sour cream in a small bowl and whisk until combined. Whisk the egg mixture into the chocolate mixture until combined and glossy. Sift over the flour, cocoa and baking powder and stir until combined. Pour into prepared pan. Bake for 1 hour 10 minutes or until crumbs cling to a skewer when inserted into the centre. Set aside for 30 minutes to cool in the pan before transferring to a wire rack to cool completely.

4 Meanwhile, to make the ganache, place chocolate, sour cream, Guinness and golden syrup in a heatproof bowl over a saucepan of simmering water (make sure the bowl doesn't touch the water). Cook, stirring often, for 6-7 minutes or until melted and smooth. Set aside, stirring occasionally, for 1½ hours or until thick and spreadable. Spread the ganache over the cake.

★★★★★

Made this cake into cupcakes for St Patrick's Day at work. It was an absolute hit!! Such a moist and dense cake!

JESSIE

● GLUTEN FREE ● MAKE AHEAD ● FREEZABLE ● EASY ● KID FRIENDLY

Pina colada
CUPCAKES

Bookmark this recipe for your next fabulously fun fiesta!

MAKES 12 | **PREP** 30 mins (+ cooling time) **COOKING** 1 hour 20 mins

150g butter, at room
  temperature
155g (¾ cup) raw caster
  sugar
1 tsp finely grated lime rind
3 eggs
150g (1 cup) self-raising flour
45g (½ cup) desiccated
  coconut
100g (½ cup) drained
  crushed pineapple in
  syrup, syrup reserved
2 tbs coconut cream

rum & pineapple syrup
125ml (½ cup) reserved
  pineapple syrup
2 tbs caster sugar
2 tbs white rum

coconut buttercream
125g butter, chopped at
  room temperature
380g (2½ cups) icing sugar
  mixture
80ml (⅓ cup) coconut cream
½ tsp coconut essence

pineapple flowers
2 tbs caster sugar
2 tbs water
1 pineapple, peeled

1 For the pineapple flowers, preheat oven to 120°C/100°C fan forced. Line twelve 125ml (½ cup) muffin pans with foil. Line 12 holes of an empty egg carton with foil. Combine sugar and water in a saucepan over high heat. Cook, stirring, for 2 minutes or until slightly thickened. Use a serrated knife to slice pineapple into twenty-four 2mm-thick slices. Brush sugar syrup over slices. Place slices, in 1 layer, on a wire rack over a baking tray. Bake for 1 hour or until pineapple is dry to touch. Place half the warm pineapple slices in prepared muffin pans and the remaining warm pineapple slices in the prepared carton to dry and set.

2 Preheat oven to 180°C/160°C fan forced. Line twelve 125ml (½ cup) muffin pans with paper cases.

3 Use electric beaters to beat the butter, sugar and rind in a bowl until pale and creamy. Add the eggs, 1 at a time. Beat well after each addition. Add the flour, coconut, crushed pineapple and coconut cream, in alternating batches. Divide

among prepared pans. Bake for 20 minutes or until skewer inserted into the centres comes out clean. Stand cupcakes in pans.

4 Meanwhile, for the syrup, place reserved pineapple syrup and sugar in a saucepan over low heat. Cook, stirring, for 1 minute or until sugar dissolves. Increase heat to high. Bring to the boil. Cook for 5 minutes or until syrup thickens slightly. Remove from heat. Add the rum. Stir to combine. Brush hot syrup over hot cakes. Set aside to cool completely.

5 For the buttercream, use electric beaters to beat the butter in a bowl until very pale. Gradually add the icing sugar and coconut cream, beating until well combined. Add coconut essence and beat to combine.

6 Use a piping bag with a large plain nozzle to pipe the buttercream over cupcakes. Top cupcakes with a large pineapple flower. Spread the base of each small pineapple flower with a little buttercream and place in centre of each large flower to secure.

● GLUTEN FREE ● MAKE AHEAD ● FREEZABLE ● EASY ● KID FRIENDLY

Gooey blueberry & white CHOCOLATE CAKE

SERVES 4 **PREP** 25 mins **COOKING** 1 hour 20 mins

200g (2 cups) frozen blueberries, plus extra, thawed, to serve (optional)

1 tbs cornflour

225g (1½ cups) self-raising flour

1 tsp baking powder

200g unsalted butter, chopped, at room temperature

220g (1 cup) caster sugar

1 tsp vanilla extract

3 eggs

240g (1 cup) ricotta

2 tbs milk

100g white chocolate, chopped

Icing sugar, to dust

1 Preheat oven to 170°C/150°C fan forced. Grease an 11 x 23cm loaf pan (base size). Line with baking paper, allowing the paper to overhang the 2 long sides.

2 Place the blueberries in a bowl and toss with the cornflour. Set aside until required.

3 Sift the flour, baking powder and a pinch of salt into a separate bowl. Set aside until needed.

4 Use electric beaters to beat the butter, sugar and vanilla in a bowl until pale and creamy. Add the eggs, 1 at a time, beating well after each addition. Add the ricotta and beat until well combined. Add the flour mixture, in batches, alternating with the milk, beating until combined.

5 Use a large metal spoon to fold the blueberry mixture and chocolate into the batter. Transfer to the prepared pan. Bake for 1 hour 20 minutes or until a skewer inserted in the centre of the cake comes out clean. Set aside in the pan for 10 minutes to cool slightly before turning onto a wire rack to cool completely.

6 Dust the cake with icing sugar. Cut into slices. Serve with extra blueberries, if using.

COOK'S TIP

Tossing the blueberries in the cornflour prevents them 'bleeding' into the cake batter.

Try swapping the blueberries with raspberries and the white chocolate with dark chocolate.

★★★★★

Huge hit with the family. Can reheat any leftover and serve with cream.

CAMTER

 GLUTEN FREE ● MAKE AHEAD ● FREEZABLE ● EASY ● KID FRIENDLY

Neapolitan
CUPCAKES

Choc, strawberry and vanilla served up in a cute little cupcake.

MAKES 12 **PREP** 20 mins (+ cooling) **COOK** 30 mins

180g butter, chopped, at room temperature
215g (1 cup) caster sugar
¾ tsp vanilla extract
3 eggs
340g (2¼ cups) self-raising flour
250ml (1 cup) milk, plus 1½ tbs extra
1 tbs cocoa powder, sifted
Chocolate sprinkles, vanilla wafers, glacé or maraschino cherries, to decorate

strawberry icing
300g butter, chopped, at room temperature
450g (3 cups) icing sugar, sifted
3 tbs milk
1½ tbs strawberries and cream flavouring
A few drops of pink food colouring, to tint

1 Preheat oven to 180°C/160°C fan forced. Line twelve 80ml (⅓ cup) muffin pans with paper cases.

2 Use electric beaters to beat butter, sugar and vanilla in a large bowl until pale and creamy. Add eggs, 1 at a time, beating well after each addition, until combined.

3 Fold in the flour and milk separately, in 2 batches each, until well combined. Divide mixture evenly into 2 bowls and stir cocoa and extra milk into 1 bowl. Spoon level tablespoons of chocolate mixture into prepared papers and smooth, then top with a level tablespoon of vanilla mixture. Smooth tops.

4 Bake for 25-30 minutes or until a skewer inserted into the centres comes out clean. Remove from oven and stand for 5 minutes before turning onto a wire rack to cool. Remove paper cases carefully.

5 To make the strawberry icing, use electric beaters to beat the butter in a large bowl until light and fluffy. Gradually add icing sugar and beat until the mixture is very pale. Gradually add milk and flavouring, and beat until well combined. Add the pink food colouring and beat to combine.

6 Spoon icing into a piping bag fitted with a 1cm fluted nozzle and pipe swirls onto cupcakes. Decorate with sprinkles, wafers and a cherry on top.

COOK'S TIP

Push the boat out and swap the cherries for Jaffas or Maltesers.

For piping tips and tricks, see page 222.

● GLUTEN FREE ● MAKE AHEAD ● FREEZABLE ● EASY ● KID FRIENDLY

Yoghurt cake with RICOTTA CREAM

Cannellini beans bring creaminess with a fraction of the calories.

SERVES 10 **PREP** 20 mins (+ cooling) **COOKING** 40 mins

400g can no-added-salt cannellini beans, rinsed, drained

200g (¾ cup) natural yoghurt

3 tsp vanilla bean paste

4 eggs

125ml (½ cup) honey (such as single origin red gum or iron bark), plus 1 tsp, extra

40g (¼ cup) gluten-free plain flour

2 tsp gluten-free baking powder

150g almond meal

125g (½ cup) reduced-fat smooth ricotta

250g fresh strawberries, hulled, sliced

Strawberry sauce, to serve (optional, see tip)

1 Preheat oven to 180°C/160°C fan forced. Grease a 20cm round cake pan and line the base and side with baking paper.

2 Place the cannellini beans, 60g (¼ cup) yoghurt and 2 tsp vanilla in a food processor and process until smooth. Use electric beaters to beat the eggs and honey in a large bowl until pale and thickened. Add the bean mixture and beat until well combined. Sift in the flour and baking powder. Add the almond meal and gently fold until combined.

3 Pour the cake mixture into the prepared pan and smooth the surface. Bake for 40 minutes or until golden and the cake is firm when lightly touched. Set aside to cool for 10 minutes before turning onto a wire rack to cool completely.

4 When ready to serve, place the ricotta, extra honey and remaining yoghurt and vanilla in a bowl. Stir until well combined and smooth. Spread over cake just before serving. Top with fresh strawberry. Drizzle over sauce, if using.

COOK'S TIP

Have a glut of strawberries? Puree them with a dash of honey for an easy sauce.

Keep un-iced cake in an airtight container for up to 3 days. Or wrap tightly in plastic wrap and freeze for up to 1 month.

● GLUTEN FREE ● MAKE AHEAD ● FREEZABLE ● EASY ● KID FRIENDLY

Spiderweb CUPCAKES

Make tricked-up treats this Halloween with these easy cupcakes.

MAKES 12 **PREP** 30 mins (+ cooling & setting) **COOK** 25 mins

150g butter, chopped,
   at room temperature
2 tbs caster sugar
80ml (⅓ cup) honey
2 tsp vanilla bean paste
2 eggs
150g (1 cup) self-raising
   flour, sifted
70g (½ cup) cornflour, sifted
160ml (⅔ cup) milk, plus
   extra 80-100ml milk
350g pkt Queen
   Buttercream Icing
Orange and black food
   colouring, to tint

1 Preheat oven to 180°C/160°C fan forced. Line twelve 80ml (⅓ cup) muffin pans with paper cases.

2 Use electric beaters to beat the butter, sugar and honey in a large bowl until pale and creamy. Add vanilla and beat until well combined. Add eggs, 1 at a time, beating well after each addition.

3 Use a metal spoon to fold in flours and milk, in alternating batches, until just smooth. Spoon mixture among paper cases and smooth the surface. Bake for 20-25 minutes or until light golden. Set aside in the pans for 10 minutes to cool slightly, then transfer to a wire rack to cool completely. Trim tops of cakes to level.

4 Place icing in a bowl. Add extra milk. Stir until icing is spreadable. Place 2 tbs icing in a bowl and reserve. Add a little orange food colouring to remaining icing. Mix until well combined. Add a little black food colouring to reserved icing and mix until well combined.

5 Spoon the black icing into a small sealable plastic bag and snip off corner. Working with 1 cupcake at a time, spread a little orange icing over a cake to cover. Pipe concentric circles of black icing over the orange icing. Use a wooden skewer to lightly drag through icing from centre circle to make a web pattern. Repeat with remaining cupcakes. Set aside to set.

● GLUTEN FREE ● MAKE AHEAD ● FREEZABLE ● EASY ● KID FRIENDLY

Flourless chocolate Baileys
MERINGUE CAKE

Double down on deliciousness with a meringue-topped cake.

SERVES 12 **PREP** 30 mins (+ cooling) **COOKING** 60 mins

200g dark chocolate
(70% cocoa), chopped
200g butter, chopped
215g (1 cup) caster sugar
4 eggs, at room temperature
55g (½ cup) almond meal
30g (¼ cup) dark cocoa
powder, sifted, plus
extra, to dust
60ml (¼ cup) Baileys Irish
Cream liqueur
meringue topping
3 egg whites
155g (¾ cup) caster sugar
40g dark chocolate (70%
cocoa), finely chopped
chocolate sauce
60g dark chocolate
(70% cocoa), chopped
80ml (⅓ cup) thickened
cream
3 tsp Baileys Irish Cream
liqueur

1 Preheat oven to 170°C/150°C fan forced. Grease base and side of a 22cm (base size) springform pan and line with baking paper.

2 Place chocolate and butter in a heatproof bowl set over a saucepan of just simmering water (make sure the bowl doesn't touch the water). Cook, stirring, until melted and smooth. Stir in the sugar. Remove from heat. Set aside for 5 minutes to cool slightly.

3 Whisk the eggs, one at a time, into the chocolate mixture until well combined and mixture comes together. Stir in almond meal, cocoa and Baileys until combined. Pour into prepared pan. Bake for 35 minutes or until just firm in the centre. Set aside in the pan to cool completely.

4 To make the meringue topping, preheat the oven to 200°C/180°C fan forced. Place the egg white and sugar in a heatproof bowl set over a saucepan of simmering water (make sure the bowl doesn't touch the water). Cook, whisking often, for 4 minutes or until frothy and sugar has dissolved. Remove from heat and cool for 1 minute. Use electric beaters to whisk egg white mixture for 5 minutes or until thick and glossy. Whisk in chocolate on low until just combined. Spoon on top of cake and use the back of a spoon to make peaks. Bake for 10-12 minutes or until meringue is firm and crisp. Set aside to cool completely.

5 To make the sauce, place the chocolate, cream and Baileys in a heatproof bowl set over a saucepan of simmering water (make sure the bowl doesn't touch the water). Cook, stirring with a metal spoon, until melted and smooth. Remove from heat. Set aside for 30 minutes to cool and thicken slightly.

6 Dust cake with the extra cocoa and drizzle over the chocolate sauce to serve.

I've made this twice now… it's really delicious. The Baileys in the chocolate brownie base adds a rich depth of flavour.

NADIA ANDERSON

● GLUTEN FREE ● MAKE AHEAD ● FREEZABLE ● EASY ● KID FRIENDLY

Shirley Temple
CUPCAKES

These cakes are as lively as the star and her namesake mocktail.

MAKES 12 **PREP** 30 mins (+ cooling) **COOKING** 20 mins

125g butter, at room
temperature
215g (1 cup) caster sugar,
plus extra 2 tbs
1 tbs finely grated lemon
rind
2 eggs
65g (¼ cup) sour cream
60ml (¼ cup) milk
225g (1½ cups) plain flour
1 tsp baking powder
60ml (¼ cup) lemon juice
12 maraschino cherries,
to decorate
6 mini chocolate cream
wafers, halved
Icing sugar, to dust
grenadine buttercream
250g unsalted butter, at
room temperature
450g (3 cups) icing sugar
2 tbs grenadine syrup
Pinch of salt

1 Preheat the oven to 160°C/140°C fan forced.
Line twelve 125ml (½ cup) muffin pans with
paper cases.

2 Use electric beaters to beat the butter and sugar
in a bowl until pale and creamy. Add lemon rind.
Beat to combine. Add eggs, 1 at a time, beating well
after each addition. Add sour cream, milk, flour and
baking powder, in alternating batches, stirring until
just combined. Divide among prepared pans. Bake
for 20 minutes or until a skewer inserted into the
centres comes out clean.

3 Meanwhile, combine the juice and extra sugar
in a small saucepan over low heat. Cook, stirring,
for 5 minutes or until the sugar dissolves and the
syrup thickens slightly.

4 Brush hot syrup over the top of cakes. Set aside to
cool completely.

5 For buttercream, use electric beaters to beat
butter in a bowl until very pale. Add icing sugar in
batches, beating to combine. Add grenadine and
salt. Beat until smooth.

6 Use a piping bag with a 5mm star nozzle to pipe
drops of the buttercream on the cupcakes. Top
with a cherry and wafer. Dust with icing sugar.

COOK'S TIP

Learn all the tips
and tricks to
cupcake icing
with our guide on
page 222.

● GLUTEN FREE ● MAKE AHEAD ● FREEZABLE ● EASY ● KID FRIENDLY

Passionfruit, lemon & POPPY SEED CAKE

Magic happens when you combine a couple of favourites.

SERVES 8-10 **PREP** 50 mins (+ cooling time) **COOKING** 30 mins

165g butter
140g (⅔ cup) caster sugar
1 tsp vanilla extract
4 eggs
200g (1⅓ cups) self-raising
    flour, sifted
70g (½ cup) cornflour, sifted
125ml (½ cup) milk
2 tbs poppy seeds
1 tbs lemon curd
Pulp from 2 passionfruit,
    sieved, seeds discarded,
    plus extra pulp from
    1 passionfruit, to drizzle
filling
2 egg whites
70g (⅓ cup) caster sugar
250g butter, at room
    temperature, cut into
    12 pieces
165g (½ cup) lemon curd
Pulp from 2 passionfruit,
    sieved, seeds discarded

1 Preheat the oven to 180°C/160°C fan forced. Grease two 17.5cm (base size) round cake pans and line with baking paper.

2 Use electric beaters to beat the butter, sugar and vanilla in a bowl until pale and creamy. Add the eggs, 1 at a time, beating well after each addition.

3 Add the flours and milk, in alternating batches, using a large metal spoon to fold together until just combined. Gently stir through the poppy seeds. Divide mixture between the prepared pans and smooth the surface. Bake for 25-30 minutes or until a skewer inserted in the centres comes out clean. Turn the cakes onto a wire rack to cool completely.

4 For the filling, combine the egg whites and sugar in a heatproof bowl. Place over a saucepan of simmering water (don't let the bowl touch the water). Stir with a wooden spoon until the sugar dissolves (do not overcook). Remove from heat and set aside to cool. Use electric beaters to beat the egg white mixture for 2-3 minutes on medium until soft peaks form. Add the butter, 1 piece at a time, beating well after each addition, until smooth and creamy. Beat in the lemon curd and passionfruit pulp until smooth.

5 Use a serrated knife to level the tops of the cakes and cut each in half horizontally. Place 1 cake half on a plate. Spread with ⅓-½ cup of the filling. Repeat layering with cake halves and filling, finishing with cake. Spread the top and side of cake with remaining filling.

6 Combine the lemon curd and passionfruit pulp in a heatproof bowl. Microwave on High for 1 minute or until bubbling. Stir until smooth. Set aside to cool. Drizzle over the cake and spoon over extra pulp.

★★★★★

Well worth the effort. Served for Aus day & people loved it.

SASHER

● GLUTEN FREE ● MAKE AHEAD ● FREEZABLE ● EASY ● KID FRIENDLY

Triple-chocolate POKE CAKE

There's much to love about a cake with oozy pockets of chocolate.

SERVES 9 **PREP** 25 mins (+ 1½ hours cooling & 15 mins chilling) **COOKING** 35 mins

225g (1½ cups) plain flour
75g (½ cup) self-raising flour
215g (1 cup) caster sugar
50g (½ cup) cocoa powder
150g butter, melted, cooled,
    plus extra 50g butter,
    chopped
250ml (1 cup) milk, plus
    extra 2 tbs
3 eggs, lightly whisked
395g can sweetened
    condensed milk
200g dark cooking
    chocolate, chopped
Dark chocolate lattice,
    to decorate, see tip
    (optional)

chocolate icing
150g butter, chopped, at
    room temperature
2 tsp milk
100g milk chocolate,
    melted, cooled
125g (⅔ cup) icing sugar
    mixture

1 Preheat the oven to 180°C/160°C fan forced. Grease a square 20cm (base size) cake pan and line with baking paper, extending 2cm above sides.

2 Combine flours, sugar and cocoa in a large bowl. Add butter, milk and egg and use a balloon whisk to whisk until well combined. Pour into pan. Smooth surface.

3 Bake for 30 minutes or until a skewer inserted into cake comes out clean. Set aside for 30 minutes to cool slightly. Use end of a wooden spoon to poke holes in cake.

4 Stir condensed milk, chocolate and extra butter in a saucepan over low heat until smooth. Gradually pour half the sauce over cake. Tap pan on bench and fill up holes. Set aside for 1 hour to cool in pan. Use the baking paper to lift the cake onto a wire rack.

5 To make the chocolate icing, use electric beaters to beat the butter in a bowl until creamy. Add the milk and beat until combined. Add the chocolate and beat to combine. Beat in icing sugar until combined. Chill for 15 minutes.

6 Spread top of cake with icing. Stir remaining chocolate sauce and extra milk in a small saucepan over low heat until smooth. Cool slightly. Drizzle over icing. Top with the chocolate lattice decorations, if using.

COOK'S TIP

The cake can be made up to 3 days ahead to the end of Step 4. Store in an airtight container. Half an hour before serving, continue from Step 5. For the dark chocolate lattice decorations, spoon melted choc melts into a piping bag. Pipe onto a lined tray in a lattice pattern. Leave to set.

★ ★ ★ ★ ★

It was very tasty and fairly easy to make.

BUNDY SHELL

● GLUTEN FREE ● MAKE AHEAD ● FREEZABLE ● EASY ● KID FRIENDLY

Hot toddy lemon CAKE

A patterned bundt pan helps the cake catch the syrup in pockets.

SERVES 12 **PREP** 35 mins (+ cooling) **COOKING** 50 mins

315g (1½ cups) caster sugar

3 lemons, rind finely grated, 1½ tbs juiced, plus extra lemon, sliced, to decorate

1 tsp table salt

½ tsp ground cardamom

250ml (1 cup) extra virgin olive oil

3 eggs

390g (1½ cups) Greek-style yoghurt, plus extra, to serve

450g (3 cups) self-raising flour, sifted, plus extra, to dust

hot toddy syrup

125ml (½ cup) honey

60ml (¼ cup) fresh lemon juice

4 whole cloves

2 cinnamon sticks

160ml (⅔ cup) whiskey

1 Preheat oven to 180°C/160°C fan forced. Spray a 24cm (top size) 2.5L/10 cup bundt pan with oil then dust with extra flour.

2 Place the sugar, lemon rind and juice, salt, cardamom, oil, and eggs in a large bowl. Whisk until combined. Whisk in yoghurt until well combined. Add flour. Stir until just combined. (Don't worry if the mixture looks a bit lumpy.) Pour the mixture into prepared pan. Bake for 45-50 minutes or until a skewer inserted into cake comes out clean. Set aside in pan for 10 minutes to cool slightly before transferring to a wire rack to cool until warm (see tips).

3 Meanwhile, make the syrup. Place honey, lemon juice, cloves, cinnamon, 125ml (½ cup) whiskey and 60ml (¼ cup) water in a saucepan. Cook, stirring, over low heat until honey melts. Increase heat to medium. Bring to the boil. Cook, stirring occasionally, for 8-10 minutes or until thickens slightly. Remove from heat. Stir in remaining whiskey. Set aside for 5 minutes to cool slightly. Remove cloves and cinnamon, reserving cinnamon.

4 Transfer cake to a serving plate with a large lip. Pour over syrup. Top with extra lemon and reserved cinnamon. Serve with extra yoghurt.

COOK'S TIP

To make sure the cake absorbs the most syrup, pour syrup over while the cake is warm. This cake is best eaten warm but any leftovers can be served at room temperature. Replace the whiskey with rum or brandy, if you prefer.

● GLUTEN FREE ● MAKE AHEAD ● FREEZABLE ● EASY ● KID FRIENDLY

Made this as a dessert and it was moist and delicious. I actually halved the recipe and baked it in a loaf tin. Turned out perfectly. **MANDY**

Choc-banana
BUTTERFLY CAKE

This super-simple cake will evoke flutters of nostalgic delight.

SERVES 8-10 **PREP** 15 MINS (+ COOLING) **COOKING** 35 MINS

2 tbs dark cocoa powder
2 tbs boiling water
125g butter, chopped,
    at room temperature
100g (½ cup) caster sugar
2 eggs
130g (½ cup) mashed ripe
    banana
1 tsp vanilla extract
225g (1½ cups) self-raising
    flour
60ml (¼ cup) milk
300ml thickened cream
1 tbs strawberry jam
Icing sugar, to dust

1 Preheat the oven to 180°C/160°C fan forced. Grease and line the base and side of a 20cm (base size) round cake pan with baking paper.

2 Combine the cocoa and boiling water in a small bowl, stirring until smooth. Set aside to cool.

3 Use electric beaters to beat the butter and sugar in a large bowl until pale and creamy. Add the eggs, 1 at a time, beating well after each addition. Add the banana and vanilla and beat until combined.

4 Sift the flour over the banana mixture then pour in the milk. Use a spatula to fold gently until just combined.

5 Fold the cocoa mixture into the banana mixture. Transfer mixture to the prepared pan, smoothing the surface. Bake for 35 minutes or until the top springs back to a gentle touch in the centre. Set aside in the pan for 10 minutes to cool slightly then turn onto a wire rack. Immediately turn right-side up to cool completely.

6 Use a pointed serrated knife to make a cut 4cm in from the edge of the cake, angling the knife in towards the centre. Carefully lift the piece out and cut in half. Set aside.

7 Use electric beaters to whip the cream in a large bowl until firm peaks form. Fill the cake indent with whipped cream and drizzle with strawberry jam. Arrange cut cake pieces on top to resemble butterfly wings. Dust with icing sugar to serve.

COOK'S TIP

For an indulgent choc-caramel version, fold caramel sauce through the thickened cream after whipping in Step 5. Drizzle with extra caramel sauce instead of the jam.

● GLUTEN FREE ● MAKE AHEAD ● FREEZABLE ● EASY ● KID FRIENDLY

Lemon meringue CUPCAKES

The hidden lemon curd centre makes these irresistible.

MAKES 12 **PREP** 30 mins (+ chilling) **COOKING** 20 mins

125g butter, chopped, at
    room temperature
155g (¾ cup) caster sugar
2 tsp finely grated
    lemon rind
2 eggs
150g (1 cup) self-raising flour
150g (1 cup) plain flour
125ml (½ cup) milk
lemon curd
1 egg, lightly whisked
50g butter
2 tsp finely grated
    lemon rind
60ml (¼ cup) lemon juice
100g (½ cup) caster sugar
meringue
4 egg whites
215g (1 cup) caster sugar

1 Preheat the oven to 180°C/160°C fan forced. Line twelve 125ml (½ cup) muffin pans with paper cases.

2 Use electric beaters to beat the butter, sugar and lemon rind in a bowl until pale and creamy. Add eggs, 1 at a time, beating well after each addition. Add the flours and milk, in alternating batches, until just combined. Divide among prepared pans. Bake for 20 minutes or until a skewer inserted into the centre comes out clean.

3 Meanwhile, for the curd, combine the egg, butter, rind, juice and sugar in a saucepan over medium-low heat. Cook, stirring, for 2 minutes or until butter melts. Increase heat to medium. Cook, stirring constantly, for 3 minutes or until mixture boils and thickens. Remove from heat. Transfer lemond curd to a bowl. Cover with plastic wrap. Place in the fridge for 1½ hours to chill.

4 Use a small serrated knife to cut a 4cm-wide, 2-3cm-deep cone from the centre of each cupcake. Spoon lemon curd into holes.

5 For the meringue, whisk the egg whites in a clean, dry bowl until soft peaks form. Continue whisking, gradually adding sugar, 1 tbs at a time. Continue whisking until sugar dissolves.

6 Use a piping bag with a 1.5cm plain nozzle to pipe meringue over cupcakes. Use a cook's blowtorch to lightly toast the meringue.

COOK'S TIP

Don't have a blowtorch? Bake on an oven tray at 220°C/200°C fan forced, for 3-5 minutes or until meringue is toasted.

★★★★★

That lemon curd is to die for!

NAXGF

● GLUTEN FREE ● MAKE AHEAD ● FREEZABLE ● EASY ● KID FRIENDLY

Irish apple CAKE

This traditional cake is best enjoyed with a friend and a cuppa.

SERVES 10 **PREP** 10 mins (+ 10 mins cooling) **COOKING** 1 hour 10 mins

375g (2½ cups) plain flour
150g butter, chilled, chopped
155g (¾ cup) caster sugar, plus 55g (¼ cup), extra
2 tsp baking powder
½ tsp ground cinnamon
4 (about 750g) Granny Smith apples, peeled, cored, coarsely chopped (about 2-3cm pieces)
2 eggs
60ml (¼ cup) milk
Vanilla custard or double cream, to serve

1 Preheat oven to 180°C/160°C fan forced. Invert base of a 22cm (base size) round springform pan. Grease the base with melted butter then line with baking paper. Secure the base back in pan, allowing paper to overhang the edge. Grease side of pan.

2 Place the flour and butter in a large bowl. Use your fingertips to rub the butter into the flour until the mixture resembles fine crumbs. Add the sugar, baking powder and cinnamon. Stir until well combined. Add the apple and stir until well combined. Whisk together the eggs and milk in a jug. Pour the egg mixture into the flour mixture and stir until well combined. Spoon the cake mixture into prepared pan. Use the back of a spoon to firmly press and spread mixture over base. Sprinkle the top with the extra sugar.

3 Bake for 1 hour 10 minutes or until a skewer inserted into centre comes out clean. Set aside in the pan for 10 minutes to cool slightly. Transfer to serving plate and serve with custard or cream.

COOK'S TIP

This cake will keep in an airtight container for up to 3 days.

★★★★★

This cake is delicious. So moist and full of flavour. Easy to make with basic ingredients. The presentation is definitely 5 star once baked.

STARFYSH

● GLUTEN FREE ● MAKE AHEAD ● FREEZABLE ● EASY ● KID FRIENDLY

Giant salted caramel
LAVA CAKE

Indulge your sweet tooth on a slice of this decadent cake.

SERVES 12 **PREP** 20 mins (+ cooling) **COOKING** 1 hour 5 mins

200g unsalted butter, chopped
50g (½ cup) cocoa powder
2 tsp vanilla extract
450g (3 cups) plain flour, sifted
645g (3 cups) caster sugar
1½ tsp bicarbonate of soda, sifted
3 eggs, lightly whisked
185ml (¾ cup) buttermilk
Caramel popcorn, to serve

salted caramel

250ml (1 cup) thickened cream
50g unsalted butter, chopped
315g (1½ cups) caster sugar
2 tsp sea salt flakes

1 Preheat the oven to 180°C/160°C fan forced. Grease an 11cm-deep, 27cm (top size) bundt pan with oil spray.

2 Place the butter, cocoa, vanilla and 375ml (1½ cups) water in a saucepan. Cook, stirring occasionally, over medium heat, for 2-3 minutes or until butter melts. Remove from heat. Set aside to cool slightly.

3 Place the flour, sugar and bicarb in a large bowl and whisk until combined. Add the cocoa mixture, eggs and buttermilk. Whisk until smooth. Pour into the prepared pan. Bake for 45-50 minutes or until a skewer inserted into the centre comes out clean. Set aside, in pan, for 10 minutes to cool slightly before transferring to wire rack to cool completely.

4 To make the caramel, place the cream and butter in a microwave-safe bowl. Microwave on Medium for 2 minutes or until butter is melted. Add sugar and 125ml (½ cup) water to a small saucepan. Heat over low heat until sugar dissolves. Increase heat to medium and bring to the boil. Cook, without stirring, for 10 minutes or until golden. Remove from heat. Carefully add the cream mixture and salt flakes and whisk to combine. Return to medium heat, whisking occasionally, for 3 minutes or until thickened. Transfer to a bowl. Set aside to cool completely.

5 Transfer cake to a serving plate with a large lip. Fill centre with salted caramel, letting sauce slightly overflow and drip down sides of the cake. Top with caramel popcorn to serve.

COOK'S TIP

Both the cake and the caramel can be made a day ahead. Keep each in an airtight container.

● GLUTEN FREE ● MAKE AHEAD ● FREEZABLE ● EASY ● KID FRIENDLY

★★★★★

I am not a baker, but I somehow managed to nail this cake. It was moist and delicious.

KATEWARREN

15
minutes
prep

Gluten-free
BANANA CAKE

So super-moist and delicious, this really hits the sweet spot!

SERVES 10 **PREP** 20 mins **COOKING** 45 mins

110g unsalted butter, at room temperature, plus 1 tbs extra

150g (⅔ cup) raw caster sugar

2 eggs

3 medium ripe bananas, mashed

150g (1 cup) gluten-free plain flour

1½ tsp gluten-free baking powder

½ tsp bicarbonate of soda

1 tsp ground cinnamon

100g (1 cup) almond meal

70g (⅓ cup) brown sugar

80ml (⅓ cup) pure cream

Sliced banana, to serve

cream cheese icing

250g cream cheese, at room temperature

1 tsp finely grated lemon rind

60g (⅓ cup) pure icing sugar, sifted

1 tbs fresh lemon juice

1 Preheat oven to 180°C/160°C fan forced. Line the base and side of a 20cm (base size) round cake pan.

2 Use electric beaters to beat the butter and caster sugar in a large bowl until pale and creamy. Add eggs, 1 at a time, beating well after each addition. Stir in the mashed banana. Sift together the flour, baking powder, bicarbonate of soda and cinnamon. Fold the flour mixture and almond meal into the banana mixture until just combined.

3 Pour mixture into prepared pan and smooth surface. Bake for 40-45 minutes, covering with foil if browning too quickly, or until a skewer inserted into the centre comes out clean. Set aside for 10 minutes to cool slightly before transferring to a wire rack to cool completely.

4 Meanwhile, to make a caramel sauce, stir the brown sugar, cream and extra butter in small saucepan over medium heat. Bring to a gentle simmer and cook for 2-3 minutes or until thickened slightly. Transfer to a bowl and set aside to cool completely.

5 To make the icing, use electric beaters to beat the cream cheese and rind in a bowl until smooth. Add the sugar and lemon juice and beat until well combined.

6 Spread the icing over the cake to cover. Decorate with the banana slices and drizzle with caramel sauce.

COOK'S TIP

For a lighter alternative, you could halve the cream cheese icing and just spread it over the top of the cake.

● GLUTEN FREE ● MAKE AHEAD ● FREEZABLE ● EASY ● KID FRIENDLY

★★★★★

I thought this recipe was great! Lovely and moist and great to have in the freezer when my coeliac friend drops around :)

HEALTHCOOK

15
minutes
prep

Basque burnt
CHEESECAKE

You're just four steps and five ingredients away from one of our faves.

SERVES 6 **PREP** 15 mins (+ cooling) **COOKING** 50 mins

600g cream cheese
4 eggs
1¼ cups (275g) caster sugar
300ml double thick cream
1 tbs plain flour

1 Preheat the oven to 200°C. Grease and line the base and sides of a 23cm springform cake pan with baking paper, so the paper comes 2cm above the rim of the pan.

2 Beat the cream cheese using electric beaters until smooth and creamy. Add the eggs, 1 at a time, beating well after each addition. Gradually beat in the sugar, then the cream, then add the flour and beat until smooth.

3 Pour the cheesecake batter into the prepared pan and tap the pan gently on a flat surface to remove any air bubbles.

4 Bake for 50 minutes or until the top is dark brown, and cake is set but with a slight wobble in the centre and a skewer inserted into the centre comes out clean. Remove from the oven and leave to cool completely before removing from the pan. This cake is best eaten within a few hours of baking.

COOK'S TIP

Dress up your cheesecake with fresh raspberries and a light dusting of icing sugar.

This is an amazing recipe! I have made this at least 10 times now and it's a winner at every function.

JULIAGOH

● GLUTEN FREE ● MAKE AHEAD ● FREEZABLE ● EASY ● KID FRIENDLY

Lemon meringue
CONCORDE CAKE

This is a cheat's version of an old-school French mousse cake.

SERVES 12 **PREP** 35 mins (+ 1 hour cooling) **COOKING** 1 hour 5 mins

4 egg whites
270g (1¼ cups) caster sugar
600ml thickened cream
2 tbs pure icing sugar
350g jar lemon curd
460g pkt double unfilled
  round sponge cakes

1 Preheat oven to 120°C/100°C fan forced. Line 2 baking trays with baking paper.

2 Whisk the egg whites and caster sugar in a large heatproof bowl until combined. Place the bowl over a saucepan of simmering water (make sure bowl doesn't touch water). Whisk until the sugar dissolves and mixture reaches 70°C on a cook's thermometer. Remove from heat. Transfer mixture to another large bowl. Use electric beaters on high speed to beat for 10 minutes or until mixture reaches room temperature. Carefully spoon into a piping bag fitted with a 1cm plain nozzle. Pipe long logs of meringue onto prepared trays. Bake for 1 hour or until crisp and dry. Turn off oven. Leave trays in oven, with door slightly ajar, for 1 hour or until cooled completely.

3 Meanwhile, use electric beaters to beat cream and icing sugar in a bowl until firm peaks form. Reserve a heaped cupful of the cream mixture and one-quarter of the curd. Use a large serrated knife to cut each cake in half horizontally. Place 1 cake layer, cut-side up, on a serving plate and spread over one-third of the remaining cream mixture to cover, then one-third of the remaining curd. Repeat layering with remaining cake layers, cream mixture and curd, finishing with a cake layer, cut-side down. Spread reserved cream mixture over top and side of layered cake.

4 Break meringue into differing lengths (none shorter than height of cake). Press meringue upright around side of cake. Use a spoon to gently spread reserved curd over the top.

COOK'S TIP

Meringue pieces can be made up to 2 days ahead. Store in an airtight container.

● GLUTEN FREE ● MAKE AHEAD ● FREEZABLE ● EASY ● KID FRIENDLY

Louise CAKE

Louise must have been a sweet girl to get a cake named after her.

SERVES 8 **PREP** 45 mins (+ cooling) **COOKING** 1 hour

125g unsalted butter, chopped, at room temperature
100g (½ cup) caster sugar
2 tsp vanilla extract
3 eggs yolks, at room temperature
150g (1 cup) plain flour
1½ tsp baking powder
20g (¼ cup) desiccated coconut
80ml (⅓ cup) milk
350g fresh or frozen raspberries, plus extra, to decorate (see tip)

meringue
3 egg whites, at room temperature
215g (1 cup) caster sugar
1 tsp cornflour
1 tsp white vinegar
1 tsp vanilla extract
20g (¼ cup) desiccated coconut

1 Preheat oven to 180°C/160°C fan forced. Grease a 21cm (base size) round springform pan. Line base and side with baking paper, allowing paper to overhang 5cm above side.

2 Use electric beaters to beat butter, sugar and vanilla in a large bowl until pale and creamy. Add egg yolks, 1 at a time, beating well after each addition. Sift flour and baking powder into a bowl. Add coconut and stir until combined. With beaters on low speed, add flour mixture and milk to butter mixture in alternating batches, until just combined. Spoon mixture into prepared pan. Smooth the surface. Bake for 25 minutes or until a skewer inserted into centre comes out clean.

3 To make the meringue, use electric beaters to whisk egg whites in a clean, dry bowl until soft peaks form. Add sugar, 1 tbs at a time, whisking constantly, until thick and glossy. Add cornflour, vinegar and vanilla. Whisk until well combined.

4 Transfer two-thirds of meringue mixture to another bowl. Fold in coconut until combined.

5 Top the cake layer with raspberries then evenly top with coconut meringue. Top with the plain meringue and use the back of a spoon to create peaks. Bake for 35 minutes or until crisp. Set aside in pan for 10 minutes to cool slightly. Carefully transfer the cake to a wire rack to cool completely.

6 Place the cake on a serving plate and top with extra raspberries to serve.

COOK'S TIPS

If using frozen raspberries in the cake, thaw completely then drain on paper towel before use. It's best to use fresh raspberries to decorate, as frozen may bleed into the meringue. This is best on the day it's made, but can be prepared up to 2 days ahead. Store in an airtight container in the fridge, before decorating.

● GLUTEN FREE ● MAKE AHEAD ● FREEZABLE ● EASY ● KID FRIENDLY

Cherry ripple black
FOREST CAKE

The choc-cherry sauce is the 'cherry on the top' of this classic.

SERVES 14 **PREP** 40 mins (+ cooling time) **COOKING** 1 1/2 hours

200g unsalted butter, at
  room temperature
200g (1 cup, firmly packed)
  brown sugar
200g dark cooking
  chocolate, melted, cooled
2 eggs
190g (1¼ cups) self-raising
  flour
55g (½ cup) almond meal
125ml (½ cup) buttermilk
30g (¼ cup) cocoa powder
300ml ctn double cream
250ml (1 cup) thickened
  cream
160g (½ cup) black cherry
  jam
60ml (¼ cup) Jim Beam
  Black Cherry Bourbon
140g (⅔ cup) drained
  morello cherries
Chocolate curls, to decorate
  (see tip)

choc-cherry sauce
100g dark cooking
  chocolate, chopped
60ml (¼ cup) thickened
  cream
1 tbs Jim Beam Black
  Cherry Bourbon

1 Preheat oven to 160°C/140°C fan forced. Grease a 20cm (base size) round cake pan with melted butter. Line the base and side with baking paper.

2 Use electric beaters to beat the butter and sugar in a bowl until pale and creamy. Beat in the melted chocolate and eggs. Fold in the flour, almond meal, buttermilk and cocoa until well combined. Spoon into the prepared pan and smooth the surface. Bake for 1 hour 20 minutes or until a skewer inserted into the centre comes out clean. Set aside in the pan to cool slightly before transferring the cake to a wire rack to cool completely.

3 For the choc-cherry sauce, stir all the ingredients in a small saucepan over low heat for 5 minutes or until melted and smooth. Set aside cool slightly.

4 Use electric beaters to beat the combined cream in a large bowl until firm peaks form. Fold in the jam to create a swirled effect. Cut the cake horizontally into 3 even layers. Place the cake base on a plate and brush the cut surface with half the bourbon. Spoon over half the cream mixture and sprinkle with half the cherries. Top with another cake layer. Repeat with the remaining bourbon, cream mixture and cherries. Top with remaining cake layer.

5 Drizzle the choc-cherry sauce over the cake and top with chocolate curls.

★★★★★

*The cake was amazing! Really fluffy and moist.
Loved the cream centre layers.*

ELLENTILEY

● GLUTEN FREE ● MAKE AHEAD ● FREEZABLE ● EASY ● KID FRIENDLY

Carrot cake
CHEESECAKE

We love a good mash-up and there's everything right with this one.

SERVES 8 **PREP** 30 mins (+ cooling & chilling) **COOKING** 1 hour

105g (¾ cup) pecans
225g (1½ cups) self-raising
  flour
155g (¾ cup) caster sugar
½ tsp ground cinnamon
½ tsp mixed spice
½ tsp bicarbonate of soda
210g (1½ cups) carrots,
  peeled, coarsely grated
95g (½ cup) raisins, coarsely
  chopped
2 eggs, lightly whisked
160ml (⅔ cup) vegetable oil
250ml (1 cup) thickened
  cream
175ml (¾ cup) double cream
Sea salt flakes, to serve
cheesecake
2 x 250g pkt cream cheese,
  at room temperature
155g (¾ cup) caster sugar
2 tsp vanilla extract
2 eggs

1 Preheat the oven to 180°C/160°C fan forced. Grease a 22cm (base size) springform pan. Line the base and side with baking paper, allowing paper to extend 2cm above the side.

2 To make cheesecake, use electric beaters to beat cream cheese, sugar and vanilla in a bowl until smooth. Beat in eggs until combined.

3 To make carrot cake, coarsely chop 70g (½ cup) of the pecans. Place in a large bowl. Add the flour, sugar, cinnamon, mixed spice and bicarb. Mix until well combined. Stir in the carrot and raisins. Add the eggs and oil. Stir to combine.

4 Spoon two-thirds of the carrot cake mixture into the prepared pan. Spoon over half the cheesecake mixture. Spoon over the remaining carrot cake mixture. Top with the remaining cheesecake mixture. Bake for 50-60 minutes or until the filling is set and lightly browned. Turn off oven. Leave the cake in the oven, with the door slightly ajar, for 2 hours or until cooled slightly. Place in the fridge for 3 hours to cool completely.

5 Use electric beaters to beat the thickened and double cream together in a bowl until firm peaks form. Spread over the cake. Coarsely chop the remaining pecans and sprinkle around the edge of the cake. Sprinkle the pecans with a little salt to serve.

COOK'S TIP

Pecans are the traditional choice for carrot cake, but you could decorate with toasted walnuts, almonds, macadamias or pepitas to put a twist on a timeless classic.

★★★★★

So good, we loved this cake. Easy to make, will make again.

JENILY

● GLUTEN FREE ● MAKE AHEAD ● FREEZABLE ● EASY ● KID FRIENDLY

Honey & blackberry swirl
CHEESECAKE

Talk about wow factor – this has it in both looks and taste.

SERVES 12 **PREP** 15 mins (+ thawing & chilling) **COOKING** 55 mins

250g frozen blackberries
1 tbs caster sugar
250g pkt Arnott's Ginger
   Nut biscuits
100g Arnott's Butternut
   Snap Cookies
125g butter, chopped,
   melted
2 x 250g pkt cream cheese,
   chopped, at room
   temperature
300g ctn sour cream
⅓ cup creamed honey
70g (⅓ cup) caster sugar,
   extra
3 eggs
Double cream, to serve

1 Place blackberries in a bowl and sprinkle with the sugar. Set aside, stirring every hour, for 4 hours or until the berries have thawed and sugar has dissolved and made a syrup.

2 Use tongs or a slotted spoon to transfer half of the berries to a separate bowl. Pour the remaining berries and syrup into a sieve set over a bowl. Use the back of a spoon to press through the juice. Discard the seeds.

3 Release the base of a 22cm (base size) springform pan and invert. Line the base with baking paper and secure in the pan, allowing the edges to overhang.

4 Keep the Ginger Nut biscuits in the packet and use a rolling pin or meat mallet to pound slightly to roughly break up. Process the cookies in a food processor until finely crushed. Add butter and process until well combined. Transfer the biscuit mixture to the prepared pan. Use

a straight-sided glass to spread and press the biscuit mixture firmly over the base and side of the pan, leaving a 1cm border at the top. Place in the fridge for 30 minutes to chill.

5 Preheat oven to 160°C/140°C fan forced. Process the cream cheese and sour cream in the clean bowl of a food processor until smooth. Add honey and extra sugar and process until well combined. Add the eggs and process until well combined.

6 Pour the cream cheese mixture into the pan. Drizzle ¼ cup of the blackberry puree over the top of the cheesecake and use a skewer to create a swirl effect. Bake for 55 minutes or until the centre wobbles slightly. Turn oven off. Leave cheesecake in the oven, with the door slightly ajar, for 2 hours or until cooled completely. Place in fridge for 4 hours to chill. Serve with a dollop of cream, the reserved berries and a drizzle of the remaining puree.

● GLUTEN FREE ● MAKE AHEAD ● FREEZABLE ● EASY ● KID FRIENDLY

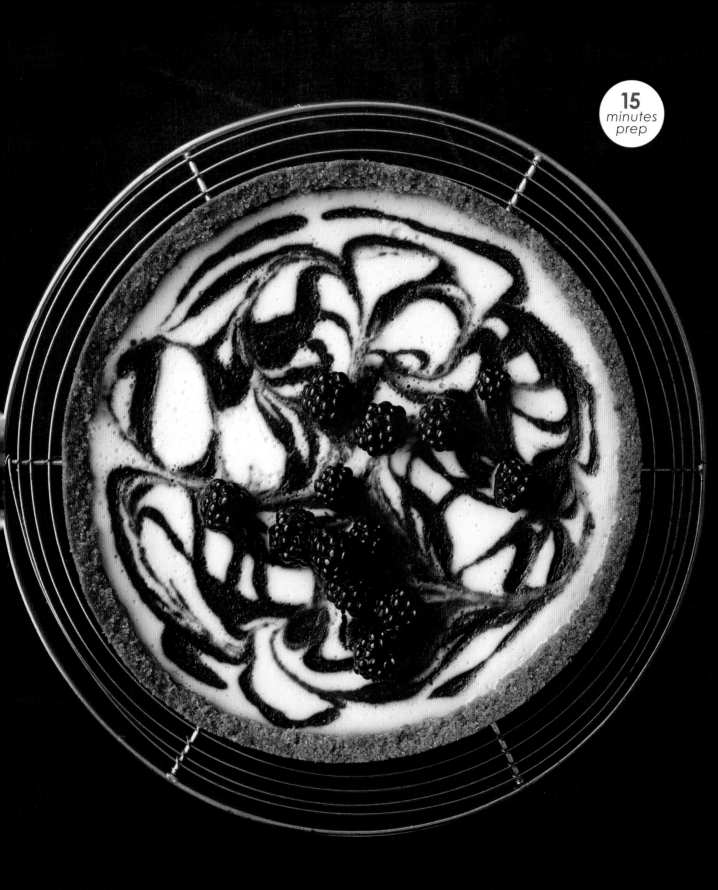

Traditional Victoria
SANDWICH CAKE

The queen of the cakes and still a fan fave, the Victoria sponge.

SERVES 8 **PREP** 20 mins (+ cooling) **COOKING** 20 mins

200g butter, chopped,
 at room temperature
200g caster sugar
4 eggs
1 tsp vanilla extract
200g (1⅓ cups) self-raising
 flour
160g (½ cup) strawberry jam
300ml thickened cream,
 whipped to firm peaks
Icing sugar, to dust
Fresh strawberries, to serve

1 Preheat oven to 180°C/160°C fan forced. Grease two 20cm (base size) round cake pans and line the bases with baking paper.

2 Use electric beaters to beat the butter and sugar in a small mixing bowl until pale and creamy. Beat in the eggs one at a time, beating well after each addition. Beat in the vanilla. Transfer the mixture to a large mixing bowl.

3 Sift the flour over the butter mixture and use a silicon spatula to fold through until evenly combined. Be careful not to overmix. Divide the mixture evenly between the prepared pans.

4 Bake for 20 minutes or until lightly golden and springy to a gentle touch. Cool in the pans for 5 minutes, then run a knife around the edge of the cakes to loosen and turn out onto wire racks. Carefully invert cakes on rack so it is right way up and set aside to cool completely.

5 Place one of the cakes on a serving plate and spread with the jam. Dollop with the whipped cream and place the other cake gently on top. Dust with icing sugar. Serve with fresh strawberries.

COOK'S TIP

This is traditionally served with strawberry jam but you can twist up the flavours with blackberry or raspberry jams. Try swirling the jam through the cream for a striking look.

● GLUTEN FREE ● MAKE AHEAD ● FREEZABLE ● EASY ● KID FRIENDLY

PIMPED-UP PARTY

WE LOVE AN EXCUSE TO LEVEL UP OUR CAKES TO OTT STATUS. CHOOSE FROM THESE WILD AND WACKY CREATIONS TO FIND YOUR PERFECT PARTY MATCH.

Ice-cream cone CAKE

An ice-cream cake with a difference... no ice-cream, all cake!

SERVES 15 **PREP** 1 hour 30 mins (+ cooling, setting & chilling) **COOKING** 30 mins

200g unsalted butter, chopped, at room temperature

285g (1⅓ cups) caster sugar

2 tsp vanilla extract

4 eggs

490g (3¼ cups) self-raising flour

310ml (1⅓ cups) milk

4 waffle cones, cut in half lengthways

50g dark chocolate, melted

Pink oil-based food colouring, to tint

White chocolate, melted, tinted pink, to drizzle

Queen Strawberry Flavoured Crunch and Persian fairy floss, to decorate

meringue buttercream

310ml (1¼ cups) bought pasteurised liquid egg whites

500g (2⅓ cups) caster sugar

650g unsalted butter, chopped, at room temperature

1 tbs vanilla extract

200g fresh strawberries, hulled, finely chopped, plus extra, halved, to decorate

1 Preheat oven to 170°C/150°C fan forced. Grease three 18cm (base size) round cake pans. Line bases and sides with baking paper. Use electric beaters to beat butter, sugar and vanilla until pale and creamy. Add eggs, 1 at a time, beating well after each addition until combined. Add flour and milk, in alternating batches, beginning and ending with flour, until combined. Divide among prepared pans. Smooth surface. Bake for 30 minutes until a skewer inserted into centres comes out clean. Set aside in pans for 5 minutes before transferring to a wire rack to cool completely.

2 Meanwhile, make buttercream. Use a whisk to combine egg whites and sugar in a heatproof bowl. Place over a saucepan of simmering water (make sure bowl doesn't touch water). Cook, stirring often with a whisk, for 3-5 minutes until hot to touch (place a small amount on a saucer, if hot to touch, it's ready). Transfer mixture to a stand mixer with whisk attachment. Whisk on high speed for 10 minutes or until almost room temperature. Switch to paddle attachment. On low speed, gradually add butter, beating well after each addition until smooth and creamy. Beat in vanilla and pinch of salt until combined. Transfer 2 cupfuls to a bowl. Fold through berries.

3 Line a tray with baking paper. Dip tops of cones in dark chocolate. Transfer to prepared tray. Place in freezer for 5-10 minutes or until set.

4 Trim to level top of cakes. Use a little plain buttercream to secure 1 cake, top-side up, to a cake board. Spoon 1 cupful plain buttercream into a piping bag fitted with a 1cm plain nozzle. Pipe a ring around top edge of cake. Cover middle with half the berry buttercream. Repeat layering with another cake, plain buttercream and remaining berry buttercream. Top with final cake, top-side down. Spread a thin layer of plain buttercream over side and top of cake (this is called a crumb coat). Place in fridge for 20 minutes. Place half remaining plain buttercream in a bowl. Tint with colouring. Transfer to a piping bag fitted with a 1cm plain nozzle. Spoon remaining into a piping bag fitted with a 1cm plain nozzle.

5 Pipe rings of buttercream, in alternating colours, around cake, starting from base and working up. Use an offset palette knife to smooth and create stripes. Switch nozzle on pink buttercream to a 1cm fluted one.

6 Press cones into side of cake. Pipe buttercream on top of cones. Decorate with pink choc, Crunch extra berries and pink fairy floss.

● GLUTEN FREE ● MAKE AHEAD ● FREEZABLE ● EASY ● KID FRIENDLY

Banana split CAKE

Dessert dreams do come true with this OTT super sundae creation.

SERVES 20-25 **PREP** 1 hour 30 mins (+ cooling & 15 mins freezing) **COOKING** 35 mins

450g (3 cups) self-raising flour
½ tsp bicarbonate of soda
½ tsp table salt
250g unsalted butter, chopped, at room temperature
285g (1⅓ cups) caster sugar
4 eggs, at room temperature
2 tsp vanilla extract
200ml sour cream
1½ cups (about 3-4 large) mashed ripe banana, plus extra, to decorate
180g (1 cup) mini dark chocolate chips
Chocolate sauce, maraschino cherries, crushed peanuts, fresh strawberries and wafer rolls, to decorate

buttercream
300g bought pasteurised liquid egg whites
485g (2¼ cups) caster sugar
650g unsalted butter, chopped, at room temperature
½ tbs vanilla extract
50g mini dark chocolate chips, melted, cooled slightly
1 tsp strawberry essence
Pink and yellow gel food colouring, to tint

1 Preheat oven to 180°C/160°C fan forced. Grease and line 3 round 20cm cake pans. Sift flour, bicarb and salt in a bowl.

2 Use a stand mixer with paddle attachment to beat butter and sugar in a bowl until pale and fluffy. Add eggs, 1 at a time, beating well after each addition. Beat in vanilla. With mixer on low speed, add flour mixture and sour cream in alternating batches, beginning and ending with flour, until just combined. Fold through banana and choc chips. Divide among pans. Smooth tops. Bake for 35-40 minutes until a skewer inserted into centre of cakes comes out clean. Set aside for 10 minutes to cool slightly. Turn onto wire rack to cool completely.

3 Meanwhile, to make buttercream, use a balloon whisk to combine whites and sugar in a large heatproof bowl. Place bowl over a saucepan of simmering water (make sure bowl doesn't touch water). Cook, whisking often, for 3-5 minutes until hot to touch (transfer a small amount to a saucer and if mixture is hot, it is ready). Transfer to a stand mixer with whisk attachment. Whisk on high for 10 minutes or until almost room temperature. Switch to paddle attachment. Reduce speed to low. Gradually add butter, beating well after each addition, until smooth and creamy. Add vanilla and a pinch of salt. Beat until well combined.

Transfer 1 cupful of buttercream to a bowl. Add melted choc. Stir to combine. Place 1 cupful of remaining buttercream in a separate bowl. Add strawberry essence and a few drops of pink colouring. Stir to combine. Place 1½ cupfuls of buttercream in a third bowl. Tint with yellow colour. Set aside.

4 Line a baking tray with baking paper. Use an ice-cream scoop to scoop 4 balls of chocolate buttercream and place 2cm apart on prepared tray. Repeat with strawberry and vanilla buttercreams. Spoon remaining vanilla buttercream into a piping bag fitted with a fluted nozzle and set aside at room temperature. Place baking tray in freezer for 15 minutes until the scoops are very firm.

5 Meanwhile, use a serrated bread knife to level top of each cake. Use a little vanilla buttercream to secure 1 cake, base-side down, onto a cake board. Spread reserved yellow buttercream over top of cake. Repeat with another cake layer and yellow buttercream. Top with cake, base-side up. Spread yellow buttercream all over cake. Use an offset palette knife or cake scraper to smooth.

6 Arrange buttercream scoops on top of cake. Pipe swirls of reserved vanilla buttercream on top and decorate with chocolate sauce, cherries, peanuts, strawberries, wafer rolls and extra banana.

● GLUTEN FREE ● MAKE AHEAD ● FREEZABLE ● EASY ● KID FRIENDLY

Toblerone mountain
MUD CAKE

Reach new baking peaks with this fudgy Toblerone-inspired cake.

SERVES 16-20 **PREP** 45 mins (+ cooling & 1 hour 45 mins chilling) **COOKING** 1 hour 5 mins

250g butter, chopped
200g Toblerone, chopped
430g (2 cups) caster sugar
4 eggs
125ml (½ cup) milk
2 tsp vanilla extract
150g (1 cup) self-raising flour
150g (1 cup) plain flour
50g (½ cup) cocoa powder
Different-sized Toblerones,
 to decorate
Icing sugar, to dust
filling
150g Toblerone, chopped
25g butter, chopped
60ml (¼ cup) thickened
 cream
icing
400g milk chocolate,
 finely chopped
60g butter, chopped
165ml (⅔ cup) thickened
 cream

1 Preheat oven to 150°C/130°C fan forced. Grease two 20cm square cake pans. Line bases and sides with baking paper. Place butter, Toblerone, caster sugar and 160ml (⅔ cup water) in a saucepan. Stir over low heat until sugar dissolves and mixture is mostly smooth and combined. Transfer to a large bowl. Set aside, stirring occasionally, until cooled slightly.

2 Add eggs, milk and vanilla to bowl. Whisk to combine. Sift in flours and cocoa. Fold gently to combine. (Be careful not to overmix.) Divide between prepared pans. Use a spatula to smooth surfaces. Bake for 1 hour or until a skewer inserted into centres comes out clean. Set aside in pans for 20 minutes to cool slightly. Turn onto a wire rack to cool completely.

3 Meanwhile, to make filling, place all ingredients in a saucepan over low heat. Stir until melted and combined. Transfer to a bowl. Place in fridge, stirring often, for 45 minutes, until a spreadable consistency.

4 To make icing, place all ingredients in a saucepan over low heat. Stir until melted and well combined. Place in the fridge, stirring occasionally, for 1 hour or until spreadable.

5 Place 1 cake, base-side down, on a serving platter or board and spread the filling over the cake top. Place remaining cake, base-side up, on top. Spread icing over top and side of cake. Break Toblerone bars into neat pieces and arrange on top. Dust with icing sugar and serve.

COOK'S TIP

Make cakes a day ahead. Make the recipe up to the end of step 2 then store cooled cakes in airtight containers in a cool dry place. Finish the recipe from step 3 on the day of serving.

● GLUTEN FREE ● MAKE AHEAD ● FREEZABLE ● EASY ● KID FRIENDLY

★ ★ ★ ★ ★

Delicious cake, and I will be using the topping on all chocolate cakes from now on. **SARAHNT**

Ricotta cannoli
CAKE

Be transported to Italy at the first bite of this epic cannoli cake.

SERVES 15 **PREP** 1 hour (+ cooling & chilling) **COOKING** 45 mins

375g (2½ cups) plain flour

1 tbs baking powder

1 tsp bicarbonate of soda

1 tsp salt

400g (2 cups, firmly packed) brown sugar

170g butter, melted

3 eggs

1 tbs vanilla extract

375ml (1½ cups) buttermilk

2 x 180g pkt dark chocolate, chopped

8 mini hollow cannoli shells

2 x 80g pkt pistachio kernels, chopped

ricotta cream

240g (1 cup) fresh ricotta

100g cream cheese, at room temperature

1 small orange, juiced

1 tsp vanilla extract

230g (1½ cups) pure icing sugar, sifted, plus extra, to dust

500ml (2 cups) thickened cream

1 Preheat oven to 180°C/160°C fan forced. Grease three 18cm (base size) round cake pans. Line each base and side with baking paper.

2 Sift flour, baking powder, bicarb and salt into a bowl. Combine sugar and butter in a large bowl. Stir in eggs and vanilla until well combined. Gently fold flour mixture and buttermilk, in alternating batches, into egg mixture until just combined. Fold in 140g (1 cup) chocolate until combined. Divide among pans. Bake for 30-40 minutes or until a skewer inserted in centres comes out clean. Cool in pans for 10 minutes. Transfer to wire racks to cool completely.

3 Place 175g (1¼ cup) chocolate in a microwave-safe bowl. Microwave, stirring every 30 seconds, for 1-2 minutes until melted and smooth. Line 2 baking trays with baking paper. Dip ends of 4 cannoli into chocolate. Place on a prepared tray in fridge for 10 minutes.

4 Place pistachio on remaining prepared tray. Use a serrated knife to trim top off each cake to level. Use a palette or flat-bladed knife to spread a thin layer of melted chocolate around side of 1 cake. Roll edge in pistachio.

Press pistachio into any gaps to fill. Transfer to rack to set. Repeat with remaining cakes. Spread cut surface of 1 cake with a thin layer of chocolate. Sprinkle with pistachio and press gently to secure nuts. Set aside.

5 To make ricotta cream, place ricotta and cream cheese in a bowl. Use electric beaters to beat until smooth. Add juice, vanilla and sugar. Beat until well combined and smooth. Use clean beaters to beat cream in a bowl until firm peaks form. Fold into ricotta mixture, in 3 batches, until combined. Transfer 2 cups to a piping bag fitted with a fluted nozzle.

6 Finely chop the remaining chocolate. Reserve the pistachio-topped cake. Place 1 remaining cake, cut-side up, on a serving plate. Top with half the remaining ricotta mixture, half the chopped chocolate and half the pistachio. Repeat with remaining cake, ricotta cream, chocolate and pistachio. Top with the reserved cake. Pipe ricotta cream into the cannoli shells. Pipe rosettes of remaining ricotta cream around top edge of the cake. Top with cannoli. Dust with extra sugar.

● GLUTEN FREE ● MAKE AHEAD ● FREEZABLE ● EASY ● KID FRIENDLY

Champagne cocktail CAKES

Individual cakes are delightfully perfect for a Champagne affair.

MAKES 12 **PREP** 1 hour (+ cooling) **COOKING** 25 mins

300g (2 cups) self-raising flour

100g plain flour

300g butter, chopped, at room temperature

330g caster sugar

3 tsp vanilla extract

320g bought pasteurised liquid egg whites

200ml sparkling white wine

80ml (⅓ cup) fresh passionfruit pulp, strained (from about 4 passionfruit)

Mixed white cachous and edible flowers, to decorate

Swiss meringue buttercream

250g bought pasteurised liquid egg whites

315g (1½ cups) caster sugar

500g butter, cut into 2cm pieces, at room temperature

1 Preheat oven to 180°C/160°C fan forced. Lightly grease 18 x 100ml straight-sided silicone muffin pans with oil. Sift self-raising and plain flours into a bowl. Gently stir to combine.

2 Use a stand mixer with paddle attachment to beat butter, sugar and vanilla for 10 minutes or until pale and creamy. Beat in half the egg whites. Gradually add flour mixture, alternating with wine and remaining egg whites. Mix until just combined. Divide among prepared pans. Smooth surface. Bake for 25 minutes or until a skewer inserted into centres comes out clean. Set aside for 5 minutes to cool slightly before turning onto a wire rack to cool completely. Use a serrated bread knife to trim and level top of each cake, then halve horizontally to make 36 cake layers.

3 Meanwhile, to make buttercream, combine egg whites and sugar in a large heatproof bowl. Place over a saucepan of simmering water (making sure bowl doesn't touch water) and cook, stirring occasionally, for 4 minutes or until mixture is hot to the touch. To test, transfer a small amount to a saucer and if mixture is hot to touch, it is ready. Remove bowl from heat and transfer mixture to a stand mixer with whisk attachment. Whisk on high for 10 minutes or until almost at room temperature. Replace the whisk with paddle attachment. Set speed to low

and add butter, 1 piece at a time, beating well after each addition and increasing speed to medium halfway through, until mixture is smooth and creamy. (Do not rush this process. It can take up to 30 minutes.)

4 Place 2 cups buttercream and passionfruit in a bowl. Use electric beaters to beat until combined. Place in a piping bag. Place 2½ cups remaining buttercream in another piping bag. Snip 1cm off end of bags.

5 Place 1 cake layer on a board. Pipe a ring of plain buttercream around top edge. Working from centre, pipe passionfruit buttercream in a spiral inside buttercream ring until top is covered and level. Place another cake layer on top. Pipe another layer of buttercreams. Finish with a third cake layer, cut-side down. Run an offset palette knife around side to smooth any buttercream poking out side. Carefully spread plain buttercream up, down and over cake to cover. Use palette knife to scrape off excess, allowing some cake to show through to create a naked effect. Repeat with remaining cake layers, and plain and passionfruit piping bags to make 12 cakes.

6 Place half remaining plain buttercream in plain buttercream piping bag and remainder in a clean piping bag. Snip 5mm of end of bags. Use to pipe big and small 'balls' on cakes. Top with cachous and flowers.

● GLUTEN FREE ● MAKE AHEAD ● FREEZABLE ● EASY ● KID FRIENDLY

Jersey Caramel mascarpone
SPONGE CAKE

Bring sweet nostalgia to your event with Jersey Caramels.

SERVES 10 **PREP** 45 mins (+ cooling) **COOKING** 35 mins

2 x 150g pkt Jersey
  Caramels, plus extra,
  sliced, to decorate
60ml (¼ cup) milk
250g unsalted butter,
  chopped, at room
  temperature
155g (¾ cup) raw
  caster sugar
2 tsp vanilla bean paste
4 eggs
225g (1½ cups) self-raising
  flour
½ tsp baking powder
mascarpone icing
150g pkt Jersey Caramels
2½ tbs milk
400g mascarpone
375ml (1½ cups) thickened
  cream
2 tsp vanilla bean paste

1 Preheat the oven to 180°C/160°C fan forced. Grease the bases and sides of two 20cm (base size) round cake pans. Line with baking paper.

2 Place 1 packet of Caramels and the milk in a small saucepan over medium-low heat. Cook, stirring often, for 5 minutes or until Caramels are melted and smooth. Transfer to a heatproof bowl. Set aside to cool completely.

3 Use electric beaters to beat the butter, sugar and vanilla in a large bowl until pale and creamy. Add the eggs, 1 at a time, beating well after each addition (mixture may look curdled). Add the flour, baking powder and caramel mixture. Beat on low speed until just combined. Divide the mixture between prepared pans and smooth the surface. Bake for 25-30 minutes or until the cakes spring back when lightly touched. Set aside for 10-15 minutes to cool in pans before transferring to a wire rack to cool completely.

4 Meanwhile, for the mascarpone icing, place Caramels and milk in a small saucepan over medium-low heat. Cook, stirring, for 5 minutes or until melted and smooth. Transfer to a bowl. Set aside to cool completely.

5 Place mascarpone, cream and vanilla in a large bowl. Add 60ml (¼ cup) of cooled caramel mixture. Reserve remaining caramel mixture. Use a balloon whisk to beat until mixture thickens slightly and is spreadable. Be careful not to overbeat. Finely chop remaining packet of Caramels and set aside.

6 To assemble, cut each cake in half horizontally. Place the base of 1 cake on a serving plate. Spread with one-quarter of the mascarpone icing. Sprinkle with one-third of the finely-chopped Caramels. Repeat layering with remaining cake, mascarpone icing and chopped Caramels, finishing with mascarpone icing. Top with extra Caramels and drizzle with reserved caramel mixture.

● GLUTEN FREE ● MAKE AHEAD ● FREEZABLE ● EASY ● KID FRIENDLY

Zesty lemon & white CHOCOLATE CAKE

Pastel painted chocolate panels really take the cake!

SERVES 12 **PREP** 1 hour 20 mins (+ cooling) **COOKING** 45 mins

450g (3 cups) self-raising flour, sifted

50g (⅓ cup) custard powder, sifted

430g (2 cups) caster sugar

1 tbs finely grated lemon rind

4 eggs

250ml (1 cup) milk

150g butter, melted, cooled

80ml (⅓ cup) vegetable oil

160ml (⅔ cup) fresh lemon juice

Yellow and purple oil-based food colouring, to tint

60ml (¼ cup) boiling water

100g (⅓ cup) lemon curd

2 x 290g pkt white chocolate melts, melted

Edible flowers, to decorate

mock Swiss meringue buttercream

125ml (½ cup) bought pasteurised liquid egg whites

600g (4 cups) icing sugar mixture

500g butter, chopped, at room temperature

1 tbs vanilla extract

1 Preheat oven to 170°C/150°C fan forced. Grease two 20cm (base size) round cake pans and line bases with baking paper.

2 Place flour, custard powder and 315g (1½ cups) caster sugar in a bowl. Make a well in centre. Whisk rind, eggs, milk, butter, oil and half the lemon juice in a bowl until combined.

3 Stir egg mixture into flour mixture until combined. Tint yellow with colouring. Divide between prepared pans. Smooth surface. Bake for 40-45 minutes or until a skewer inserted into centres comes out clean. Turn onto a rack to cool completely.

4 Meanwhile, combine the boiling water, remaining juice and remaining sugar in a jug. Stir until dissolved. Set aside to cool slightly.

5 To make buttercream, combine egg whites and sugar in a heatproof bowl. Place over a saucepan of simmering water (make sure bowl doesn't touch water). Cook, stirring with a spoon, for 4 minutes or until hot to the touch. (To test, place a small amount on a saucer and if hot to touch, it's ready.) Transfer mixture to a stand mixer with whisk attachment. Whisk on high speed for 10 minutes or until almost room temperature. Switch to paddle attachment. On low speed, gradually add butter, beating well after each addition and increasing to medium halfway through, until smooth and creamy. (It may curdle, keep beating and it'll come together.) Add vanilla and beat until combined.

6 Trim to level top of each cake. Cut each in half horizontally. Use a little buttercream to secure 1 cake, cut-side up, to a cake board. Drizzle over a little lemon syrup. Spread over one-third of curd then ½ cupful buttercream to cover. Repeat layering cakes, syrup, curd and buttercream, finishing with final cake, cut-side down. Spread a little buttercream over side and top to cover (this is called a crumb coat). Spoon remaining buttercream into a piping bag fitted with a 1cm fluted nozzle.

7 Place about ¼ cupful melted white choc in a small bowl. Tint purple with colouring. Transfer to a small sealable plastic bag.

8 Cut baking paper into two 12 x 38cm strips. Use a spatula to spread remaining white choc evenly over strips. Snip 1 corner of bag. Drizzle purple choc over white choc. Working quickly, use back of a spoon to smooth over choc to create marbled effect. Set aside for 1-2 minutes. Slide strips onto another baking paper sheet. Set aside until almost set. Cut each strip crossways into 3cm-wide rectangles.

9 Starting from centre, pipe remaining buttercream on top of cake in a circular pattern. Press choc strips to side of cake. Top with flowers.

● GLUTEN FREE ● MAKE AHEAD ● FREEZABLE ● EASY ● KID FRIENDLY

Hot chocolate marshmallow CAKE

You'll warm to this fudgy, marshmallow-smooshed layer cake.

SERVES 20 **PREP** 1 hour (+ cooling & chilling) **COOKING** 55 mins

300g (2 cups) self-raising flour

150g (1 cup) plain flour

70g (⅔ cup) cocoa powder

400g unsalted butter, chopped, at room temperature

315g (1½ cups) caster sugar

4 eggs

375ml (1½ cups) milk

Assorted white marshmallows, to decorate

marshmallow crème

1 egg white

185ml (¾ cup) glucose syrup

125g (¾ cup) pure icing sugar, sifted

2 tsp vanilla extract

chocolate buttercream

300g unsalted butter, chopped, at room temperature

450g (3 cups) pure icing sugar, sifted

35g (⅓ cup) cocoa powder, sifted

2 tbs milk

hot chocolate fudge sauce

180g dark chocolate, chopped

125ml (½ cup) thickened cream

1 Preheat oven to 180°C/160°C fan forced. Grease two 20cm (base size) round cake pans. Line the bases and sides with baking paper. Sift the flours and cocoa powder into a large bowl.

2 Use a stand mixer with paddle attachment to whisk the butter and sugar until pale and creamy. Add the eggs, 1 at a time, whisking well after each addition. With the mixer on low speed, add the flour mixture and milk in alternating batches, beginning and ending with flour, until just combined. Divide the cake mixture between the prepared pans and smooth the surfaces. Bake for 45-50 minutes or until a skewer inserted into the centres comes out clean. Set aside in pans for 10 minutes to cool slightly before turning onto a wire rack to cool completely.

3 To make the marshmallow crème, use a stand mixer with whisk attachment to whisk egg white, syrup and a pinch of salt in a bowl on high speed for 5 minutes or until thick and doubled in volume. Reduce speed to low. Beat in icing sugar until combined. Beat in vanilla. Transfer to a bowl. Chill until required.

4 To make the chocolate buttercream, use a stand mixer with paddle attachment on medium-high speed to beat butter in a bowl for 6-8 minutes or until pale and

creamy. Reduce speed to low. Add icing sugar, cocoa powder and milk. Beat until well combined. Increase the speed to medium-high and beat for 3-4 minutes or until fluffy. Transfer 1 cup to a piping bag fitted with a 1cm-wide plain nozzle.

5 Use a serrated bread knife to trim and level the top of each cake. Cut each cake in half horizontally. Pipe a little buttercream in the centre of a serving plate. Place 1 cake, cut-side up, on the plate. Spread a layer of buttercream over the top of the cake. Pipe a ring of buttercream around the edge. Fill with ¼ cup of the marshmallow crème. Repeat layering with the cake, buttercream and marshmallow crème, finishing with the final cake, base-side up. Spread the remaining buttercream over top and side of the cake. Place in the fridge for 20 minutes to chill.

6 Meanwhile, to make the hot chocolate fudge sauce, place the chocolate in a small heatproof bowl. Bring the cream to a simmer in a small saucepan over medium heat. Remove from heat and pour over the chocolate. Set aside for 2 minutes then stir until smooth and glossy. Fold ¼ cup marshmallow crème into the chocolate.

7 Decorate the top of the cake with assorted marshmallows. Drizzle with the warm fudge sauce to serve.

● GLUTEN FREE ● MAKE AHEAD ● FREEZABLE ● EASY ● KID FRIENDLY

★★★★★

*This was fun and actually pretty simple to make! I did cheat and
buy the buttercream though.* **EMSIE_B**

Clinkers layer CAKE

Cut into a surprisingly crunchy Clinker-studded centre.

SERVES 15 **PREP** 2 hours (+ cooling & 6 hours chilling) **COOKING** 40 mins

400g Cadbury Clinkers, 120g (1 cup) roughly chopped
300g (2 cups) plain flour
1¾ tsp baking powder
1 tsp salt
315g (1½ cups) caster sugar
2 eggs
250ml (1 cup) milk
185ml (¾ cup) vegetable oil
1 tbs vanilla extract

cheesecake
400g cream cheese, at room temperature
140g (⅔ cup) caster sugar
2 tsp vanilla extract
Pink gel or liquid food colouring, to tint
3 tsp gelatine powder
250ml (1 cup) thickened cream, whipped to firm peaks

buttercream
560g unsalted butter, chopped, at room temperature
600g (4 cups) pure icing sugar, sifted
1 tbs vanilla extract
Pink gel or liquid food colouring, to tint

1 Grease an 18cm (base size) round springform pan. Line base and side with baking paper.

2 To make cheesecake, use electric beaters to beat cheese, sugar and vanilla in a bowl until smooth. Add a few drops of food colouring. Beat until well combined. Place 2 tbs water in a microwave-safe bowl. Sprinkle with the gelatine and stir to combine. Microwave for 10 seconds (do not overheat). Use a fork to whisk until gelatine dissolves. Beat into cheese mixture until well combined. Fold in whipped cream, in 3 batches, until combined. Fold through chopped Clinkers. Pour mixture into prepared pan and smooth the surface. Cover with plastic wrap. Place in the fridge for 6 hours, or overnight, until set.

3 Preheat oven to 180°C/160°C fan forced. Grease two 18cm (base size) round cake pans. Line bases and sides with baking paper. Sift flour, baking powder and salt into a bowl.

4 Use electric beaters on medium speed to beat sugar and eggs in a bowl for 3 minutes or until thickened and well combined. Beat in milk, oil and vanilla until just combined. With mixer on low speed, gradually add the flour mixture, beating until just combined. Divide between prepared pans. Bake for 40 minutes or until a skewer inserted into centres comes out clean. Set aside in pans for 10 minutes to cool slightly before transferring to a wire rack to cool completely.

5 To make buttercream, use electric beaters on medium-high speed to beat butter in a bowl for 6-8 minutes or until pale and creamy. Add icing sugar, vanilla and a pinch of salt. Reduce speed to low. Mix until combined. Increase speed to medium-high and beat for 6-8 minutes or until fluffy. Add a few drops of food colouring to tint. Beat until well combined.

6 Coarsely crush 6 whole Clinkers. Slice each of remaining Clinkers crossways into 4 pieces.

7 Trim top of each cake to level if needed. Use a little buttercream to secure 1 cake, base-side down, on a serving plate. Spread ½ cup of buttercream over top of cake. Remove cheesecake from fridge. Release from pan. Remove baking paper. Invert cheesecake on top of buttercream layer. Spread ½ cup of buttercream over top of cheesecake. Top with remaining cake, base-side up. Spoon 1½ cups of buttercream into a piping bag fitted with a fluted nozzle. Spread remaining buttercream over top and side of cake. Use a palette knife to smooth cake to remove excess buttercream, if necessary.

8 Attach sliced Clinkers to the buttercream on side of cake. Pipe buttercream rosettes around top of cake. Sprinkle with crushed Clinkers.

● GLUTEN FREE ● MAKE AHEAD ● FREEZABLE ● EASY ● KID FRIENDLY

Lamington pavlova CAKE

Two Aussie faves unite to make one Austastic treat.

SERVES 10-12 **PREP** 1 hour (+ cooling & chilling) **COOKING** 1 hour 5 mins

500g pkt frozen raspberries
2 tbs caster sugar
600ml ctn thickened cream
¼ tsp vanilla bean paste
Fresh raspberries and pure
  icing sugar, to serve
sponge cake
5 eggs, at room temperature
155g (¾ cup) caster sugar
½ tsp vanilla bean paste
150g (1 cup) plain flour,
  sifted
1 tsp baking powder, sifted
230g (1½ cups) pure icing
  sugar
30g (¼ cup) cocoa powder
170g (2 cups) desiccated
  coconut
pavlova
3 egg whites, at room
  temperature
155g (¾ cup) caster sugar
1½ tsp cornflour
1 tsp white vinegar
½ tsp vanilla bean paste

1 Preheat oven to 180°C/160°C fan forced. To make the sponge cake, grease two 20cm (base size) round cake pans and line the bases and sides with baking paper. Use electric beaters to beat the eggs and sugar in a large bowl until thick and pale. Beat in the vanilla bean paste. Use a large metal spoon to gently fold in the flour and baking powder until well combined. Divide evenly between the prepared pans and smooth the surface. Bake for 20 minutes or until the cakes spring back in the centre. Set aside in pans for 5 minutes before turning the cakes out onto a wire rack to cool completely.

2 Place icing sugar and cocoa in a bowl. Add 90ml water. Mix until combined. Transfer to a large shallow bowl or dish. Place half the coconut on a baking tray, spreading it out over just half of the tray. Line a separate large baking tray with baking paper and set aside. Dip one cake into the chocolate icing, turning to coat well all over. Allow excess to drain off, then roll sides in the coconut to coat, using the remaining 1 cup coconut to sprinkle over the top and base of the cake to coat completely. Transfer to prepared tray. Repeat with remaining cake. Place in the fridge for 1 hour or overnight to set.

3 To make pavlova discs, preheat oven to 120°C/100°C fan forced. Grease two 20cm (base size) round cake pans. Line bases and sides with baking paper. Use electric beaters to beat egg whites in a bowl until firm peaks form. Add sugar, 1 tbs at a time, beating well after each addition, until thick and glossy. Beat in cornflour, vinegar and vanilla until combined. Divide evenly between the 2 pans. Smooth surface. Bake for 40 minutes until dry to touch and pale golden. Set aside to cool for 30 minutes then remove from pans.

4 Place raspberries, caster sugar and 2 tbs water in a saucepan over medium-high heat. Cook, stirring, for 3 minutes or until berries are just heated through and mixture is slightly saucy. Transfer to a bowl. Set aside to cool completely.

5 Use electric beaters to beat the cream and vanilla in a bowl until soft peaks form.

6 Place 1 lamington cake on a serving plate. Top with 1 of the pavlova discs, half the cream and half the raspberry compote. Top with the remaining lamington cake then remaining pavlova disc, cream and raspberry compote. Top with the fresh raspberries and dust with icing sugar before serving.

● GLUTEN FREE ● MAKE AHEAD ● FREEZABLE ● EASY ● KID FRIENDLY

★★★★★

Delicious and easy to make. Absolutely delicious, best assembled just before eating as pavlova may collapse under the weight of the cake.

LOULOUCAN

Chequerboard
WAFER CAKE

This two-tone cake was created as an ode to Crème Wafer Minis.

SERVES 12 **PREP** 1 hour (+ cooling) **COOKING** 1 hour 15 mins

375g (2½ cups) plain flour
½ tsp baking powder
¼ tsp bicarbonate of soda
230g unsalted butter, chopped, at room temperature
430g (2 cups) caster sugar
6 eggs
1 tbs vanilla extract
250g sour cream
Pink gel or liquid food colouring, to tint
2 x 175g pkt Crème Wafer Minis

buttercream
5 egg whites
270g (1¼ cups) caster sugar
340g unsalted butter, chopped, at room temperature
2 tsp vanilla extract

1 Preheat oven to 160°C/140°C fan forced. Grease two 7cm deep, 14 x 24cm (base size) loaf pans. Line bases and sides with baking paper, allowing long sides to overhang.

2 Sift flour, baking powder and bicarb into a bowl. Use electric beaters to beat butter and sugar in a separate bowl until pale and creamy. Add eggs, 1 at a time, beating well after each addition. Add vanilla and beat until combined. Gently fold flour mixture into butter mixture, alternating with sour cream, until just combined.

3 Pour half the cake mixture into 1 prepared pan. Smooth the top. Add a little food colouring to tint the remaining cake mixture pink then pour into remaining pan. Smooth top. Bake for 1 hour 10 minutes or until a skewer inserted into centre of cakes comes out clean. Set aside for 10 minutes to cool slightly before transferring to a wire rack to cool completely.

4 To make the buttercream, use a balloon whisk to combine egg whites and sugar in a large heatproof bowl. Place bowl over a saucepan of simmering water (make sure bowl doesn't touch the water). Cook, stirring often with the whisk, for 3-5 minutes or until hot to the touch (to test, transfer a small amount to a saucer and if mixture is hot, it is ready). Remove bowl from heat and transfer mixture to a stand mixer with the whisk attachment (you can also use electric beaters). Whisk on high speed for 10 minutes or until almost room temperature. Switch to paddle attachment. Reduce speed to low. Gradually add butter, beating well after each addition, until pale and creamy. Add vanilla and a pinch of salt. Beat until combined. Transfer 1 cup buttercream to a piping bag fitted with a 1cm plain round nozzle.

5 Use a large serrated knife to trim and level top of each cake. Cut each cake in half horizontally. Layer alternate slices of pink and vanilla cake on top of each other, using a little buttercream between each layer to adhere. Use knife to level sides of cake if necessary. Evenly slice cake lengthways into 4 long pieces.

6 To assemble, spread a little of the buttercream into the centre of a serving plate or cake board. Lay a slice of cake flat. Cover with a little buttercream. Layer with remaining cake slices, alternating colours to form a chequerboard pattern and covering each layer with a thin layer of buttercream. Spread remaining buttercream over top and sides of cake. Use an offset palette knife or cake scraper to smooth the sides and top. Pipe peaks of the reserved buttercream over the top of the cake in rows to cover. Arrange wafers in a chequerboard pattern over the top of the buttercream peaks.

● GLUTEN FREE ● MAKE AHEAD ● FREEZABLE ● EASY ● KID FRIENDLY

Chocolate freckle CAKE

Add a sprinkle of fun to any party with this freckly extravaganza.

SERVES 20 **PREP** 1 hour 30 mins (+ chilling) **COOKING** 1 hour 35 mins

450g (3 cups) plain flour
645g (3 cups) caster sugar
90g (¾ cup) cocoa powder
3 tsp bicarbonate of soda
1½ tsp baking powder
1 tsp salt
3 eggs
375ml (1½ cups) buttermilk
375ml (1½ cups) vegetable oil
375ml (1½ cups) boiling water
2 tsp vanilla extract
120g (½ cup) hundreds and thousands
Bought chocolate freckles in assorted sizes, to decorate (or scan QR code below)
dark chocolate ganache
400g dark chocolate, broken into pieces
300ml ctn thickened cream
buttercream
560g unsalted butter, chopped, at room temperature
600g (4 cups) pure icing sugar, sifted
1 tbs vanilla extract

1 Preheat oven to 180°C/160°C fan forced. Grease two 18cm round cake pans. Line bases and sides with baking paper. Whisk together flour, sugar, cocoa, bicarb, baking powder and salt in a large bowl. Add eggs, buttermilk, oil, water and vanilla. Whisk until well combined and smooth. Divide half mixture between pans. Bake for 40-45 minutes until a skewer inserted into centre of cakes comes out clean. Set aside for 10 minutes to cool slightly, before transferring to a wire rack to cool completely. Grease and reline pans. Divide remaining mixture between pans. Bake for 40-45 minutes or until a skewer inserted into centre of cakes comes out clean. Set aside for 10 minutes to cool slightly. Transfer to a wire rack to cool completely.

2 To make ganache, process chocolate until finely chopped. Place cream in a saucepan over medium heat. Bring just to the boil. With motor running, slowly add cream to chocolate. Process until smooth. Transfer to a bowl. Place in fridge, stirring occasionally, for 20-30 minutes or until thickened.

3 To make the buttercream, use electric beaters to beat butter in a large bowl until pale and creamy.

Add icing sugar, vanilla and a pinch of salt. Beat until for 6-8 minutes or until pale and creamy.

4 Use a large serrated knife to trim top of each cake. Use a little buttercream to secure 1 cake, base-side down, on a serving board. Reserve ¼ cup ganache. Spread one-third of remaining ganache over cake top. Sprinkle with one-third of hundreds and thousands. Repeat layering with cake, ganache and hundreds and thousands. Top with remaining cake, base-side up. Spread buttercream over top and side to cover and smooth, removing excess buttercream. Spoon remaining buttercream into a piping bag fitted with a fluted nozzle. Place cake in fridge for 20 minutes to chill.

5 To assemble the cake, place reserved ganache in a small microwave-safe bowl. Microwave on high for 10-15 seconds or until melted. Set aside for 2-3 minutes to cool slightly. Remove the cake from the fridge. Use a teaspoon to gently pour drips of warm chocolate ganache from top edge of cake. Decorate cake with chocolate freckles, using the reserved buttercream to secure freckles to the cake, as necessary.

● GLUTEN FREE ● MAKE AHEAD ● FREEZABLE ● EASY ● KID FRIENDLY

Lemon curd coconut PAVLOVA CAKE

Like sunshine on a rainy day, this zingy little number is bright and fresh.

SERVES 12 **PREP** 45 mins (+ cooling & setting) **COOKING** 2 hours 35 mins

160ml (⅔ cup) grapeseed oil

200g (¾ cup) Greek-style yoghurt

2 tbs fresh lemon juice

1 tbs finely grated lemon rind

3 eggs

75g (½ cup) self-raising flour

85g (1 cup) desiccated coconut

155g (¾ cup) caster sugar

300ml ctn double cream

125ml (½ cup) thickened cream

Edible flowers, to decorate

lemon curd

2 eggs

100g (½ cup) caster sugar

85g unsalted butter, melted, cooled

160ml (⅔ cup) fresh lemon juice

2 tsp finely grated lemon rind

candied lemon

100g (½ cup) caster sugar

1 lemon, cut into 5mm-thick slices

pavlova

5 egg whites, at room temperature

215g (1 cup) caster sugar

2 tsp cornflour

1 tsp white vinegar

1 tsp vanilla extract

1 Preheat the oven to 180°C/160°C fan forced. Release the base of a 20cm (base size) springform pan and invert. Line the base with baking paper, allowing a 4cm overhang. Secure the base, paper side up, back in the pan. Grease the side of the pan with olive oil spray.

2 Place oil, yoghurt, lemon juice, rind and eggs in a large bowl. Use a balloon whisk to whisk until well combined. Add flour, coconut and sugar and whisk until combined. Pour into prepared pan. Bake for 50 minutes or until a skewer inserted into centre comes out clean. Set aside.

3 Meanwhile, for the lemon curd, whisk eggs, sugar, butter, lemon juice and rind in a large microwave-safe glass bowl until combined. Microwave on Medium, stirring every minute, for 4-6 minutes or until a smooth, thick curd forms. Set aside to cool completely. Stir in 1 tbs water.

4 For the candied lemon, place a wire rack over a baking tray. Stir the sugar and 125ml (½ cup) water in a frying pan over low heat until the sugar dissolves. Increase heat to medium and add the lemon slices. Gently simmer, turning halfway, for 10-15 minutes or until lemon slices are translucent. Transfer to the wire rack. Set aside for at least 1 hour to set.

5 For the pavlova, reduce the oven temperature to 150°C/130°C fan forced. Use electric beaters with a whisk attachment to whisk the egg whites in a bowl until firm peaks form. Gradually add the sugar, beating well after each addition, until the mixture is thick and glossy. Beat in the cornflour, vinegar and vanilla.

6 Place large spoonfuls of meringue on top of the cake, leaving a 2cm border around the edge. Bake for 10 minutes. Reduce the oven temperature to 100°C/80°C fan forced and bake for a further 1 hour 35 minutes or until the pavlova is crisp and dry. Turn the oven off and leave the pavlova-topped cake in the oven, with the door closed, until it has cooled completely.

7 Use a balloon whisk to whisk the double cream and thickened cream together in a large bowl until soft peaks form.

8 Carefully remove the cake from the pan and place on a serving platter or cake board. Spread the top of the pavlova with the lemon curd and whipped cream. Top with the candied lemon and flowers.

● GLUTEN FREE ● MAKE AHEAD ● FREEZABLE ● EASY ● **KID FRIENDLY**

★★★★★

Everything worked very well. Stunning and delicious! Everyone loved it.

KERRI

Pink lemonade brushstroke CAKE

Pretty as a picture but a sight tastier, this is a work of edible art.

SERVES 20 **PREP** 45 mins (+ cooling, setting & chilling) **COOKING** 55 mins

375g unsalted butter, at
  room temperature
315g (1½ cups) caster sugar
2 tsp vanilla extract
5 eggs, at room temperature
565g (3¾ cups) self-raising
  flour
250ml (1 cup) pink
  lemonade
2 tbs grenadine
225g Wilton Bright White
  Candy Melts
75g Wilton Orange
  Candy Melts
150g Wilton Pink
  Candy Melts
Fresh flower, to decorate
swiss meringue buttercream
4 egg whites
215g (1 cup) caster sugar
400g butter, chopped, at
  room temperature
2 tsp grenadine

1 Preheat oven to 180°C/160°C fan forced. Line the base and side of a round 18cm (base size) and a round 22cm (base size) cake pan.

2 Use electric beaters to beat butter, sugar and vanilla in a bowl until pale and creamy. Add the eggs, 1 at a time, beating well after each addition. Use a large metal spoon to fold in flour, lemonade and grenadine until combined. Divide between prepared pans. Smooth surface of each. Place both cakes in oven – bake smaller cake for 45 minutes or until a skewer inserted into the centre comes out clean, and the larger cake for 55 minutes or until a skewer inserted into centre comes out clean. Cool slightly, then turn onto a wire rack to cool completely.

3 Meanwhile, take 3 small microwave-safe bowls. Place 150g white candy melts in 1 bowl. Place orange candy melts and remaining white candy melts in another bowl. Place pink candy melts in the last bowl. Microwave melts, 1 bowl at a time, on Medium, stirring every minute, until melted. Line 2 trays with baking paper. Dip a 2cm-wide pastry brush in a bowl of melts. Dab the brush on a lined tray, then 'paint' to create a brushstroke effect. Repeat using bowls of melts to make 'brushstrokes'

in different colours and lengths. Set aside for 15 minutes to set.

4 Meanwhile, for the buttercream, combine the egg whites and sugar in a heatproof bowl. Place over a saucepan of simmering water (don't let bowl touch the water). Use a balloon whisk to stir for 8-10 minutes or until sugar dissolves and mixture reaches 70°C on a cook's thermometer. Transfer to a clean bowl. Use electric beaters to beat for 5 minutes or until firm peaks form and the mixture is almost at room temperature. Gradually add the butter, beating well after each addition, until mixture is thick and smooth. Add grenadine. Beat until well combined.

5 Use a serrated knife to halve cakes horizontally. Place a large cake layer, cut-side up, on a serving plate. Spread with a little buttercream. Continue layering with remaining large cake layer and small cake layers, spreading buttercream between layers. Spread half the remaining buttercream in a thin layer over top and sides of cake (don't worry if there are crumbs). Place in fridge for about 15 minutes to chill.

6 Spread remaining buttercream over top and side of cake, leaving some cake exposed. Decorate with 'brushstrokes' and top with a flower.

● GLUTEN FREE ● MAKE AHEAD ● FREEZABLE ● EASY ● KID FRIENDLY

Neapolitan KitKat LAYER CAKE

The choc, strawberry and vanilla flavour has stood the test of time.

SERVES 10-12 **PREP** 45 mins (+ cooling & 30 mins chilling) **COOKING** 40 mins

375g unsalted butter, at
  room temperature
485g (2¼ cups) caster sugar
3 tsp vanilla extract
5 eggs, at room temperature
565g (3¾ cups) self-raising
  flour, sifted
375ml (1½ cups) milk, plus
  2 tbs, extra
200g (¾ cup) Greek-style
  yoghurt
¼ tsp Queen Raspberry
  Baking Paste
Pink food colouring, to tint
50g (½ cup) cocoa powder
100g dark cooking
  chocolate, chopped
60ml (¼ cup) thickened
  cream
170g pkt Raspberry
  Cheesecake Duo KitKat,
  to decorate (see tip)
170g pkt KitKat, to decorate
100g (½ cup) Neapolitan
  M&M's (see tip)

vanilla buttercream
250g butter, at room
  temperature
2 tsp vanilla extract
450g (3 cups) icing sugar
  mixture, sifted
2 tbs milk

1 Preheat the oven to 180°C/160°C fan forced. Grease 3 round 20cm (base size) cake pans and line bases and sides with baking paper.

2 Use electric beaters to beat the butter, sugar and vanilla in a large bowl until pale and creamy. Add eggs, 1 at a time, beating well after each addition. Add the flour, milk and yoghurt and beat until smooth. Divide the batter evenly among 3 bowls.

3 Pour 1 portion of the batter into a prepared pan. Smooth the surface. Add the raspberry baking paste and a few drops of pink food colouring to another portion of batter. Stir until well combined. Pour into another prepared pan. Smooth the surface. Add cocoa powder and extra 2 tbs milk to the remaining portion of batter. Stir until well combined. Pour into remaining prepared pan. Smooth surface.

4 Bake the cakes for 30-35 minutes or until a skewer inserted into the centres comes out clean. Turn onto wire racks to cool completely.

5 For buttercream, use electric beaters to beat butter and vanilla in a bowl until pale and creamy. Beat in icing sugar and milk, in alternating batches, until smooth and creamy.

6 Place the chocolate cake on a serving plate. Spread top with a little buttercream. Top with the pink cake. Spread top with a little buttercream. Top with vanilla cake. Spread remaining buttercream over the top and side of cake to coat. Place the cake in the fridge for at least 30 minutes to chill.

7 Place the chocolate and cream in a microwave-safe bowl. Microwave, stirring every 30 seconds, until smooth. Cool slightly. Pour over top of cake and use a palette knife to spread to the edge, allowing it to drip down the sides. Decorate the top of the cake with KitKat and M&M's.

COOK'S TIP

The Raspberry Duo KitKat and Neapolitan M&M's were limited release. You can replace them with regular KitKat and M&M's.

● GLUTEN FREE ● MAKE AHEAD ● FREEZABLE ● EASY ● KID FRIENDLY

Brilliant cake recipe! The cake was perfect, an almost mud cake-like texture and not too sweet. **JODITELHA**

Fairy bread
LAYER CAKE

There are hundreds and thousands of reasons why you need this!

SERVES 20 **PREP** 45 mins (+ cooling & chilling) **COOKING** 25 mins

10 eggs
215g (1 cup) caster sugar
150g (1 cup) plain flour
150g (1 cup) self-raising flour
125g pkt Dollar 5s sprinkles
Pink gel food colouring,
   to tint
Hundreds and thousands, to
   decorate
Pink Persian fairy floss, to
   decorate
buttercream
750g butter, at room
   temperature
1.35kg (9 cups) icing sugar
   mixture
80ml (⅓ cup) milk
pink chocolate ganache
180g white chocolate,
   broken into squares
80ml (⅓ cup) thickened
   cream
Pink gel food colouring,
   to tint

1 Preheat the oven to 180°C/160°C fan forced. Grease four 5cm-deep, round 20cm (base size) cake pans. Line bases with baking paper.

2 Use electric beaters to beat eggs in a large bowl until pale. Add the sugar and beat for 8-10 minutes or until the mixture is thick and glossy. Sift the plain flour and self-raising flour into a bowl. Use a large metal spoon to gently fold the flour mixture into the egg mixture. Add 1 tbs of each of the 5 colours in the Dollar 5s sprinkles packet and gently fold through, being careful not to overmix. Divide evenly among the prepared pans and gently smooth the surface of each. Bake for 20 minutes or until golden brown and the cakes spring back when lightly touched. Cool in the pans for 10 minutes, then turn onto wire racks to cool completely.

3 To make the buttercream, use electric beaters to beat the butter in a large bowl until pale and creamy. Gradually add the icing sugar, beating until well combined. Add the milk and beat until light and fluffy.

4 To assemble, reserve 1 cup buttercream. Transfer 3 cups buttercream to a separate bowl and tint pink with food colouring. Place a cake on a cake stand. Spread 1 cup pink buttercream over the top. Repeat layering with remaining cakes and pink buttercream. Spread a thin layer of the remaining white buttercream over the top and side of the cake. Smooth with a metal spatula. Place in the fridge for 20 minutes to set. Gently mix 1 tsp of each of the 5 colours in the Dollar 5s sprinkles through the remaining white buttercream. Cover the top and side of the cake with the rainbow buttercream and use a metal spatula to smooth the surface. Chill the cake while you prepare the ganache.

5 For the ganache, place the chocolate and cream in a microwave-safe bowl and microwave for 1 minute, stirring halfway, until melted and smooth. Tint pink with food colouring and set aside to cool until ganache just begins to thicken.

6 Pour the ganache evenly over the top of the chilled cake, using the back of a metal spoon to gently spread it to the edge and allowing it to drip down the side of the cake. Place in the fridge for 15 minutes to set.

7 Spoon the reserved 1 cup buttercream into a piping bag with a 1cm plain nozzle and pipe peaks around the top edge of the cake. Decorate with the remaining the hundreds and thousands. Just before serving, top with the fairy floss.

● GLUTEN FREE ● MAKE AHEAD ● FREEZABLE ● EASY ● KID FRIENDLY

Strawberry lime
MARGARITA CAKE

Fancy up your next fiesta with this cocktail-infused extravaganza.

SERVES 15-20 **PREP** 40 mins (+ cooling & 20 mins chilling) **COOKING** 45 mins

300g (2 cups) plain flour
1¾ tsp baking powder
1 tsp table salt
250g fresh strawberries, plus
    extra, halved, to decorate
315g (1½ cups) caster sugar
2 eggs
250ml (1 cup) milk
185ml (¾ cup) vegetable oil
2 tbs fresh lime juice
2 tbs finely grated lime rind
3 limes, thinly sliced, plus
    lime wedge, to serve
margarita syrup
100g (½ cup) caster sugar
2 tbs fresh lime juice
60ml (¼ cup) tequila
buttercream
5 egg whites
270g (1¼ cups) caster sugar
340g unsalted butter,
    chopped, at room
    temperature
100ml tequila
1 tbs fresh lime juice
Green and yellow gel food
    colouring, to tint

1 Preheat oven to 180°C/160°C fan forced. Grease three 15cm (base size) round cake pans. Line bases and sides with baking paper. Sift flour, baking powder and salt into a bowl. Reserve 3 strawberries. Hull and cut remaining into 1-2cm pieces.

2 Use electric beaters on medium to beat sugar and eggs in a bowl for 3 minutes or until thick and creamy. Beat in milk, oil, juice and rind until combined. Reduce speed to low. Add flour mixture. Beat until just combined. Divide among pans. Smooth surface. Bake for 35 minutes or until a skewer inserted into centres comes out clean. Set aside for 5 minutes to cool slightly. Turn onto a sheet of baking paper.

3 To make syrup, stir sugar, juice and 60ml (¼ cup) water in a small saucepan over medium heat until sugar dissolves. Increase heat to medium-high. Bring to a simmer. Reduce heat to low. Simmer for 5 minutes or until syrup thickens slightly. Remove from heat. Stir in tequila. Prick warm cakes all over with a skewer. Drizzle over syrup.

4 To make buttercream, combine egg whites and sugar in a large heatproof bowl. Place over a pan of simmering water (make sure bowl doesn't touch water). Whisk until sugar dissolves and reaches 70°C on a cook's thermometer. Use electric beaters on high to whisk for 10 minutes

or until almost at room temp. On low speed gradually add butter, beating well after each addition, until smooth. Add tequila, juice and a pinch of salt. Beat until combined. Use colouring to tint. Transfer ½ cupful to a piping bag fitted with a 1cm-wide nozzle.

5 Line a baking tray with paper towel. Thinly slice reserved berries. Arrange on tray with lime slices. Gently press to remove moisture.

6 Use a serrated knife to trim and level top of each cake. Pipe a little buttercream in centre of a serving plate. Place 1 cake, base-side down, on top. Spread a layer of buttercream over top of cake. Pipe a ring of buttercream around edge to create a dam. Fill with half the chopped strawberries. Top with second cake. Repeat to make another buttercream layer and dam, and fill with remaining chopped berries. Top with remaining cake. Thinly spread buttercream over top and side to create a crumb coat. Place in fridge for 20 minutes to chill.

7 Use a palette knife to spread buttercream around middle of cake. Leave top and bottom thirds exposed. Reserve a few lime slices. Press remaining sliced fruit onto this buttercream layer. Spread remaining buttercream above and below fruit. Use palette knife or cake scraper to smooth buttercream. Top with reserved lime and extra berries.

● GLUTEN FREE ● MAKE AHEAD ● FREEZABLE ● EASY ● KID FRIENDLY

White velvet CAKE

From white Christmas, to winter wonderland, this takes the cake!

SERVES 12 **PREP** 1 hour (+ cooling & setting) **COOKING** 45 mins

8 eggs, at room
   temperature, separated
220g (1 cup) caster sugar
250ml (1 cup) canola oil
160ml (⅔ cup) water
1 tbs vanilla bean paste
300g (2 cups) plain flour
1 tsp baking powder
1 tsp cream of tartar
white chocolate
buttercream
500g butter, chopped, at
   room temperature
750g icing sugar mixture
2 tbs milk
300g white chocolate,
   melted, cooled
decorations
250g Dr. Oetker Ready-
   rolled Icing White
150g (1 cup) royal icing
   mixture
35ml cold water
10 large white marshmallows
Edible silver colour mist
   spray, to decorate
Edible silver glitter, to
   decorate

1 Preheat the oven to 170°C/150°C fan forced. Line the bases of two round 20cm (base size) cake pans with baking paper.

2 Place the egg yolks, pinch of salt and 70g (⅓ cup) sugar in a large bowl. Use a balloon whisk to whisk until combined. Whisk in the oil, water and vanilla. Sift the flour and baking powder over the mixture. Use a large metal spoon to fold until combined.

3 Use electric beaters to beat egg whites and cream of tartar in a bowl until soft peaks form. Gradually add remaining sugar, 1 tbs at a time, beating well after each addition until sugar dissolves. Stir one-third of the egg white mixture into the flour mixture to loosen, then gently fold in the remaining meringue.

4 Divide mixture among the prepared pans. Smooth tops. Bake for 45 minutes or until cakes spring back when lightly touched in the centre. Place 2 wire racks on the bench with even-sized glasses or cans under each corner to allow air to circulate. Transfer cake pans to the racks. Set aside for 5 minutes or until the cakes sink slightly. Invert cakes onto racks, without removing the pans, for 10 minutes. Turn pans right side up. Carefully run a palette knife around the edge of each cake to loosen.

Remove glasses or cans from under racks and turn cakes onto racks. Set aside to cool completely.

5 To make buttercream, use electric beaters to beat butter in a large bowl until pale. Gradually add icing sugar and milk, in alternating batches, beating well after each addition. Add chocolate. Beat until combined.

6 Cut each cake in half horizontally. Place 1 cake base on a plate. Spread with 1 cup buttercream. Repeat with 2 more layers, spreading each with 1 cup buttercream icing. Place the final layer on top. Spread 1-1½ cups buttercream over top and side of cake. Place in fridge for 1 hour. Keep the remaining buttercream in a cool place (not the fridge).

7 Meanwhile, roll out ready-rolled icing. Use snowflake cutters to cut out snowflakes and set aside until firm.

8 Spread remaining buttercream over cake for a second coating. Place in the fridge for 30 minutes to set. Use electric beaters to beat royal icing mixture and water in a bowl until smooth. Spread over top of cake and carefully towards edges so it drizzles slowly down the sides. Set aside for about 1 hour or until set. Lightly spray marshmallows with silver spray. Sprinkle with glitter. Top the cake with the marshmallows and the snowflakes.

● GLUTEN FREE ● MAKE AHEAD ● FREEZABLE ● EASY ● KID FRIENDLY

I made this cake for a birthday and everyone loved it!! **MADDY123**

Nutella TORTE

This choc-hazelnut cake is a simply stunning crowd-pleaser.

SERVES 10-12 **PREP** 55 mins (+ cooling, 15 mins setting & 30 mins chilling) **COOKING** 25 mins

8 eggs, separated

380g (2½ cups) icing sugar mixture, sifted

150g (1 cup) self-raising flour

2 tbs dark cocoa powder

80g (⅔ cup) hazelnut meal

75g hazelnuts

80g dark chocolate (80% cocoa), melted

250g butter

90g (⅓ cup) smooth peanut butter

125ml (½ cup) Frangelico liqueur

240g (¾ cup) Nutella

chocolate topping

100g dark chocolate (80% cocoa), chopped

1 tbs Frangelico liqueur

20g butter

1 Preheat the oven to 190°C/170°C fan forced. Grease two 20cm (base size) round cake pans and line with baking paper.

2 Use electric beaters to beat the egg whites in a bowl until firm peaks form. Gradually beat in 80g (½ cup) icing sugar, 1 tbs at a time, beating well after each addition. Add the yolks. Beat until combined.

3 Place the flour and cocoa in a sieve and sift one-third over the egg mixture. Use a large metal spoon to fold until just combined. Repeat, in 2 batches, with remaining flour mixture. Fold in the hazelnut meal until just combined. Divide mixture among pans and smooth the surface. Bake for 15-20 minutes or until a skewer inserted in the centres comes out clean. Transfer to a wire rack to cool.

4 Meanwhile, line a tray with baking paper. Use a fork to dip the hazelnuts into the melted chocolate and shake off excess. Place on prepared tray. Place in the fridge for 10-15 minutes to set.

5 Use electric beaters to beat the butter and peanut butter in a bowl until pale and creamy. Gradually add the remaining icing sugar, 1 tbs at a time, beating well after each addition, until well combined.

6 Use a serrated knife to trim the tops of the cakes to level. Carefully cut each cake in half horizontally. Place 1 cake base on a plate and brush with 2 tbs of the liqueur. Spread with one-third of the Nutella. Top with about ⅓-½ cup of the peanut butter mixture. Repeat the layering with the cake layers, liqueur, Nutella and peanut butter mixture, finishing with a cake layer. Spread the top and side of the cake with the remaining peanut butter mixture and place in the fridge for 30 minutes to chill.

7 For the topping, combine ingredients in a heatproof bowl. Microwave for 1 minute. Stir until smooth. Cool slightly.

8 Pour the chocolate topping over the cake, spreading to the edges. Tap the cake gently on the bench to flatten the top, allowing the topping to drip down the side of the cake. Cut a few of the chocolate hazelnuts in half. Use both the halved and whole chocolate hazelnuts to decorate edge of the top of the cake.

● GLUTEN FREE ● MAKE AHEAD ● FREEZABLE ● EASY ● KID FRIENDLY

Coconut ice CAKE

We dedicate this cake to one of our fave childhood treats.

SERVES 10 **PREP** 45 mins (+ cooling) **COOKING** 50 mins

50g desiccated coconut
400ml can coconut milk
1 tbs coconut essence
270g (1¾ cups) plain flour
2½ tsp baking powder
250g unsalted butter,
　chopped, at room
　temperature
285g (1⅓ cups) caster sugar
3 eggs
Rose pink liquid food
　colouring, to tint
500ml thickened cream
100g pure icing sugar, sifted
200g coconut flakes
Coconut ice, mini meringues
　and mini marshmallows,
　some halved, to decorate

1 Preheat oven to 180°C/160°C fan forced. Grease two 7cm-deep, 14 x 24cm (base size) loaf pans. Line bases and sides with baking paper.

2 Place the desiccated coconut, 250ml (1 cup) coconut milk and 1 tsp coconut essence in a small saucepan over low heat until just heated through. Set aside to cool. Place the remaining coconut milk in the fridge to chill. Sift the flour and baking powder into a bowl. Add a pinch of salt.

3 Use a stand mixer with the paddle attachment or electric beaters to beat the butter and caster sugar in a large bowl until pale and fluffy. Add eggs, 1 at a time, beating well after each addition. With the mixer on low speed, add the flour mixture and coconut milk mixture in alternating batches, beginning and ending with the flour, until just combined. Pour half the cake mixture into 1 prepared pan. Smooth the surface. Add a little food colouring to tint the remaining cake mixture pink then pour into remaining pan. Smooth the surface. Bake for 40-45 minutes or

until a skewer inserted into the centre of the cakes comes out clean. Set aside in the pans for 10 minutes to cool slightly before turning onto a wire rack to cool completely.

4 Use a stand mixer with the whisk attachment or electric beaters to beat the cream, chilled coconut milk, icing sugar and remaining coconut essence in a large bowl until firm peaks form.

5 Use a serrated bread knife to trim and level the top of each cake. Cut each cake in half horizontally. Place 1 pink cake layer, base-side down, on a cake board or serving platter and spread ½ cupful of coconut milk mixture over top of the cake. Repeat layering with the remaining pink cake followed by the plain cakes, spreading ½ cupful of coconut milk mixture between each layer. Spread the remaining coconut milk mixture over the top and side of the whole cake. Gently press the coconut flakes over the top and side of the cake. Decorate the top with coconut ice, meringues and marshmallows.

● GLUTEN FREE ● MAKE AHEAD ● FREEZABLE ● EASY ● KID FRIENDLY

Skittles pastel CAKE

Love your lollies? This colourful creation is for you!

SERVES 25 **PREP** 1 hour 30 mins (+ cooling) **COOKING** 1 hour 20 mins

600g (4 cups) plain flour
3½ tsp baking powder
2 tsp salt
645g (3 cups) caster sugar
4 eggs, at room temperature
500ml (2 cups) milk
375ml (1½ cups) vegetable oil
1 tbs vanilla extract
Pink, blue, orange and yellow gel food colouring, to tint
5 x 190g pkt Skittles

buttercream
560g unsalted butter, chopped, at room temperature
600g (4 cups) pure icing sugar, sifted
1 tbs vanilla extract

1 Preheat oven to 180°C/160°C fan forced. Grease two 18cm (base size) round cake pans. Line bases and sides with baking paper. Sift the flour, baking powder and salt into a bowl.

2 Use electric beaters on medium speed to beat the caster sugar and eggs in a large bowl for 3 minutes or until thickened and well combined. Beat in the milk, oil and vanilla until just combined. With the mixer on low speed, gradually add the flour mixture, beating until just combined. Divide the cake mixture among 4 bowls.

3 Tint one bowl with a few drops of pink colouring. Gently fold to combine. Pour into 1 prepared pan and smooth the surface. Repeat with the blue colouring and remaining cake pan. Bake for 40 minutes or until a skewer inserted into the centres comes out clean. Set aside in the pans for 10 minutes to cool slightly before turning onto a wire rack to cool completely. Grease and line the pans again. Repeat with the orange colouring for 1 pan and yellow colouring for the remaining pan. Set aside all cakes to cool completely.

4 To make the buttercream, use electric beaters on medium-high speed to beat butter in a large bowl for 6-8 minutes or until pale and creamy. Add the icing sugar, vanilla and a pinch of salt. Reduce speed to low and mix until combined. Increase speed to medium-high and beat for 6-8 minutes or until pale and creamy.

5 Use a large serrated knife to level the top of each cake if needed. Use a little of the buttercream to secure the yellow cake, base-side down, on a serving platter or board. Spread ½ cup of the buttercream over the top of the cake. Repeat with the orange and blue cake layers and 1 cup of buttercream. Top with pink cake, base-side up. Spread 2 cups of the buttercream over top and side of the cake to cover. Use a large palette knife to smooth the top and side of cake and remove any excess buttercream, if necessary. Spoon the remaining buttercream into a piping bag fitted with a fluted nozzle.

6 Starting at the base of the cake and working your way up, arrange Skittles in a graphic pattern, gently pressing into the buttercream to secure. Pipe ruffled peaks around the top edge of the cake with the reserved buttercream. Top each buttercream peak with a Skittle.

● GLUTEN FREE ● MAKE AHEAD ● FREEZABLE ● EASY ● KID FRIENDLY

Hundreds & thousands BISCUIT CAKE

These old-school bikkies make the perfect pink decoration.

SERVES 25 **PREP** 1 hour (+ cooling) **COOKING** 45 mins

450g (3 cups) plain flour
1 tbs baking powder
½ tsp table salt
230g unsalted butter, chopped, at room temperature
370g (1¾ cups) caster sugar
4 eggs
1 tbs vanilla extract
250ml (1 cup) buttermilk, at room temperature
200g pkt Arnott's Hundreds & Thousands biscuits
Hundreds and thousands, to decorate

buttercream
330g unsalted butter, chopped, at room temperature
375g cream cheese, chopped, at room temperature
750g (5 cups) icing sugar mixture, sifted
2 tsp vanilla extract
Pink gel food colouring,

1 Preheat oven to 180°C/160°C fan forced. Grease two 20cm (base size) square cake pans. Line the bases and sides with baking paper. Sift flour, baking powder and salt into a bowl.

2 Use a stand mixer with the paddle attachment or electric beaters to beat the butter and sugar in a large bowl until pale and fluffy. Add eggs, 1 at a time, beating well after each addition. Add vanilla and beat until combined. With the mixer on low speed, add flour mixture and buttermilk in alternating batches, beginning and ending with the flour, until just combined. Divide the cake mixture evenly between the prepared pans and smooth the surface. Bake for 40-45 minutes or until a skewer inserted into the centre of the cakes comes out clean. Set aside in pans for 10 minutes to cool slightly before turning onto a wire rack to cool completely.

3 Meanwhile, to make the buttercream, use a stand mixer with the whisk attachment or electric beaters on medium speed to beat the butter in a large bowl until pale and creamy. Gradually add cream cheese and whisk until smooth. Scrape the bottom and side of the bowl then add half the icing sugar and half the vanilla. Whisk on low speed until combined. Add the remaining icing sugar and vanilla. Whisk on low speed until combined. Increase speed to medium-high and whisk for a further 5 minutes or until fluffy. Add a little food colouring to tint the buttercream pale pink.

4 Place 4 biscuits in a food processor and process until coarsely crushed. Transfer to a bowl with 1 cupful of the buttercream and mix until combined.

5 Use a serrated bread knife to trim and level the top of each cake. Use a little plain buttercream to secure 1 cake layer, base-side down, onto a cake board or serving platter. Spread the crushed biscuit buttercream over the top of the cake. Place the remaining cake, base-side up, on top. Spread the plain buttercream over the top and sides of the whole cake. Use an offset palette knife or cake scraper to smooth the sides and top.

6 Spoon the plain buttercream into a disposable piping bag and snip a 1cm off the end of a corner. Pipe small peaks of buttercream on top of the cake and arrange 20 remaining biscuits on top, gently pressing to secure. Decorate sides of the cake with hundreds and thousands.

● GLUTEN FREE ● MAKE AHEAD ● FREEZABLE ● EASY ● KID FRIENDLY

German chocolate
CAKE

A levelled up chocolate cake experience with caramel and nuts.

SERVES 12 **PREP** 40 mins (+ cooling & 30 mins chilling) **COOKING** 1 hour 30 mins

645g (3 cups) caster sugar
450g (3 cups) plain flour
95g (1 cup) cocoa powder
3 tsp bicarbonate of soda
1½ tsp baking powder
1 tsp table salt
3 eggs
375ml (1½ cups) buttermilk
375ml (1½ cups) vegetable oil
375ml (1½ cups) boiling water
2 tsp vanilla extract
150g pecans
McKenzie's Moist Flakes Coconut and caramel spread, to decorate

coconut pecan filling
215g (1 cup) caster sugar
250ml (1 cup) evaporated milk
3 eggs yolks, lightly whisked
125g unsalted butter, chopped
130g (2 cups) McKenzie's Moist Flakes Coconut
150g pecans, chopped
1 tsp vanilla extract

chocolate buttercream
450g unsalted butter, chopped, at room temperature
600g (4 cups) pure icing sugar, sifted
50g (½ cup) cocoa powder, sifted
2 tbs milk

1 Preheat oven to 180°C/160°C fan forced. Grease two 18cm (base size) round cake pans. Line the bases and sides with baking paper.

2 Whisk together caster sugar, flour, cocoa, bicarb, baking powder and salt in a large bowl. Add the eggs, buttermilk, oil, boiling water and vanilla. Whisk until well combined and smooth. Divide half of the mixture evenly between prepared pans. Bake for 40-45 minutes or until a skewer inserted into centres comes out clean. Set aside in the pans for 10 minutes to cool slightly before transferring to a wire rack to cool completely. Grease and reline pans. Repeat the process, using the remaining cake mixture to bake 2 more cakes.

3 Meanwhile, to make the coconut pecan filling, place the caster sugar, evaporated milk and egg yolk in a large saucepan. Whisk until combined. Add the butter. Place over medium heat. Cook, stirring constantly, for 4-5 minutes or until the butter melts. Continue to cook, stirring constantly, for another 10 minutes or until the mixture starts to boil and thicken. Remove from heat and stir through the coconut, pecan and vanilla until combined. Transfer to a bowl and set aside to cool completely.

4 To make chocolate buttercream, use a stand mixer with paddle attachment on medium-high speed to beat the butter for 6-8 minutes or until pale and creamy. Reduce speed to low. Add icing sugar, cocoa and milk. Beat until well combined. Increase speed to medium-high and beat for 3-4 minutes until fluffy. Spoon 1 cupful of the buttercream into a piping bag fitted with a 1cm plain nozzle. Spoon another 1 cupful into a piping bag fitted with a large fluted nozzle.

5 Use a large serrated knife to trim and level the top of each cake. Pipe a little buttercream in the centre of a serving plate. Place 1 cake, cut-side up, on the plate. Use the plain nozzle piping bag to pipe a ring of buttercream around the top edge of cake. Fill with one-third of the coconut pecan filling. Repeat layering with the remaining cakes, buttercream and coconut pecan filling, finishing with the final cake, base-side up. Place in the fridge for 30 minutes to chill.

6 Spread remaining buttercream over top and side of cake. Use an offset palette knife or cake scraper to smooth top and side. Reserve a few pecan halves then roughly chop the remainder. Gently press the chopped pecans around base of cake. Use the fluted nozzle piping bag to pipe swirls of buttercream around the top edge of the cake. Decorate the swirls with reserved pecan halves and coconut flakes. Drizzle caramel spread over top and side of cake to serve.

● GLUTEN FREE ● MAKE AHEAD ● FREEZABLE ● EASY ● KID FRIENDLY

Pink velvet watercolour CAKE

This requires a higher level of competency but worth the effort!

MAKES 50 cake fingers **PREP** 1 hour (+ cooling & overnight chilling) **COOKING** 1 hour 20 mins

675g (4½ cups) plain flour

1½ tsp bicarbonate of soda

180g butter, chopped, at room temperature

645g (3 cups) caster sugar

375ml (1½ cups) vegetable oil

6 eggs, at room temperature, separated

1½ tbs vanilla extract

1½ tsp white vinegar

2 tsp rose pink liquid food colouring

375ml (1½ cups) buttermilk, at room temperature

250g pkt cream cheese, at room temperature

1 quantity Swiss meringue buttercream (see page 306)

Queen Hot Pink Food Colour Gel, to tint

50g dark chocolate melts

25ml thickened cream

Fresh flowers, wired, taped, to decorate

1 Preheat the oven to 180°C/160°C fan forced. Line the bases and sides of three 15cm (base size) round cake pans with baking paper. Sift flour and bicarb into a bowl.

2 Use a stand mixer with a paddle attachment to beat butter and sugar for 2 minutes until combined. Add oil. Beat until combined and smooth. Add half the yolks. Beat until just combined. Repeat with remaining yolks. Beat in vanilla and vinegar until combined. Beat in rose pink colouring. Gradually add flour mix, alternating with buttermilk. Mix until just combined.

3 Use electric beaters to whisk egg whites in a bowl until soft peaks form. Fold into cake mixture until just combined. Divide between prepared pans. Smooth surface. Bake for 1 hour 15 minutes until a skewer inserted into centres of cakes comes out clean. Cool slightly. Turn each cake onto a sheet of plastic wrap. Remove paper from sides, leaving paper on bases. Wrap each cake in plastic wrap. (This keeps cake moist.) Place in fridge overnight.

4 Use a serrated bread knife to level cakes. Halve each horizontally.

5 Use electric beaters to beat cheese in a bowl until smooth and creamy. Add ½ cup buttercream. Beat until well combined. Beat in 1 cup buttercream until well combined. Set aside.

6 Place remaining buttercream in a bowl. Add pink gel to tint pale pink.

Spoon into a piping bag. Snip 1cm off end. Pipe 1 tbs onto centre of a cake board. Place a cake layer, cut-side up, on top. Spread top with ½ cup cheese mixture to cover. Repeat layering cakes and cheese mixture, finishing with cake.

7 Pipe pink buttercream on top of cake. Spread to cover. Starting from bottom of cake, pipe a ring of pink buttercream around cake. Continue piping rings all the way up. Run a cake scraper around side to blend. Use an offset palette knife to scrape buttercream off scraper into a bowl. Reserve. Repeat blending buttercream 2 more times until smooth. Use palette knife to push buttercream from top edge of cake into centre to neaten. Place cake in fridge for 1 hour until firm.

8 To create watercolour effect, add pink food colour gel to bowl of reserved buttercream. Starting from bottom of cake, use a palette knife to spread pink buttercream up side, using less pressure as you reach middle. Run scraper around to blend. Repeat two more times until look is achieved. Place in fridge for 2 hours until very cold.

9 Place choc melts and cream in a microwave-safe bowl. Microwave for 20 seconds. Stir. Microwave for 10 seconds. Stir. Repeat until smooth. Remove cake from fridge. Pour drips of chocolate mixture from top edge of cake. Place in fridge for 1 hour until set. Decorate with flowers.

● GLUTEN FREE ● MAKE AHEAD ● FREEZABLE ● EASY ● KID FRIENDLY

Lamington & Iced VoVo
CAKE

A true-blue beauty featuring two Aussie favourites.

SERVES 15 **PREP** 1 hour (+ cooling & chilling) **COOKING** 40 mins

285g (1⅓ cups) caster sugar
200g butter, chopped, at
  room temperature
2 tsp vanilla extract
4 eggs
490g (3¼ cups) self-raising
  flour
310ml (1⅓ cups) milk
2 x 85g pkt raspberry
  jelly crystals
250ml (1 cup) boiling water
130g (1½ cups) desiccated
  coconut
100g (1½ cups) shredded
  coconut
315g (1 cup) raspberry jam
6 Arnott's Iced VoVo biscuits,
  halved diagonally
marshmallow filling
315g (1½ cups) caster sugar
165ml (⅔ cup) hot water
2 tbs gelatine powder
1 tsp vanilla extract

1 Preheat oven to 170°C/150°C fan forced. Grease three 18cm (base size) round cake pans and line bases with baking paper.

2 Use electric beaters to beat the sugar, butter and vanilla in a bowl until pale and creamy. Add the eggs, 1 at a time, beating well after each addition until just combined. Add the flour and milk. Beat until well combined. Divide among prepared pans and smooth surfaces. Bake for 30 minutes or until a skewer inserted into centres comes out clean. Set aside in pans for 5 minutes before turning onto wire racks to cool completely.

3 Meanwhile, place the jelly crystals and boiling water in a large bowl and stir until crystals dissolve. Stir in 500ml (2 cups) water. Place in the fridge for 1 hour or until mixture is consistency of egg whites.

4 Combine the desiccated and shredded coconut on a large tray. Carefully dip each cake in jelly then in coconut, pressing gently on top, base and side of cakes. Transfer to trays. Place in the fridge for 20 minutes to set.

5 Spread 2 tbs jam over top of each cake, leaving a 2cm border. Spoon remaining into a piping bag fitted with a 5mm plain nozzle.

6 To make the marshmallow filling, place the sugar and hot water in a saucepan over medium heat. Cook, stirring, for 3 minutes or until sugar dissolves and mixture is clear. Place the gelatine and 160ml (⅔ cup) water in a jug. Use a fork to stir until well combined. Pour into pan. Stir for 2-3 minutes until gelatine dissolves and mixture is clear. Pour into the bowl of a stand mixer. Set aside for 30 minutes to cool to room temperature.

7 Beat the marshmallow mixture on high speed for 6-10 minutes or until very thick. Add the vanilla and beat for 1 minute. Spoon into a piping bag fitted with a 1cm plain nozzle. Pipe small peaks around edge of each cake then cover the middle of 2 cakes with the remaining marshmallow. Set aside for 20 minutes or until the marshmallow has set.

8 Pipe jam around edge of each cake. Stack cakes, finishing with the cake not fully covered with marshmallow. Decorate with biscuits.

● GLUTEN FREE ● MAKE AHEAD ● FREEZABLE ● EASY ● KID FRIENDLY

Choc-mint forest NAKED CAKE

Celebrate nature with this forest green mint-choc marvel.

SERVES 16 **PREP** 1 hour (+ cooling & chilling) **COOKING** 1 hour 30 mins

200g dark chocolate, chopped
200g butter, chopped
125ml (½ cup) boiling water
215g (1 cup) caster sugar
150g (1 cup) self-raising flour
120g (⅔ cup) potato flour
35g (⅓ cup) cocoa powder
390g can sweetened condensed milk
185ml (¾ cup) buttermilk
4 eggs

mint buttercream
400g butter, chopped, at room temperature
230g (2½ cups) icing sugar mixture
1 tbs milk
Green food colouring, to tint
Peppermint essence, to taste

chocolate drizzle
100g dark chocolate, chopped
1 tbs liquid glucose
125ml (½ cup) pouring cream

decorations
Nestle Aero Peppermint, halved diagonally
Cadbury Flake, halved
Yoghurt-coated craisins
Meringue kisses, dusted with cocoa
Darrell Lea Mint Chocolate Balls, halved
Peppermint Crisp, crushed
Chocolate crisp pearls
Coloured sugar crystals

1 Preheat the oven to 170°C/150°C fan forced. Grease 2 deep 17.5cm (base size) round cake pans. Line the bases and sides with baking paper.

2 Combine chocolate, butter and boiling water in a heatproof bowl. Microwave for 1-2 minutes or until melted and smooth. Combine sugar, flours and cocoa powder in a large bowl. Make a well in the centre. Add chocolate mixture, condensed milk, buttermilk and eggs. Use a balloon whisk to whisk until combined and smooth. Divide evenly between the prepared pans and bake for 50-55 minutes or until a skewer inserted into the centres of the cakes comes out clean. Set aside in pans on a wire rack to cool completely.

3 For the mint buttercream, use electric beaters to beat the butter in a bowl until softened. Gradually add the icing sugar, beating until pale and creamy. Add the milk and beat until smooth. Add a few drops of green food colouring and peppermint essence. Beat until well combined. Reserve ½ cup buttercream in a separate bowl.

4 To assemble, use a large serrated knife to trim the tops of the cakes to level. Cut the cakes in half horizontally. Place cake half on a serving plate or stand. Spread over one-fifth of the buttercream. Top with another cake half, pressing gently but firmly to secure. Repeat layering with the remaining cake halves and half of the remaining buttercream, finishing with a cake half, base-side up. Spread a thin layer of buttercream over the top and side of the assembled cake. Place in fridge for 15 minutes or until just firm. Spread the remaining buttercream over the top and side, allowing some of the side to show through. Place in fridge to chill.

5 For the chocolate drizzle, combine the chocolate, glucose and cream in a heatproof bowl. Microwave for 1 minute. Stir until melted and smooth. Set aside to cool to room temperature.

6 Pour the chocolate drizzle over the centre of the cake. Use a palette knife to carefully spread to the edge, allowing it to drizzle down the side of the cake and set.

7 Spoon reserved buttercream into a piping bag fitted with a 5mm round nozzle. Pipe buttercream peaks onto top of the cake. Use decorations to top cake with Aero, Flake, craisins, meringue kisses, Mint Chocolate Ball halves, Peppermint Crisp, crispy chocolate pearls and sugar crystals to create a 'forest' effect.

● GLUTEN FREE ● MAKE AHEAD ● FREEZABLE ● EASY ● KID FRIENDLY

★★★★★

Great recipe, easy to follow and one of the best cakes I have ever made.
GPNELSON

Strawberries & cream
NAKED CAKE

The barely there buttercream adds rustic charm to this cake.

SERVES 12 **PREP** 1 hour (+ cooling, standing & chilling) **COOKING** 50 mins

300g unsalted butter, at
    room temperature
315g (1½ cups) caster sugar
1 vanilla bean, split, seeds
    scraped
5 eggs, at room temperature
550g (3⅔ cups) self-raising
    flour
200g sour cream
185ml (¾ cup) milk
250g strawberries, hulled,
    finely chopped
250ml (1 cup) thickened
    cream, whipped
160g (½ cup) strawberry jam
Fresh flowers, to decorate
Small strawberries and
    leaves, to decorate
buttercream
350g unsalted butter,
    chopped, at room
    temperature
1 tsp vanilla extract
600g (4 cups) icing sugar
    mixture, sifted
chocolate drizzle
200g white chocolate,
    finely chopped
125ml (½ cup) thickened
    cream
1 tbs liquid glucose
Pink food gel, to tint
basil sugar
4 large fresh basil leaves
55g (¼ cup) caster sugar

1 Preheat oven to 180°C/160°C fan forced. Grease the bases and sides of three 5cm-deep, 20cm (base size) round cake pans and line with baking paper.

2 Use electric beaters to beat butter, sugar, vanilla and a pinch of salt in a bowl until pale and creamy. Add the eggs 1 at a time, beating well after each addition. Add half the flour and half the combined sour cream and milk. Beat on low until just combined. Repeat with remaining flour and combined sour cream and milk until just combined. Stir in the chopped strawberries. Divide mixture among prepared pans. Smooth the surface.

3 Bake for 38-45 minutes or until a skewer inserted in the centres of the cakes comes out clean. Stand in pans for 15 minutes. Turn onto wire racks to cool completely.

4 Meanwhile, for the buttercream, use electric beaters to beat the butter and vanilla in a bowl until pale and creamy. Gradually add icing sugar and beat until smooth and combined. Spoon half the buttercream into a piping bag fitted with a 1.5cm plain nozzle.

5 Place 1 cake on a serving plate. Pipe a high, thick border of the buttercream around edge of cake. Fill the centre with half the whipped cream. Use the back of a spoon to make indents in the cream and spoon in half the jam. Top with another cake and repeat with another border of buttercream, then the remaining cream and jam. Top with the remaining cake. Pipe or spread enough of the remaining buttercream to evenly cover the top and the side of the cake. Use a palette knife or cake scraper to smooth over the outside of the cake, allowing some of the cake to show through. Place in the fridge for 1 hour to chill.

6 Meanwhile, for the chocolate drizzle, melt the chocolate, cream and glucose in a microwave-safe bowl in the microwave on Medium, stirring every 30 seconds, until smooth. Tint with pink colouring. Set aside to cool slightly, stirring often. Spread over the top of the cake and allow to drip down the side. Set aside to set.

7 For the basil sugar, place basil and 1 tbs sugar in a mortar. Pound with a pestle until finely crushed. Stir in remaining sugar. Pass through a coarse sieve and discard solids.

8 Decorate the cake with a sprinkle of basil sugar, the fresh flowers, strawberries and leaves.

● GLUTEN FREE ● MAKE AHEAD ● FREEZABLE ● EASY ● KID FRIENDLY

Hummingbird naked CAKE

Pretty up your cake with pineapple flowers and carrot roses.

SERVES 16 **PREP** 1 hour (+ cooling, chilling & setting) **COOKING** 3 hours 10 mins

265g (1¾ cups) self-raising
  flour
200g (1 cup, firmly packed)
  brown sugar
70g (⅔ cup) desiccated
  coconut
1 tsp bicarbonate of soda
1 tsp ground cinnamon
½ tsp ground nutmeg
440g can crushed pineapple
  in natural juice
1 large carrot, peeled,
  coarsely grated
2 bananas, mashed
70g (½ cup) chopped
  pecans
185ml (¾ cup) vegetable oil
4 eggs
1 small whole pineapple,
  ends trimmed, peeled
Sugar crystals, to decorate
sweet carrot roses
1 carrot, peeled
215g (1 cup) caster sugar
buttercream
250g cream cheese,
  chopped at room
  temperature
80g butter, chopped, at
  room temperature
195g (1¼ cups) icing sugar
italian meringue
155g (¾ cup) caster sugar
2 egg whites, at room
  temperature
Pinch cream of tartar

1 Preheat oven to 170°C/150°C fan forced. Grease three 20cm (base size) round cake pans. Line bases and sides with baking paper.

2 Combine flour, sugar, coconut, bicarb, cinnamon and nutmeg in a bowl. Make a well in centre. Add crushed pineapple and its juice, carrot, banana, pecan, oil and eggs. Stir until combined. Divide among pans. Bake for 35 minutes until a skewer inserted into centres comes out clean. Set aside in pans to cool completely.

3 Reduce oven to 120°C/100°C fan forced. Line 3 large baking trays with baking paper. Cut pineapple into 2.5mm-thick slices. Place in a single layer on trays. Bake for 1 hour. Turn over. Bake, turning once more, for 45-60 minutes or until almost dried. Set aside on trays to cool completely. Carefully peel off trays and scrunch centres together to create 'flowers'. Set aside on cleaned, lined trays to set.

4 For carrot roses, use a peeler to peel carrot into ribbons. Pat dry. Line a baking tray with baking paper. Place sugar and ½ cup water in a saucepan over low heat. Heat, stirring, until sugar is dissolved. Bring to boil. Simmer for 5 minutes. Add carrot. Simmer for 10-15 minutes or until almost translucent. Use tongs to shake carrot ribbons over saucepan to remove excess syrup. Place flat on tray and set aside to cool. When cool enough

to handle but still pliable, roll into rose shapes. Set aside on cleaned, lined tray to cool completely and set.

5 For buttercream, use electric beaters to beat cheese and butter in a bowl until smooth. Gradually add sugar. Beat until pale and creamy.

6 To assemble, place 1 cake on a serving plate or board. Spread over ¼ of frosting. Top with another cake. Spread over ⅓ remaining frosting. Top with remaining cake, base side up. Spread remaining frosting over top and side of cake, allowing some side to show. Place in the fridge to chill.

7 For meringue, place sugar and 2 tbs water in a saucepan over low heat. Heat, stirring, until sugar is dissolved, brushing side of pan with a wet pastry brush to prevent crystals forming. Increase heat to medium-high. Heat, without stirring, for 3-4 minutes or until syrup reaches 115°C (soft ball stage) on a sugar thermometer. While it continues to cook, use electric beaters to beat egg whites and cream of tartar in a bowl until soft peaks form. When syrup reaches 120°C (hard ball stage) and with beaters on low, gradually add to egg mix. Increase speed to high. Beat for 10 minutes or until thick, glossy and cool.

8 Spoon meringue over cake. Use a cook's blowtorch to caramelise. Decorate with pineapple and carrot flowers. Sprinkle with sugar crystals.

● GLUTEN FREE ● MAKE AHEAD ● FREEZABLE ● EASY ● KID FRIENDLY

Eton mess CAKE

A not-so-messy reinvention of this best-of-British-summer treat.

SERVES 12 **PREP** 30 mins (+ cooling & chilling) **COOKING** 1 hour 10 mins

225g (1½ cups) self-raising flour

75g (½ cup) plain flour

215g (1 cup) caster sugar

3 eggs, at room temperature

150g unsalted butter, chopped, at room temperature

160ml (⅔ cup) milk

2 tsp vanilla extract

400g strawberries, hulled and sliced

Mini meringues, to decorate

Icing sugar mixture, to dust

330g pkt Queen Royal Icing

Pink food colouring, to tint

Freeze-dried strawberries, crushed, to decorate

Sugar pearls, to decorate

Fresh flowers and strawberry plant, to decorate

cream cheese icing

500g cream cheese, chopped, at room temperature

100g unsalted butter, chopped, at room temperature

450g (3 cups) icing sugar mixture

1 Preheat the oven to 140°C/120°C fan forced. Line a 6cm-deep, 12 x 27cm (base size) loaf pan with baking paper.

2 Place the flours, sugar, eggs, butter, milk and vanilla in a bowl. Use electric beaters to beat on low speed for 30 seconds. Increase the speed to high and beat for 1-2 minutes or until mixture is thick and butter is incorporated. Spoon into prepared pan and smooth the surface. Bake for 1 hour to 1 hour 10 minutes or until a skewer inserted into the centre of the cake comes out clean. Set aside for 10 minutes to cool slightly before turning onto a wire rack to cool.

3 To make the icing, beat the cream cheese and butter in a bowl until well combined. Add the icing sugar and beat until pale and creamy.

4 Cut the cake horizontally into 3 even layers. Spread 1 layer with half the cream cheese icing. Top with half the strawberries. Repeat with the remaining icing, strawberries and cake. Place in the fridge for 30 minutes to chill.

5 Dust meringues with icing sugar. Make royal icing following packet directions, If it's too stiff to swirl, add ½ tsp extra water at a time and mix in to loosen slightly. Add a few drops of food colouring. Swirl for a marbled effect. Drizzle icing over cake. Decorate with meringues, crushed freeze-dried strawberry, sugar pearls and fresh flowers and strawberry plant.

COOK'S TIP

The cake can be made the day before. Make up to the end of step 2 and then store, whole, in an airtight container in a cool dry place. Continue from step 3 on the day of serving.

● GLUTEN FREE ● MAKE AHEAD ● FREEZABLE ● EASY ● KID FRIENDLY

Giant fairy bread
ICE-CREAM CAKE

Celebrate with the best of all worlds with this ice-cream cake combo.

SERVES 12 **PREP** 30 mins (+ 3 hours freezing, cooling & 10 mins chilling) **COOKING** 50 mins

2L vanilla ice-cream,
   softened slightly
60ml (¼ cup) milk
125g butter, chopped
100g (½ cup) caster sugar
220g white chocolate,
   chopped, plus extra
   75g, melted
2 eggs, lightly whisked
150g (1 cup) plain flour
50g (⅓ cup) self-raising flour
40g (⅓ cup) hundreds and
   thousands, plus extra,
   to decorate
½ bought rectangular
   plain sponge cake
white chocolate ganache
140g white chocolate,
   chopped
60ml (¼ cup) thickened
   cream

1 Line a 20cm (base size) round cake pan with plastic wrap. Place ice-cream in prepared pan. Smooth surface. Place in freezer for 3 hours or until firm.

2 Preheat oven to 180°C/160°C fan forced. Grease another 20cm (base size) round cake pan. Line base and side with baking paper.

3 Combine the milk, butter, sugar and 120g chocolate in a saucepan over low heat. Cook, stirring, for 5 minutes or until sugar has dissolved and chocolate has melted. Transfer to a large bowl. Set aside for 10 minutes to cool.

4 Whisk egg and flours into cooled chocolate mixture until just combined. Gently stir in sprinkles and remaining chopped chocolate. Pour mixture into prepared pan. Bake for 40 minutes or until crumbs cling to a skewer inserted into centre. Set aside in pan to cool completely.

5 To make ganache, combine chocolate and cream in a small saucepan over low heat. Stir for 2-3 minutes or until smooth. Transfer to a bowl. Set aside for 5 minutes to cool. Place in the fridge for 10 minutes or until thickened slightly.

6 Spread extra melted chocolate over bought sponge. Sprinkle with some extra sprinkles. Cut into triangles. Set aside to set.

7 Use a large serrated knife to cut the cooled cake horizontally into 2 even layers. Place the ice-cream disc on 1 cake layer. Top with the remaining cake layer. Place in freezer to firm up.

8 Place extra sprinkles on a baking tray and shake to distribute evenly. Spread half the ganache over side of cake then roll in sprinkles. Place cake on a serving plate then in freezer for 30 minutes to firm up. Spread remaining ganache over top of cake. Top with sponge triangles.

COOK'S TIP

You can prepare the ice-cream disc ahead of time and keep, covered, in the freezer until ready to assemble.

● GLUTEN FREE ● MAKE AHEAD ● FREEZABLE ● EASY ● KID FRIENDLY

Mini lemon
COCONUT CAKES

Deceptively simple, these mini treats will make a big impression.

MAKES 4 **PREP** 30 mins (+ cooling & 20 mins chilling) **COOKING** 30 mins

250g unsalted butter, chopped, at room temperature
430g (2 cups) caster sugar
4 eggs
300ml ctn sour cream
1 lemon, rind finely grated, juiced
300g (2 cups) plain flour
150g (1 cup) self-raising flour
85g (1 cup) desiccated coconut
125ml (½ cup) coconut milk
400ml double cream
215g (⅔ cup) lemon curd
1 passionfruit, halved
330g pkt Queen Royal Icing
Yellow food colouring, to tint
Fresh flowers, to decorate

1 Preheat oven to 180°C/160°C fan forced. Grease two 20 x 30cm (base size) slice pans and line with baking paper.

2 Use electric beaters to beat butter and sugar in a bowl until pale and creamy. Add eggs, 1 at a time, beating well after each addition, until combined. Beat in sour cream and lemon rind. Stir in the flours, coconut, coconut milk and 2 tbs lemon juice. Divide between the prepared pans and smooth surface of each. Bake for 25-30 minutes or until golden and a skewer inserted into centres comes out clean. Set aside for 30 minutes, to cool slightly, then turn onto wire racks to cool completely.

3 Use a round 8.5cm cutter to cut out 6 discs from each cake. Whisk the cream in a bowl or until just-firm peaks form (don't overbeat or it will curdle). Transfer the cream to a piping bag fitted with a 1.5cm fluted nozzle.

4 Reserve 4 cake discs. Spread the remaining 8 cake discs with lemon curd and pipe some cream over the top. Stack 1 curd-topped cake on top of another. Top with a reserved plain cake. Repeat with the remaining cakes to make 4 layered cakes. Transfer to a tray. Place in the fridge for 20 minutes to chill.

5 Place passionfruit pulp in a measuring jug. Add enough water to make 60ml (¼ cup). Place royal icing in a bowl. Add passionfruit liquid and a couple of drops of food colouring to tint pale yellow. Mix until well combined.

6 Drizzle the passionfruit icing over the top of each layered cake, allowing some to drip down the side. Top with fresh flowers.

COOK'S TIP

Turn this into an easy slab cake. Instead of cutting out discs in Step 3, leave the cakes whole. Spread the top of 1 cake with lemon curd. Pipe cream evenly over the top. Top with remaining cake. Place in the fridge for 20 minutes to chill then continue from Step 5.

● GLUTEN FREE ● MAKE AHEAD ● FREEZABLE ● EASY ● KID FRIENDLY

Raspberry apple
MARBLE CAKE

Guests will marvel at this marble creation, which tastes a treat.

SERVES 16 **PREP** 1 hour (+ chilling & setting) **COOKING** 1 hour

200g white chocolate, finely chopped

200g butter, chopped

125ml (½ cup) boiling water

215g (1 cup) caster sugar

150g (1 cup) self-raising flour

75g (½ cup) plain flour

45g (½ cup) desiccated coconut

200g (1 cup) unsweetened pie fruit apple

4 eggs

200g (¾ cup) Greek yoghurt

125g punnet raspberries

330g pkt Queen Royal Icing

80ml (⅓ cup) cold water

Assorted pink and purple food pastes, to tint

Pastel-coloured cachous and sugar crystals, to decorate

raspberry buttercream

350g butter, chopped, at room temperature

300g (2 cups) icing sugar mixture

115g (⅓ cup) raspberry jam

marble bark

200g white chocolate melts

Assorted pink and purple food pastes, to tint

1 Preheat the oven to 170°C/150°C fan forced. Grease 2 deep 17.5cm (base size) round cake pans. Line the bases and sides with baking paper.

2 Place chocolate, butter and boiling water in a microwave-safe bowl. Microwave for 2 minutes or until melted and smooth. Combine sugar, flours and coconut in a large bowl. Make a well in centre. Add chocolate mixture, apple, eggs and yoghurt. Use a balloon whisk to whisk until smooth. Divide between pans. Bake for 50-55 minutes or until golden and firm to touch. Set aside in pans on a rack to cool completely.

3 For buttercream, use electric beaters to beat butter in a bowl until softened. Gradually add icing sugar, beating until pale and creamy. Beat in jam until just smooth (don't overbeat, as icing may split).

4 To assemble, use a large serrated knife to half cakes horizontally. Place 1 piece of cake on a serving plate or board. Spread over one-fifth of buttercream. Scatter over one-third of raspberries, pressing gently into buttercream. Top with another piece of cake, pressing to secure. Repeat layering with half the remaining buttercream and remaining cake and raspberries, finishing with a layer of cake, base-side up. Spread a thin layer of buttercream over top and side of cake, allowing some cake to show

through. Reserve remaining buttercream. Place cake in fridge for 15 minutes or until just firm. Spread reserved buttercream over top and side of cake. Place in fridge to chill.

5 Meanwhile, for marble bark, line a baking tray with baking paper. Place chocolate in a heatproof bowl. Microwave on Medium, stirring every 30 seconds, until melted and smooth. Pour over prepared tray and use a palette knife to spread slightly. Dip a skewer or toothpick into each food paste. Lightly swirl through chocolate to create a marbled effect. Leave to set. Break into pieces.

6 Use a balloon whisk to whisk royal icing mixture and cold water in a bowl until thick, slightly airy and increased in volume (icing shouldn't be too runny). Dip a skewer or toothpick into pink food pastes and lightly swirl through icing to create a marbled effect. Repeat with a clean skewer or toothpick and the purple food pastes (see opposite). Place cake on a wire rack over a baking tray. Carefully pour icing over cake to cover, allowing excess to run off. While runny, use a clean skewer to carefully drag colours through icing to create extra marbling. Set aside until set.

7 Transfer the cake to a serving plate or cake stand. Gently press the marble bark into the top. Sprinkle with the cachous and sugar crystals.

● GLUTEN FREE ● MAKE AHEAD ● FREEZABLE ● EASY ● KID FRIENDLY

Chocolate & meringue cream
LAYER CAKE

The perfectly imperfect meringue kisses add a charming element.

SERVES 12 **PREP** 1 hour 10 mins (+ cooling & setting) **COOKING** 1 hour 25 mins

200g butter, chopped, plus
    extra 25g butter
200g dark chocolate,
    chopped, plus extra
    80g, chopped
125ml (½ cup) boiling water
225g (1 cup) white sugar
75g (½ cup) plain flour, sifted
150g (1 cup) self-raising
    flour, sifted
50g (½ cup) dark cocoa
    powder, sifted
395g can condensed milk
210g (¾ cup) thick Greek-
    style yoghurt
3 eggs
Coloured cachous and
    sprinkles, to decorate
meringue kisses
3 egg whites
Pinch of cream of tartar
165g (¾ cup) caster sugar
Assorted pink and purple
    paste food colouring
meringue cream icing
4 egg whites
215g (1 cup) caster sugar
300g butter, cut into
    12 pieces, at room
    temperature

1 Preheat the oven to 140°C/120°C fan forced. Grease 2 deep 17.5cm (base size) round pans. Line with baking paper.

2 Combine butter and chocolate in a heatproof bowl. Add water and microwave for 1-2 minutes or until melted and smooth. Cool slightly.

3 Combine sugar, flours and cocoa in a bowl. Make a well in centre and add condensed milk, yoghurt and eggs. Gradually whisk until just combined. Add half the chocolate mixture and whisk until smooth. Add remaining chocolate mixture, whisking until smooth. Divide between prepared pans. Bake for 1 hour 10 minutes to 1 hour 15 minutes or until a skewer inserted into centres comes out clean. Cool in pans for 20 minutes. Turn onto a wire rack to cool completely.

4 Meanwhile, to make kisses, preheat oven to 120°C/100°C fan forced. Line 3 baking trays with baking paper. Use electric beaters to beat egg whites and cream of tartar in a clean, dry bowl until firm peaks. Add sugar, 1 tbs at a time, beating constantly until sugar dissolves and mixture is thick and glossy. Stand 3 piping bags, fitted with a 1cm plain and two 1cm star nozzles, upright in tall glasses. Use a small paintbrush to lightly paint 5cm-long stripes of pink and purple food colouring into bags. Divide meringue mixture between bags. Pipe plain and star-shaped meringues of different sizes onto trays (colours will vary the more you pipe). Bake for 25 minutes until crisp and dry. Turn oven off and leave meringues to cool in the oven with the door ajar.

5 To make icing, combine egg whites and sugar in a heatproof bowl. Place bowl over a pan of lightly simmering water (don't let the bowl touch the water). Stir with a wooden spoon until sugar has dissolved. Be careful not to scramble egg. Transfer to an electric mixer. Beat on high until mixture forms soft peaks. Add 1 piece of butter at a time, beating well after each addition until the mixture is thick and creamy with a silky texture.

6 To assemble, trim top of each cake to level. Cut each cake into 3 horizontal layers. Place 1 layer on a cake board or serving plate. Spread with a thin layer of meringue icing. Top with another layer of cake, then icing. Repeat layering. Finish with final layer of cake. Cover top and side with remaining icing in a thin, smooth layer.

7 Combine extra dark chocolate and extra butter in a heatproof bowl. Microwave for 1-2 minutes until melted. Cool slightly. Pour over top of cake. Work quickly with a palette knife to spread to edges. Tap cake on work bench. Leave for 30 minutes to set.

8 Decorate cake with meringue kisses, cachous and sprinkles.

● GLUTEN FREE ● MAKE AHEAD ● FREEZABLE ● EASY ● KID FRIENDLY

★★★★★

I am only 12 years old and I can make this cake, it is easy to make. This cake is stunning but it is time consuming. **CHOCOLATECHIP564738**

Pink grapefruit & mascarpone CAKE

Pink grapefruit curd adds a delicate flavour to each layer.

SERVES 12 **PREP** 40 mins (+ cooling & chilling) **COOKING** 50 mins

250g ctn sour cream
100ml fresh pink or ruby
    grapefruit juice
125ml (½ cup) milk
300g unsalted butter,
    chopped, at room
    temperature
200g (1 cup, firmly packed)
    brown sugar
140g (⅔ cup) caster sugar
1 vanilla bean, split,
    seeds scraped
2 tsp finely grated pink or
    ruby grapefruit rind
5 eggs
550g (3⅔ cups) self-raising
    flour
Fresh flowers, to decorate
pink grapefruit curd
5 egg yolks
100g (½ cup) caster sugar
125ml (½ cup) strained
    fresh pink or ruby
    grapefruit juice
50g unsalted butter,
    chopped
2 tsp finely grated pink or
    ruby grapefruit rind
mascarpone icing
500g mascarpone
60g (⅓ cup) icing sugar
    mixture, sifted
1 tsp vanilla extract
300ml ctn thickened cream
Orange food gel, to tint
Dark pink food gel, to tint

1 For the curd, whisk together the egg yolks and sugar in a small saucepan. Add the juice, butter and rind. Cook over medium heat, stirring constantly, for 4-5 minutes or until thick. Remove from heat. Strain through a sieve into a bowl and set aside for 30 minutes to cool. Cover and place in the fridge for 2 hours or until chilled.

2 Meanwhile, preheat the oven to 180°C/160°C fan forced. Grease base and side of 3 round 5cm-deep, 20cm (base size) cake pans and line with baking paper.

3 Whisk the sour cream, juice and milk in a jug. Set aside. Use electric beaters to beat the butter, sugars, vanilla, rind and a pinch of salt in a bowl until pale and creamy. Add the eggs 1 at a time, beating well after each addition. Add half the flour and half the sour cream mixture. Beat on low until just combined. Repeat with the remaining flour and sour cream mixture until just combined. Divide evenly among the prepared pans and smooth the surface.

4 Bake for 40-45 minutes or until a skewer inserted into the centre of the cakes comes out clean. Cool in the pans for 15 minutes. Transfer to wire racks to cool completely.

5 For mascarpone icing, use electric beaters to beat the mascarpone, icing sugar, vanilla, 1 cup cream and ⅓ cup grapefruit curd in a bowl on medium-low speed until mixture thickens slightly (don't overbeat).

6 Place 1 cake on a serving plate and spread with 1 cup of the mascarpone icing. Spread with half the remaining curd. Top with another cake and repeat with another 1 cup icing and remaining curd. Top with the remaining cake. Place in the fridge for 15 minutes to firm slightly.

7 Divide the remaining icing in half and set aside. Tint half the remaining cream with orange food gel. Pour orange cream into 1 bowl of icing and gently stir to marble. Tint remaining cream with pink food gel. Pour the pink cream into remaining bowl of icing and gently stir to marble. Spread the pink icing around lower half of cake. Spread the orange icing over the upper half of the cake, including top. Place drops of the pink gel on a toothpick and dot around the pink side of cake. Use the end of a spatula to spread the drops and create a streaked effect. Repeat with the orange food gel. Decorate with some flowers.

● GLUTEN FREE ● MAKE AHEAD ● FREEZABLE ● EASY ● KID FRIENDLY

White chocolate
CANDY CANE CAKE

Christmas miracles are made with crushed crystals of candy cane.

SERVES 12 **PREP** 45 mins (+ cooling) **COOKING** 1 hour 50 mins

375g butter, chopped
250g white chocolate, chopped
645g (3 cups) caster sugar
375ml (1½ cups) milk
340g (2¼ cups) plain flour
115g (¾ cup) self-raising flour
3 eggs
Candy canes, crushed, to decorate
Edible gold dust, to decorate

white chocolate buttercream
300g unsalted butter, chopped, at room temperature
500g icing sugar mixture
1-2 tbs milk
300g white chocolate, melted, cooled
1-2 drops rose pink food colouring, to tint

italian meringue
315g (1½ cups) caster sugar
4 egg whites

1 Preheat oven to 160°C/140°C fan forced. Grease the bases and sides of two 20cm (base size) round cake pans and line with baking paper.

2 Combine the butter, chocolate, sugar and milk in a saucepan over low heat. Cook, stirring, for 5 minutes or until melted and smooth. Set aside for 5 minutes to cool.

3 Sift the flours over the chocolate mixture. Stir to combine. Add the eggs and stir to combine. Pour evenly among prepared pans. Bake for 1 hour 30 minutes or until a skewer inserted into the centres comes out clean. Set aside in pans to cool completely.

4 For the buttercream, use electric beaters to beat the butter in a bowl until pale and creamy. Gradually add the icing sugar and milk, in alternating batches, beating well after each addition. Add the white chocolate and beat until smooth and combined. Add 1-2 drops food colouring to tint pale pink.

5 Use a serrated knife to trim the top of cakes to level. Cut each cake in half horizontally. Place 1 cake base on a plate. Spread with one-third of the buttercream. Repeat layering with the remaining cake layers and buttercream, finishing with cake.

6 For the Italian meringue, stir the sugar and 60ml (¼ cup) water in a saucepan over low heat until sugar has dissolved, brushing down the side of the pan with a wet pastry brush to prevent sugar crystals forming. Increase heat to high. Cook, without stirring, for 5-6 minutes or until mixture reaches 115°C (soft ball stage) on a sugar thermometer. While the syrup continues to cook, use electric beaters to whisk the egg whites in a bowl until firm peaks form. When the syrup reaches 120°C (hard ball stage) and with the beaters on low speed, gradually add syrup to egg white mixture. Increase speed to high. Whisk for 10 minutes or until thick, glossy and cool. Spread half the meringue over top and side of cake. Place remaining meringue in a piping bag fitted with a large plain nozzle. Pipe peaks over top of cake. Sprinkle with the crushed candy canes and gold dust.

● GLUTEN FREE ● MAKE AHEAD ● FREEZABLE ● EASY ● KID FRIENDLY

INDEX

USE OUR HANDY TWO-PART INDEX TO FIND
THE PERFECT BAKE EVERY TIME – VIA ALPHABETICAL ORDER
OR BAKING TREAT TYPE.

Sweet As Baking Cookbook
ALPHABETICAL INDEX

Looking for your favourite treat? Here's a list of every recipe in this book to make it easier to find the ones you want to bake again and again.

Sweet As Baking Cookbook
INDEX BY TYPE

Get your bake on quickly and easily with our handy index by chapter / type, for whatever you're in the mood to bake.

CUPCAKES & CAKES

PIMPED-UP PARTY

CREDITS

editor-in-chief Brodee Myers
executive editor Dani Bertollo
food director Michelle Southan
creative director Harmony Southern
book art director Samantha Yates
book sub editor Imogen Rafferty

managing director – food and travel Fiona Nilsson

HarperCollins*Publishers* Australia
publishing director Brigitta Doyle
head of Australian non-fiction Helen Littleton

CONTRIBUTORS

Recipes

Alison Adams, Cynthia Black, Claire Brookman, Lucy Busuttil, Kim Coverdale, Dixie Elliot, Chrissy Freer, Sarah Hobbs, Jessica Holmes, Louise Keats, Kathy Knudsen, Cathie Lonnie, Amanda Lennon, Gemma Luongo, Liz Macri, Lucy Nunes, Miranda Payne, Elisa Pietrantonio, Matt Preston, Kerrie Ray, Tracy Rutherford, Michelle Southan, Katrina Woodman

Photography

Guy Bailey, Jean Cazals, Chris L. Jones, Vanessa Levis, Nigel Lough, Al Richardson, Jeremy Simons, Brett Stevens

HarperCollins*Publishers*

Australia • Brazil • Canada • France • Germany • Holland • India • Italy Japan • Mexico • New Zealand • Poland • Spain • Sweden • Switzerland United Kingdom • United States of America

HarperCollins acknowledges the Traditional Custodians of the land upon which we live and work, and pays respect to Elders past and present.

First published, Australia in 2024
by HarperCollinsPublishers Australia Pty Limited
Level 19, 201 Elizabeth Street, Sydney NSW 2000
ABN 36 009 913 517
harpercollins.com.au
Copyright © NewsLifeMedia 2024

A catalogue record for this book is available from the National Library of Australia.

ISBN 978 1 4607 6574 6 (hardback)

Colour reproduction by Splitting Image Colour Studio, Wantirna, Victoria. Printed and bound in China by 1010.

THANK YOU

At taste.com.au HQ, we've always been passionate about baking, in fact we believe the sweeter, the better. So it was with huge enjoyment that we sifted through the thousands of tried and tested recipes to bring you this beautiful compendium of baking greats.

We'd like to thank everyone on the taste team who contributed to this book – from our foodies to photographers, stylists, editors, designers and the digital team. Each recipe is a result of their amazing dedication and hard work.

A huge thank you as well to Brigitta Doyle and Helen Littleton, our partners at HarperCollins. We're very thankful for your expertise and support.

We'd also like to thank all those passionate bakers of taste.com.au! Numbering in their thousands every day, they come to plan, cook and share the reviews, ratings and genius recipe twists and tips that make taste.com.au that essential resource for all Australians.